Building Applications in the Cloud

Building Applications in the Cloud

Concepts, Patterns, and Projects

Christopher M. Moyer

♦♦Addison-Wesley

Upper Saddle River, NJ • Boston • Indianapolis • San Francisco
New York • Toronto • Montreal • London • Munich • Paris • Madrid
Cape Town • Sydney • Tokyo • Singapore • Mexico City

The publisher offers excellent discounts on this book when ordered in quantity for bulk purchases or special sales, which may include electronic versions and/or custom covers and content particular to your business, training goals, marketing focus, and branding interests. For more information, please contact:

U.S. Corporate and Government Sales
(800) 382-3419
corpsales@pearsontechgroup.com

For sales outside the United States please contact:

International Sales
international@pearson.com

Visit us on the Web: informit.com/aw

Library of Congress Cataloging-in-Publication Data:

Howard, Ken, 1962-
  Individuals and interactions : an agile guide / Ken Howard, Barry Rogers.
      p. cm.
  Includes bibliographical references and index.
  ISBN 978-0-321-71409-1 (pbk. : alk. paper) 1. Teams in the workplace. 2. Communication. I. Rogers, Barry, 1963- II. Title.
  HD66.H695 2011
  658.4'022 -- dc22

                                         2011001898

ISBN-13: 978-0-321-72020-7
ISBN-10: 0-321-72020-2

Text printed in the United States on recycled paper at R.R. Donnelley & Sons, Crawfordsville, Indiana.

First printing April 2011

Editor-in-Chief
Mark Taub

Acquisitions Editor
Trina MacDonald

Development Editor
Michael Thurston

Managing Editor
Kristy Hart

Senior Project Editor
Lori Lyons

Copy Editor
Apostrophe Editing Services

Indexer
Ken Johnson

Proofreader
Sheri Cain

Technical Reviewers
Kevin Davis
Mocky Habeeb
Colin Percival

Publishing Coordinator
Olivia Basegio

Cover Designer
Chuti Prasertsith

Cover Illustrator
Lynn A. Moyer
www.designbylynn.com

Compositor
Nonie Ratcliff

❖

*To my wonderful wife Lynn,
without whom this book would never
have been finished.*

❖

Table of Contents

III: Projects

8   A Simple Weblog   229

Preface

After a few months working as a developer in a small start-up company migrating existing services to the cloud, I started realizing that there was way too much work to be done just by myself. I started looking around for other developers like myself that could assist me, or replace me if I were to find a better and more exciting opportunity elsewhere. I quickly realized that there are so few people that actually fully comprehend the level of complexity it requires to develop a cloud-based application, and almost all these people were happy with their current companies.

I began to create a series of blog posts about working with cloud-based platforms, still available at http://blog.coredumped. org, but soon realized that I could quite literally spend an entire year writing up everything there is to know. This documentation would be better placed in a reference book than simply scattered throughout several blog posts, so I decided to write this book.

The Purpose of This Book

This book isn't designed as a tutorial to be read through from cover to cover. It's not a guide for how to build an application for the cloud, but instead it's designed as a reference point for when you have specific questions. When your boss hands you a new project and tells you to make it scale, check the patterns discussed in this book to see what fits. When you work on a project and you find a specific problem that you don't know how to handle, pick up this book. If you're trying to start on a new project, and you have a perfect idea, but you don't know how to scale it, pick up this book. If you're trying to modify an existing project to scale in the cloud, pick up this book. If you don't know what kinds of applications you can build with cloud computing, pick up this book.

This book doesn't invent many new patterns but simply shows you the tricks and new techniques that you need to consider while running them in the cloud. Although you can use any patterns discussed in this book in any sort of clustering environment, they're designed to take full advantage of the services provided by cloud computing.

How This Book Should Be Used

This book is divided into three parts. Everyone should read Part I, "Concepts," for a basic understanding of cloud computing. In Part II, "Patterns," you can skip to the patterns you're most interested in. If you've never developed any sort of cloud-based application, you may want to go over the example applications in Part III, "Projects," so that you can see exactly what kinds of applications are best suited for this type of system.

Part I, "Concepts"

Part I is designed to give you a general concept of how to develop in the cloud. It's designed to be read from start to finish and is broken into different key chapters important to development:

- Chapter 1, "Fundamentals of Cloud Services"—Provides a basic set of fundamental ideals when working with cloud-based solutions. This is an absolute must read for any developer beginning with this book.

- Chapter 2, "Making Software a Service"—Provides a basic set of instructions for providing Software as a Service (SaaS). It includes details on why this is a good idea and some basics as to how to properly construct your SaaS.

- Chapter 3, "Cloud Service Providers"—Provides some specific examples of services offered by cloud providers.

Part II, "Patterns"

Part II functions more like a reference manual and provides you with a problem and the pattern that solves that problem:

- Chapter 4, "Designing an Image"—Includes basic patterns for use in building your basic image that is the basis for the rest of your application.

- Chapter 5, "Designing an Architecture"—Includes the patterns used for interacting with external systems, not systems offered by your cloud provider.

- Chapter 6, "Executing Actions on Data"—Includes the patterns used to execute code segments against your data.

- Chapter 7, "Clustering"—Includes the patterns used within a basic framework designed to take advantage of multiserver deployments.

Part III, "Projects"

Part III includes examples of real-world applications of the patterns provided throughout this book. These chapters use the same overall hello world tutorial, but in two different ways:

- Chapter 8, "A Simple Weblog"—Details how to build a simple weblog from scratch, not using any existing frameworks.

- Chapter 9, "A Weblog Using Marajo"—Details how to build a weblog using the Marajo cloud-based Web framework.

Conventions Used in This Book

Throughout this book you occasionally see bold words. These words represent a new term, followed by the definition. If you find a term in the book that you don't know, see the Glossary for a full listing of definitions.

Words listed in italic highlight key important ideas to take away from the section. These are usually used to highlight important keywords in a topic, so if you're skimming over a section looking for something specific, this should help you find exactly what you need.

Where to Begin

The first question for most people now is, where do you start? How do you quickly begin developing applications? What if you don't want to go through and read about all these things you could do and simply want to get into the meat of how things work?

By picking up this book, you're already on the right track. You already know that you can't simply go to a cloud provider and start launching servers and expect to get exactly what you want out of them. People who just pick up a cloud provider and don't do enough research beforehand typically end up with lots of problems, and usually end up blaming the cloud provider for those problems. This is like buying a stick-shift car without first knowing how to drive it and then complaining to the dealership for selling it to you. If you don't first do some research and preparation, you shouldn't be surprised when you have problems with the cloud. If you're not a developer, you probably would be better suited to using a third party to manage your cloud; but if you're reading this book, I'm going to assume that you're interested in more than just "let that guy handle it."

Acknowledgments

I'd like to thank my peer and mentor Mitch Garnaat for all his help and inspiration to push me to cloud computing. I'd also like to thank the team at Amazon Web Services for pushing the market forward and constantly bringing out new products that make everything in this book possible.

About the Author

Chris Moyer is a recent graduate of RIT, the Rochester Institute of Technology, with a bachelor's degree in Software Engineering. Chris has more than five years experience in programming with a main emphasis on cloud computing. Much of his time has been spent working on the popular *boto* client library, used for communicating with Amazon Web Services. Having studied under the creator of *boto*, Mitch Garnaat, Chris then went on to create two web frameworks based on this client library, known as *Marajo* and *botoweb*. He has also created large scaled applications based on those frameworks.

Chris is currently Vice President of Technology for Newstex, LLC, where he manages the technological development of migrating applications to the cloud, and he also manages his own department, which is actively maintaining and developing several applications. Chris lives with his wife, Lynn, in the New York area.

Introduction

Before diving into how to develop your cloud applications, you need to understand a few key concepts behind cloud computing. The term **cloud computing** has been around for only a few years, but the concepts and patterns behind how to use it have been in use since the dawn of the computing age.

What Is Cloud Computing?

There are literally hundreds of definitions for cloud computing, and most of them make little to no sense at all to anyone other than the people that originally created them. Most companies call their virtual hosting environments **clouds** simply because it connotes power, speed, and scalability. In reality, a cloud is little more then *a cluster of computational and storage resources that has almost limitless expandability*. Most cloud offerings also charge you only by what you use.

The advantage to running your application in a cloud computing environment is typically a lower cost because you have no initial investment for most services, and you don't have to pay for expensive IT staff. Although this is a great reason to switch over to using cloud computing services, it's not the only one. Cloud computing also offers you the advantage of *instantly scaling* any application built using the proper design patterns. Additionally, it offers you the ability to offload your work to the people that have been managing it best for years. It would take a full-trained staff much longer to react to the increased demand because it has to go out and purchase new hardware. In contrast, when you work with a cloud-based platform, you can simply request more hardware usage time from the large pool of available resources. Because these cloud services are typically provided by larger corporations, they can afford to have the staff available all the time to keep their systems running at peak performance.

If you've ever had a server fail in the middle of the night and have to get it back up and running, then you know how much of a pain it can be to get someone to fix it. By offloading your physical servers to the cloud, you can stop worrying about systems management and start working on your applications.

The goal of any entrepreneur is to build a booming business with millions of customers, but most people don't have enough initial capital to build a server farm that can scale to that sort of potential. If you're just starting up a business, you don't even know if it's going to take off. But say your business does take off suddenly, and now you have to quickly scale your web-based application from handling 20 customers to handling 20,000 customers overnight.

In a traditional environment in which you host your own servers, this could mean you need to not only get a faster pipe out of your server farm, but you also actually need to purchase new or faster servers and build them all up and hope they all work together well. You then need to worry about data management and all sorts of other fun and interesting things that go with maintaining your own cluster. If you had been using a cloud, you'd have simply run a few API calls to your cloud vendor and had 40 new machines behind your application within minutes. In a week if that number drops down to 200 customers, you can terminate those unused instances. You'd have saved money because you didn't have to buy them outright.

The Evolution of Cloud Computing

There's been talk lately about how cloud computing and other new software architectures have been designed similar to how things were designed in the past, and that perhaps we've actually taken a step backward. Although there may be some similarities between how things were done in the past and how things are done now, the design techniques are actually quite different. Following is a brief history of application development.

The Main Frame

In the beginning, there was the mainframe. The mainframe was a single supercomputer with the fastest processing chips money could buy, and they were a prized commodity. They were so large and took so much cooling and electricity that typically even large businesses wouldn't even have one locally to work with, so you had to communicate with it remotely via a **dumb terminal**, a special computer with almost no resources other then to connect to the mainframe (see Figure I.1). Eventually these mainframe's got smaller, but you were still forced to interact with them via these thin clients.

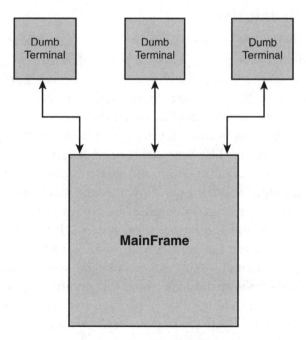

Figure I.1   The mainframe.

These mainframes were designed to run a single process quickly, so there was no need to even think about parallel processing; everything was simply done in sequence. Mainframes needed a complicated scheduling system so that they could allot a given amount of time to any single process but enable others to interject requests in between.

This method of client-server interaction was a huge leap forward from the original system with only one interface to a computer. In many cases, this is still a widely used architecture, although the dumb terminals have been replaced with **thin clients**, which was actually software designed to run on standard computers, not providing much functionality apart from simply connecting to the mainframe. A good example of a thin client still in use today is the modern web browser.

The PC Revolution

As robust as the first mainframes were, they were actually less powerful than a modern digital wrist watch. Eventually technology evolved past the powerful mainframe and into smaller and more powerful devices that were actually housed in an average-sized room. These new devices revolutionized the way software was built, by enabling application developers to run everything locally on the client's system. This meant that your Internet connection speed was no longer a bottleneck and was completely removed from the equation, and the only slowness you would ever see was from your own personal computer. As machines got faster, software continued to demand more from local systems. PCs today, however, are overpowered for most average tasks. This led to the interesting prospect of multitasking, where a single system can be used to run multiple tasks at the same time. Originally, tasking was simply handled by a more advanced version of the scheduler used in the mainframe but eventually became replaced with hardware threading, and even multiprocessor systems.

Many developers refused to adapt to this new multitasking technology, but some did. Those that did developed massively scaled systems that could run in fractions of the time of a single-process system, taking full advantage of the hardware at hand. This would help aid in the next big leap in technology, the fast Internet.

The Fast Internet

Previously the concern was with network latency and throughput, but eventually the telecommunications industry caught up with the rest of the market. What previously took minutes to send over-the-wire now takes seconds, or even fractions of seconds. With the introduction of the largest infrastructure system ever created, the Internet was born and provided enough throughput and band-width to make us rethink how our systems were architected. Many people had come to terms with the idea that software needed to be threaded, but now they took it one step further—developing **clustering**.

Clustering took the idea of processing in parallel to a new level. Instead of simply processing things in parallel on the same machine, clustering is the concept of processing things in parallel on *multiple machines* (see Figure I.2). All these personal computers had much more power than was being used, and most of the time they were entirely idle.

As an example, a few years ago a graphics design company was looking into buying a few servers to run its graphics processing. Graphics manipulation, conversion, and processing is one of the most processor-intensive things required from a computer, so usually it can't be done on local systems without bogging them down or taking a long time. Instead of buying expensive hardware to run and maintain graphics processing, this company decided to take a revolutionary approach.

Its solution was to use the unused processing power on the local systems for graphics processing. It designed a simple queue service that would accept jobs and a simple client interface that ran on every PC in the office that would accept and process jobs only when the computers had downtime. This meant that during off-hours or other periods when employees weren't using their com-puters, the jobs could be completed, and no additional expensive hardware was required! This idea of distributed computing across commodity hardware created a new way to develop software applications.

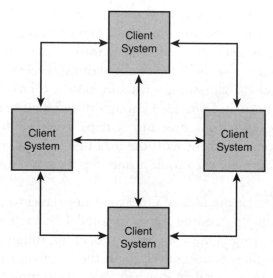

Figure I.2   The cluster system.

The Cloud

Then Amazon released its concept of cloud computing. The idea of a cloud is almost identical to the distributed processing concept, except it uses dedicated systems instead of employees' systems to run the processing jobs (see Figure I.3). This ensures that you'll always have the capacity required to run your jobs. Although it is more expensive (although not much so), you don't have to provide upfront capital to purchase the extra systems; instead you can instantly acquire a few more servers for temporary usage. Again, this revolutionized the way people thought about software and how to design it. However, haven't you seen this approach before?

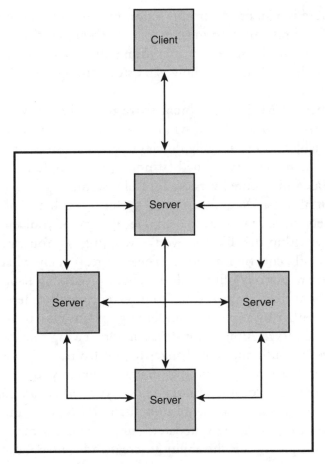

Figure I.3   The cloud system.

Indeed, it does look similar to the original mainframe architecture; from a purely black-box perspective, it's almost identical. The big difference is how the server actually achieves its processing capabilities by combining the best of both architectures into one.

HTML5 and Local Storage

But really, can't we do better? Isn't there some new technology coming out that will enable us to merge these two separate systems better?

Yes, there is. Client-server interaction mostly involves web applications. The problem with most modern web applications is that they have to ask the server for everything; they can't run any processing locally, and they certainly can't store enough data locally in a usable format.

In comes HTML5 with a **local storage option**, a way to store application-level information within the browser. This new technology enables you to literally distribute every trusted action between client and server. The best non-web example is **Mercurial**, a distributed version control system.

Mercurial doesn't require a central server to push and pull change-sets from, but instead keeps a local copy of your entire repository within the directory you're working on. You can continue to work, check in, revert, update, merge, branch, whatever, even if you're entirely offline. All the client processing happens locally. If you then want to share your changes with others, you can do so either by manually transferring update files, or using a central sync server. Although it does support having one default sync server to push and pull changes to and from, that's not its limit. It can push and pull from as many servers as you'd like without breaking your local repository. These sync servers are simply designed to provide an authenticated distribution point and ensure that the data its providing is updated only by trusted sources.

What this provides is the ability to create a local application on a clients system that synchronizes its database with your central server and then enables you to perform regular tasks on it. Because you only get information from your central server that you have access to, you can open your server up and let any client connect to it, and you can just plop your permissions on top and only let the client see what you want it to see from the database. Unlike the old client-server interaction, your central server's full power is used, and your client's full power is used. Anything requiring massive processing (such as processing graphics) can still run on the server side so that you don't bog down your client's systems, but simple things such as searching through a database and rendering records into visuals can all happen locally on your client!

The biggest question for the new-age application is where to put each bit of functionality. The best answer to this is through trial-and-error. Other than for security, there's no true set of rules on what should be processed where; it's just a matter of seeing what your client is capable of. For example, some clients are capable of running XSLT natively in their browsers, but some don't do it correctly. If you can convince your clients to simply not use unsupported browsers, you can probably offload all of that to them, but you may need to allow your server to run it if you need to support all browsers.

The Dawn of Mobile Devices

Why are we moving away from an all-client infrastructure? Quite simply, it's because of Apple. Smart phones (such as Blackberrys) had previously been thought of for only large businesses, and even then it was usually just for email. There are two different scales of devices: the mobile touch pad and the mobile smart phone. These devices have revolutionized the way you think of the client-server interaction because you can pick up where you left off with one device on another.

Now look at Netflix for a good example. Netflix has recently announced that it will support both the iPhone and the iPad for viewing movies. Additionally, it recently made available Netflix on console gaming systems, and even on some TVs. It also provides specific streaming boxes if you don't want to buy either of these things. The best thing Netflix offers is the ability to pause a movie and resume play on any other device. You can start watching a movie on your way home from the airport, and pick it up again on your TV when you get home!

So what does that mean in the general sense? Quite simply, users want a seamless interaction between their PC and their mobile devices. They don't want to have two totally different systems, just two different interfaces. They want to pick up right where they left off on their desktop when they move to their laptop or iPad. They want to have everything synced automatically for them without having to copy files. They also want to have offline support so that when they go into one of those pesky areas where there's no AT&T coverage, they can still continue to work, and the system will simply sync the tasks when it can. These are all things that every developer needs to be thinking about when designing their systems.

Threading, Parallel Processing, and Parallel Computing

Whenever dealing with large applications, you often need to split processes into multiple segments to speed things up. Typically this is done by a simple process of **threading**, which is using the language's internal capabilities to process bits of code simultaneously. Threading uses shared memory; you have access to exactly the same information in each thread without having to handle anything else. You have to worry about locking and using semaphores or some other methodology to prevent your application from having problems when accessing the same data. For example, if you have two threads of execution that each increment a single variable by one, they could both read the data at the same time, increment it by one, and then write that back. In this instance, instead of the ending value of the variable being incremented by 2, it would only be incremented by 1 because you didn't properly lock to ensure that only one thread was operating on that bit of data at the same time. This problem of simultaneous write-ability can also be seen in other forms of segmenting code, but in threading, several built-in methods handle locking for you. Threading typically relies on a scheduler built into the language; code is technically not running at the same time, but instead it's given little bits of time to execute in between other threads.

Parallel processing, on the other hand, doesn't have shared memory. Instead of using the language's built-in capabilities of running code in a scheduler, you're actually using the operating system's capability of executing multiple processes, possibly on different CPUs. Because of how this processing is handled, you can't simply share variables, but you can share resources such as files and other data on the physical machine. Although you don't have the ability to use semaphores anymore for locking, you still have the native filesystem, and you can use file-locks to prevent your code from overlapping writes. Although this is a much better way to separate out bits of code that can run asynchronously, you still need to build one giant supercomputer to process a lot of data because even the most advanced commodity hardware usually tops out at about 12 virtual cores.

The most complex of asynchronous design is parallel computing. Instead of simply splitting your code into different processes and relying on the attached filesystem and other native sources on your local machine, each machine is a large processing unit with a lot of memory to spare. Although you can use the local filesystem as an extension of the RAM for extra storage, you shouldn't rely on it being there in each process, and it can't be used to share data between processes. Because each process could be on an entirely different system, you need to focus on putting any shared data on some other shared datasource. Typically this is a form of database or shared filesystem. This method of design also scales almost infinitely because it's only limited to how many machines you can run at the same time, and how much bandwidth the machines have between them and the shared data sources. Using this methodology, you don't need to build a supercomputer, but you can instead use smaller processing units in a clustered manor to expand almost infinitely. It also enables you to scale and rescale on-the-fly by simply starting and stopping extra servers whenever the demand changes. This is the typical design used behind almost all cloud-based applications.

How Does Cloud-Based Development Differ from Other Application Development?

Unlike server-based application development, cloud-based application development is focused on splitting the two things that every application needs: compute power and data storage. Essentially, this is the data and compute power to manipulate that data. Data can also be sorted into different levels: shared and nonshared. Nonshared data is like RAM, small, fast, and accessible but can be removed at any point. Although not all cloud computing environments throw away all your data on a local system when you take it down, it's generally a good idea to think of anything on a local system exactly as you would RAM, and assume that after you're done with that specific thread of execution, it will be gone forever. Any data you want to persist or share between processes needs to be stored in some other form, either a database or a data store.

You can't use the local filesystem to send messages between processes when they need to communicate. For example, if you need to fire off new processes or send a message for an existing process to do something, you have to handle that by using a queue, not just making a file somewhere. If your cloud computing service doesn't offer it's own queue service (such as Simple Queue Service with Amazon Web Services), you can do the exact same thing with a locking database (such as MySQL or MsSQL).

The most typical thing that's stored in RAM or on local filesystems is session data in Internet applications. Because all cloud applications have some component of the Internet to it (even if you're not making a browser-based application, you're still talking to your application over some Internet protocol), this is an important bit of design to think about. If at all possible, your application should be exactly like the HTTP or HTTPS protocols, completely sessionless. If you do need to store session data, you need to store it in a shared database, not something local because when you're properly scaling your application, you don't know which process the user will access next, nor do you know which server that process is on. You don't even know if the process that first handled that request is even running because you're operating on a constantly scaling system that could be changing, adapting, and even recovering from failures.

Although the cloud can be used to implement legacy code and save you money, in general you probably want to change things around instead of simply copying existing systems. It's a good idea to use as much as your cloud provider has to offer, which includes using any shared database systems, queuing systems, and computing systems. All cloud providers offer a **compute cloud**, a utility to execute code against data, but most also offer hosted databases and storage. Some cloud providers even provide queuing systems that can help you send messages between processes.

The most important thing to remember when developing a cloud-based application is that *failure is inevitable*. Instead of spending hours trying to figure out why something failed, *just replace it*. It usually takes only about a minute to launch a new server, and if you've built everything properly, there won't be any data loss and little impact, if any, from the outside world. You can achieve this by using the proper patterns and design techniques outlined in Part III, "Projects.".

If you have experience developing cluster-based applications, you already have a good start to move to the cloud. The main difference between developing with cluster-based applications and cloud-based applications is using existing systems instead of building your own. For example, you may have already built your own proxy system, but many cloud providers offer their own solutions, which will cost you less and require much less maintenance work.

What to Avoid

As soon as people hear they can put their application "in the cloud," they assume the application is now simply infallible, super scalable, and will easily adapt and save money. *Just because your application is running in the cloud doesn't make it scalable or infallible.* You need to actually build your application around the cloud to take the full advantages it has to offer. Most cloud offerings use commodity hardware in a clustered fashion; it's exactly as likely to fail as any desktop put under the same pressure. *Get ready for failures.* The goal of cloud computing isn't to avoid failures but to be prepared and recover from them.

One of the worst things you can do is make everything rely on one single point of failure, such as a server responsible for maintaining some data or handing out requests. The biggest part of making an application run in the cloud is avoiding bottlenecks. In the past, the biggest bottleneck used to be physical servers, bandwidth, and money. With cloud-computing services, you suddenly are no longer limited by these, so you now can focus on other areas where things could get stuck in a bottleneck. Typically this is something like generating sequential numbers or some other non-threadable process. *Whenever possible, avoid using sequential numbers for IDs.* Instead, try using random UUIDs, which are almost guaranteed to never overlap. Switching away from requiring a single blocking thread to generate the next number in a series for IDs means that you no longer rely on a single point of failure, and you avoid that bottleneck. This process scales almost infinitely because you can simply throw more threads or processes at the service when you have more demand.

Getting Started in the Cloud

The first thing to tackle when working with cloud-based applications is creating your instance image. This is the core set of code that will be used and can either be everything you need or only the base subset of what all your instances need. The more you put into an image, the larger it will be and the slower it will start up, but if you don't put enough onto an instance, it will take even longer to install those extra features before the rest of your services can start. You can use a simple package-management system on a core image to limit what you need to update to a single image, configuring extra packages on boot, or you can build multiple images, each with its own set of packages and update each of them individually. Each cloud-provider enables you to create an image and then set specific instance-level data when running a single instance of that image. You can use this configuration data to load up extra packages, perform updates, or just simply pass in secure information that you would not want to bundle in your image.

In Amazon Web Services, this instance data is typically used to store your AWS credentials so that you can access other services from that instance.

Next, you need to decouple your data from your processing threads. You want to process all data locally and then upload your results to some shared data storage system. For Amazon Web Services, this would be Simple Storage Service (S3) for large data or SimpleDB (SDB) for small searchable data. If you prefer to use a relational database instead of SDB, you can also use MySQL in the cloud.

After you know *where* to store your data, you need to know when to process it and why you are processing it. This is typically done with a **messaging** method. If you've ever dealt with Aspect-Oriented programming languages (such as Objective-C), you know that you already deal with messaging in your programming, but most of it is handled behind the scenes. In a **message queue**, you send a message with your request for a specific processing instruction, such as a function call, to a shared and lockable data source, and other processes listen on that queue for instructions. If a process picks up an instruction it can handle, it locks that message from being read by anyone else, processes the instruction, and then pushes the resulting data to another shared data source, and finally deletes the message so that no other processes will reprocess the same instruction. If your cloud-provider doesn't offer a solution to this, you can simply use a locking database such as MySQL or MSSQL to create your own queue.

When you know how to send messages between processes, you have to manage locking between processes to ensure that multiple processes don't override each other when accessing the same data. If you use MySQL or MsSQL, you can simply use the locking capabilities provided there and lock on tables or on specific rows if possible. Be wary, though, of locking tables because this will hold up other threads, and if something goes wrong with the process that created the lock before it can free it, you'll end up in a deadlock state. You can handle this in several ways, but most of them are better documented in the manual for your respective database.

Locking in a nonrelational database, however, usually is an inexact science and involves a lot of waiting. Nonrelational databases, such as SDB, also have problems with **eventual consistency**, meaning that even if you write your own lock into a database, you'll have to wait a reasonable amount of time to make sure it wasn't overridden by someone else before you can actually assume you have the lock. Even with waiting, this isn't a guarantee because you can't actually put a time limit on "eventually." Even with the best practices, you can't reliably use any nonconsistent database for locking. Fortunately, SimpleDB now provides the option to use consistent read and write, but then you lose the advantages provided by eventual consistency.

Selecting a Cloud Pattern

After you know what you're building, you need to select the cloud patterns to use to make your application take full advantage of the cloud. This is more of an art than a science, so read over the introduction on each pattern before selecting one. You'll probably need to select multiple patterns to implement your full application, so don't try to find one pattern to fit all your needs. If you find a case study in Part II, "Patterns," that closely matches your situation, you can use that as a good starting point and build from there. You can also jump directly to Part III and find the specific pattern that fits your needs.

In general, you should try to split your application as much as possible and use the patterns as needed. Most applications can benefit from the clustering patterns in Chapter 7, "Clustering," because just about every cloud application will be based on the web patterns shown there. If you work with asynchronous processing of data, see Chapter 6, "Executing Actions on Data." If you need to access data from outside of the cloud, see Chapter 5, "Designing an Architecture." If you're just starting and you need to know how to build an instance and start developing from scratch, start at Chapter 4, "Designing an Image," and continue from there.

Implementing a Cloud Pattern

After you select your patterns, you need to put them into practice. The last section of each pattern includes details and code examples for Amazon Web Services, but this code can easily be extracted and used in almost any cloud-based system. As cloud providers continue to grow, they're also continuing to merge to provide one unified set of offerings. The **boto** python library currently supports Amazon Web Services, Google Storage, and Eucalyptus. Work is also being done to bring in the Rackspace cloud, which uses the free and open source **Open Stack** library. Because all the examples provided in this book use Python and boto, many of these examples can be easily transitioned to any number of cloud providing platforms with little or no code modifications.

Concepts

1

Fundamentals of Cloud Services

No matter what type of cloud service you choose, you can't simply expect to use your existing applications without modifications. Most applications are not designed to work in this new age of computing, and much of their architectures need to be redesigned. Before discussing the patterns and concepts required to build your applications in the cloud, first take a look at the fundamental features and functionality of cloud computing. Where did it come from? What does it mean? And what shouldn't you do with it?

Origins of Cloud Computing

There are many different ideas as to what a "cloud service" actually is. Since its original usage in the early 1990s, the term cloud computing has been expanded, and confused, up to a point at which people are now using it as a buzzword rather than to describe a service. Originally, cloud computing meant a service that provides a virtually unlimited access to computational resources (virtual machines) provided to developers as a utility just like electricity. Also like electricity, this implied that there would be multiple different providers to choose from, each giving a utility that is interchangeable with the other. Unfortunately this is not yet the case, but many providers offer similar services and some are even working toward that end goal to provide a truly utility-like service instead of proprietary services that lock you into one single provider.

Because cloud computing is still in its infancy, many people struggle with how to create applications and deploy them to this strange, new world. Unfortunately, most people get things wrong and expect to use their old ideas and patterns in the exact same ways as they did when working with traditional servers. The problem with these old patterns is that they all rely on the single supercomputer for large-scale usage. These computers are not economical, and when you want to increase your capacity, your only option is to buy a new system. What's even worse is that if a single processor in that system fails, you have no system until that one is fixed.

Many large corporations saw these issues and began to develop their own infrastructures to support scalability, reliability, and recoverability on a massive scale. They discovered that while doing so, many traditional conceptions about computing simply didn't apply. This included the idea that big, fast computers were the solution to the issue of scale. Indeed, it turned out that having many smaller computers was not only more affordable, but also helped provide that scalability and availability that they needed.

Unfortunately for most companies, to have this scalability and availability, they would need to purchase a large amount of machines upfront, costing thousands if not millions of dollars for applications that may require only a fraction of that capacity at most times. After the large dot-com bubble in the 1990s, Amazon discovered that it was using less than 10% of its overall capacity during most normal business hours just so it could have expandability for when major events happened. This burst-capacity was not used most of the time and was wasting space and money in its data centers except when it was actually needed.

Amazon then decided to sell this extra unused space to developers. It realized that its infrastructure system was not only useful to Amazon, but with a few modifications could also be useful to other developers. Amazon started by offering a simple web service that enabled users to use Amazon's unused disk space in its vast storage arrays and eventually built on that service to provide additional services, including the now-famous Elastic Compute Cloud. These services revolutionized the way people thought about computing in general, giving you the ability to think of servers as a utility rather than an appliance. This introduced the concept of **Infrastructure as a Service**, or **IaaS**. This concept makes the offering of lower level infrastructure systems available to developers.

Following in the waves of Amazon, many other large corporations began to release their own services, offering up virtual servers to clients. These companies include Google, Sun Microsystems, Microsoft, and Rackspace. Google also began to make waves in the cloud computing world by being the first to offer a **Platform as a Service**, or **PaaS**. This unique offering goes above the simple IaaS and automatically scales for you instead of requiring you to build up the framework.

What Is a Cloud Service?

Although most people today are talking only about cloud computing when they refer to cloud services, the concept exists well outside of the realm of computing alone. A **cloud service** is something provided as a utility, such as cable, Internet, or even gas. Just like there are multiple classes of utilities, there are multiple classes of cloud services.

Cloud services provide so much more then just compute resources. The first cloud services offered weren't compute resources at all; indeed, they were offering *storage*. They provided this storage in a unique web-based offering, providing you access to a system that wasn't a filesystem but simply an API that enabled you to store, retrieve, and modify **objects**, which were basically named resources. Only three core infrastructure offerings can be called cloud services: compute, storage, and connectivity. Everything else is an adaptation on top of one or more of these utilities.

Compute

Cloud computational resources are services that enable you to execute a set of instructions on a physical processor. Access can be provided as a virtual machine, platform or framework, or even an API that enables you to execute code. Any way you want to use it, these services enable you to execute a block of code against input data, which produces output data.

As the compute service is an essential building block for other services, many cloud providers actually abstract this layer and instead provide you with a framework. For example, Google released a service called AppEngine that provides you access to the compute service, but not directly. Instead, it gives you the ability to launch your application within a specialized framework that has access to the compute resource.

Storage

Storage can be thought of as the replication of either a filesystem or a database, but in reality it doesn't have to be either. Storage can either be short term or long term, but it must be **persistent**. The data must be saved outside of temporary memory and accessible even if the system you saved it on is restarted or reset. Your data may not necessarily be consistent, but you usually expect some sort of guarantee that when you save it, your changes will *eventually* go through in the order they were sent. Storage can also be for large objects such as video files and small data sets such as databases. Usually cloud providers offer multiple different types of storage; some provide query-able databases and some that provide you with a filesystem, such as a resource.

Connectivity

Another common functionality that cloud providers give you is connectivity with services or resources. Sometimes this is transparent, as with having a network adapter on your compute instance, but sometimes they also expose this underlying infrastructure to you. The biggest example of a connectivity service is load balancing, in which you are provided with a single node that can equally direct traffic to your processing nodes and automatically handle node failures. As discussed more in Part II, "Patterns," this can be a key offering to help assist you with fault tolerance.

The Legacy Pattern

The legacy pattern is a way for existing applications to be run in the cloud platform without modifying it. For example, Amazon Web Services now has a service that enables you to start and stop an instance from an Elastic Block Storage, enabling you to provide a persistent virtual machine-like environment. However, the legacy pattern is actually an antipattern, often causing more problems than it solves. It's relatively easy to make an existing application work within the cloud, but this is often where people start to have issues. People often complain about the throughput or overall performance of cloud providers because they simply don't understand the concept of **horizontal scaling**, or **scaling out**. This method of scaling involves adding more machines to an application, not adding more hardware to the same machine.

The biggest issue most people have when they first start developing cloud-based applications is that they try to fit their existing applications into cloud servers. The problem with this is that most cloud providers offer something vastly different from traditional virtual machines. In reality, most cloud providers aren't providing systems anything like a virtual machine, but are instead giving you access to **commodity hardware**; they're using consumer-grade hardware instead of supercomputers traditionally used in large-scale applications. Unfortunately, it's harder to **scale upward**, adding more hardware to a single machine or purchasing a larger machine, and instead you need to **scale out**, or add more machines to your cluster.

Your typical applications were probably designed for fast machines with a lot of hardware; however, these systems are now run using simple systems that can run on multiple systems simultaneously. In a traditional environment, when your system started to become slow, you'd simply migrate to a larger, much faster system. However, with cloud platforms this is often limiting, and you can scale up only so much before your system can't get any larger. Additionally, cloud providers often assume that all hardware has a failure rate, and instead of preventing this inevitable situation, they provide you with an easy way to recover from that failure.

When many organizations look at migrating to the cloud, they attempt to run their existing applications using the cloud providers' instances. They build up a basic image and get the largest machine available. They look at this from a cost-saving perspective and notice that they no longer need a large IT staff to maintain the hardware, and see just how much money they can save. Looking into the way cloud providers offer their services, they'll soon discover that they can launch something similar to a virtual machine, and they'll start one up, build it up to what they need by installing all their applications and their custom code, and then attach an external IP address and point their users at that system. They'll then find the various backup solutions that can be used to ensure that their data is protected.

Unfortunately, after a few months they'll typically discover their first major issue and realize that the system they set up doesn't work well within the cloud-computing environment. For example, the I/O throughput on a single instance is probably not good enough for most high-performance applications, and they'll probably notice that they have only so much throughput in both CPU and network performance. This bottleneck often quickly turns most people away from cloud-platforms and on to more traditional hosting services.

Just Because It's in the Cloud Doesn't Mean It Scales

The largest misconception about cloud computing is that if you use a cloud provider, you immediately have infinite scalability.

You can't take an existing application designed to run in a single computer environment, plop it in a cloud service, and expect it to scale. Just because you use your application in the cloud doesn't mean your application scales.

Cloud providers don't take your existing applications and make them scale; they provide you with the tools you need to *power your applications*. Just like you can't plug an oil lamp into an electric socket and expect to get light, you can't take an existing application and plug it into a cloud service and expect scalability. Not only do you need to rebuild your application, you also want to *rethink* your application. Many fundamentals that work in a single compute environment don't scale well or even work in a multiple computer infrastructure.

The ideas and concepts in this book can help you build a framework, a solid platform on which to design and build your custom application to scale with the market. Although most of these concepts have existed since long before cloud computing existed, they have new applications now that it's a real possibility. If you are familiar with how to handle parallel computing, most of these concepts will be familiar to you. If not, don't worry; the concepts are simple and easy to follow.

Failure as a Feature

Another large misconception is that if you use a cloud provider, your system will be highly reliable and always available. This is not true because most cloud providers use nothing more then commodity hardware for their underlying hardware. Although this hardware is no more or less likely to fail than your personal desktop, it's also under a lot more load, and it's used by more people. Just like you are more likely to find people speeding on a highway because there are more cars there than on any side streets, you are more likely to find failures on cloud-computing platforms than with dedicated normal hosting because cloud providers have a larger share of the market than any single, dedicated hosting company.

As most good software designers know, it's almost impossible to always ensure that there will never be any errors, and it's much more important to recover from errors than trying to prevent them entirely. When a server fails in a traditional environment, typically someone is going to get paged and have to spend hours fixing the issue. They'll have to comb through log files to discover what exactly happened, usually to find something simple, such as having a full disk or some sort of hung process. With cloud-based servers, it's as simple as terminating a failed instance and starting up a new one. The original image for these instances is traditionally read-only; any changes, including any possible vulnerabilities or compromises, will be wiped away when the machine is killed and restarted. This is similar to how a firewall works, holding a permanent copy of the base operating system so that if the system is compromised, it can simply be restarted immediately to recover.

When an issue occurs, you can simply take the compromised or broken system offline immediately, turn on a new one, and put it online without much downtime. Although most developers would be more concerned with why the system failed, most business people and customers simply want to know when the system will be back online.

A cloud-driven system enables you to have the best of both worlds. You can have your servers automatically removed from your application when they fail and have them diagnosed while a new server is brought online to replace them. This enables you to diagnose the issues you may have encountered without extending downtime to your end users. Most developers won't need to worry about being woken up at 2 a.m. because their application can now be **self-healing** and recover on its own without any manual intervention.

Consistency, Availability, and Partition Tolerance

The CAP theorem was first introduced by Eric Brewer in 2000. In his keynote speech "Principles of Distributed Computing," he proposed that there are three things that any service can provide two of, but no system can provide all three. Those three quality attributes are Consistency, Availability, and Partition Tolerance.

Consistency

When the large digital TV revolution occurred, many people in large cities noticed that their channels were coming in much clearer. However, many people in smaller cities suddenly noticed that they weren't getting anything. Where they had been at least getting some static, they now had nothing.

In many ways, digital TV is a Consistent system. Consistent systems, also known as atomic systems, are defined as systems that either are fully operational or not at all. There is no middle ground and no partial broadcast.

Almost every database currently used is consistent. In today's world, when you write something to a database, you expect to instantly retrieve that same data exactly as you just saved it. Think of a filesystem where you save a file and then can instantly read it.

The Consistent system has one major flaw; its implies that it must rely on a single point-of-failure, that is one central system that manages that set of data. Think of an incremental counter in a threaded environment. To ensure that you can increment that counter, only one of your threads may access that data at any given time; you need to support locking, typically by using some sort of semaphore. Unfortunately, your system will also be slower because the throughput of this system will have to funnel through a single point.

Unfortunately, consistent systems are also required for most applications. For example, any banking application requires this consistency to perform transactions. Consider the act of performing a purchase, where either you send money and receive goods, or you don't do either. In a consistent system, there's no way to have your purchase half-finished, where your money is taken but you have no product (or even worse, where you have the product but didn't pay). This consistency is also a safety feature to prevent unwanted circumstances. As discussed earlier, failure is always an option, so without transactions to recover, you leave yourself wide open to disaster.

Availability

When most people first start their computer, they will immediately open up a web browser and log in to read their email. In today's world, most users expect to see their email immediately, not a message stating that their system is currently down and will be up momentarily. Availability is one of the most important quality attributes in web-based systems. As previously discussed, failure is inevitable, so one good way to solve this issue is with a high-availability system that has backups and redundancy built in.

Partition Tolerance

One of the most common system deployments is to launch a single database on a massively large central server that everything else connects to. This makes your system consistent, but what about scalability? Partition Tolerance is the capability of your system to be fully operational in a partial network outage. To be fully partition-tolerant, your system must behave properly in all cases short of a total network failure. Partition Tolerance almost always goes hand-in-hand with Availability and usually is quite different from Consistency.

One common way to achieve partition tolerance to split your database into multiple different "partitions," or segments across your network, or even in different networks. This gives you the added advantage that if a single network segment goes down, it shouldn't take down your whole system. If you equally split your application across multiple different networks or network segments, your application will not rely on a single network segment and therefore can be better partition-tolerant. Partition Tolerance implies that any failure short of a *total failure* must result in the system responding correctly. That is, if a single node in your network fails, the rest of the system must accommodate and make up for that failure.

Partition Tolerance is one of the most complicated concepts to achieve. You often need to split your system into equal chunks, each capable of doing the job of the entire system. When a node fails, it must not impact the rest of the system. As long as you can connect to at least one node in the system, the entire system must function properly, and when they come back online they must also fall back into sync.

Eventual Consistency

One of the most common patterns in cloud-provider solutions is the concept of **eventual consistency**. As the CAP theorem states, you can have only two of the three quality attributes Consistency, Availability, and Partition Tolerance. Most traditional applications use a system that is simply Consistent and not Available or Partition Tolerant. Cloud-based applications trend to Availability and Partition Tolerance and are often not Consistent, *at least immediately*.

Eventual consistency enables you to provide constant and highly scalable access to your data while sacrificing immediate consistency. Your transactions are all guaranteed to happen in order, but they may not happen immediately on all nodes in the system. You cannot create things such as sequential counters because multiple different nodes may have different values. The only consistent guarantee that you have is that *eventually* all nodes will come in sync.

One major issue with eventual consistency is that people don't know how to use it. People tend to treat these databases just like regular databases and forget that they can't immediately query back and get the results they want. For example, they cannot use an eventually consistent database to store session information because that type of information is typically highly volatile.

When Amazon introduced SimpleDB, it was the first database that I had ever experienced that used eventual consistency. As my first dive into developing a framework that ran entirely off of Amazon Web Services, I attempted to make a service that would be highly Partition Tolerant by not storing any session information in a local system on each node, but instead by storing that information in SimpleDB. Unfortunately, this was a horribly wrong approach because sometimes users would have to log in several times before their data was stored in SimpleDB. In reality, it took a while before their login information was posted to SimpleDB and made available to the node that they were connecting to.

The problem is that session data isn't long term; more correctly, it's *highly volatile and temporary*. This type of storage doesn't need to be available or Partition Tolerant, but it's important that it remains consistent. This information is entirely inappropriate for eventually consistent systems. It's never a good idea to think you can build a system that is all reliant on AP systems and never have a consistent portion.

Summary

The most important takeaway from this chapter is that you can't dive right into cloud computing without first taking a good look at what you actually plan to do. The biggest mistake most people make is to assume that migrating to the cloud is something that they can do on a whim without any preparation. In reality, cloud computing is something you need to research a lot before you dive into it, or you'll end up walking away disappointed.

You shouldn't walk away from this discouraged; just be aware that migrating to the cloud *properly* is no simple task. In the end, you can end up saving a lot of money, but it is by far not a zero-cost startup procedure. You need to spend time researching, planning, and developing before making the switch to using a cloud service. Don't expect to spend only a few weeks and walk out with a fully functioning cloud deployment.

2

Making Software a Service

Developing your Software as a Service (SaaS) takes you away from the dark ages of programming and into the new age in which copyright protection, DMA, and pirating don't exist. In the current age of computing, people don't expect to pay for software but instead prefer to pay for the support and other services that come with it. When was the last time anyone paid for a web browser? With the advent of Open Source applications, the majority of paid software is moving to hosted systems which rely less on the users' physical machines. This means you don't need to support more hardware and other software that may conflict with your software, for example, permissions, firewalls, and antivirus software.

Instead of developing a simple desktop application that you need to defend and protect against pirating and cloning, you can develop your software as a service; releasing updates and new content seamlessly while charging your users on a monthly basis. With this method, you can charge your customers a small monthly fee instead of making them pay a large amount for the program upfront, and you can make more money in the long run. For example, many people pirate Microsoft Office instead of shelling out $300 upfront for a legal copy, whereas if it were offered software online in a format such as Google Docs, those same people might gladly pay $12.50 a month for the service. Not only do they get a web-based version that they can use on any computer, but everything they save is stored online and backed up. After two years of that user paying for your service, you've made as much money from that client as the desktop version, plus you're ensuring that they'll stay with you as long as they want to have access to those documents. However, if your users use the software for a month and decide they don't like it, they don't need to continue the subscription, and they have lost only a small amount of money. If you offer a trial-based subscription, users can test your software at *no* cost, which means they're more likely to sign up.

Tools Used in This Book

You need to take a look at some of the tools used throughout this book. For the examples, the boto Python library is used to communicate with Amazon Web Services. This library is currently the most full-featured Python library for interacting with AWS, and it's one I helped to develop. It's relatively easy to install and configure, so you can now receive a few brief instructions here. boto currently works only with Python 2.5 to 2.7, not Python 3. It's recommended that you use Python 2.6 for the purposes of this book.

Signing Up for Amazon Web Services

Before installing the libraries required to communicate with Amazon Web Services, you need to sign up for an account and any services you need. This can be done by going to http://aws.amazon.com/ and choosing Sign Up Now and following the instructions. You need to provide a credit card to bill you for usage, but you won't actually be billed until the end of each month. You can log in here at any time to sign up for more services. You pay for only what you use, so don't worry about accidentally signing up for too many things. At a minimum, you need to sign up for the following services:

- Elastic Compute Cloud (EC2)
- Simple Storage Service (S3)
- SimpleDB
- Simple Queue Service (SQS)

After you create your account, log in to your portal by clicking Account and then choosing Security Credentials. Here you can see your Access Credentials, which will be required in the configuration section later. At any given time you may have two Access keys associated with your account, which are your private credentials to access Amazon Web Services. You may also inactivate any of these keys, which helps when migrating to a new set of credentials because you may have two active until everything is migrated over to your new keys.

Installing boto

You can install boto in several different ways, but the best way to make sure you're using the latest code is to download the source from github at http://github.com/boto/boto. There are several different ways to download this code, but the easiest is to just click the Downloads button and choose a version to download. Although the master branch is typically okay for development purposes, you probably want to just download the latest tag because that's guaranteed to be stable, and all the tests have been run against it before bundling. You need to download that to your local disk and unpack it before continuing.

The next step will be to actually install the boto package. As with any Python package, this is done using the `setup.py` file, with either the `install` or `develop` command. Open up a terminal, or command shell on Windows, change the directory to where you downloaded the boto source code, and run

```
$ python setup.py install
```

Depending on what type of system you run, you may have to do this as root or administrator. On UNIX-based systems, this can be done by prepending `sudo` to the command:

```
$ sudo python setup.py install
```

On Windows, you should be prompted for your administrative login if it's required, although most likely it's not.

Setting Up the Environment

Although there are many ways to set up your environment for boto, use the one that's also compatible with using the downloaded Amazon Tools, which you can find at http://aws.amazon.com/developertools. Each service has its own set of command-line-based developer tools written in Java, and most of them enable you to also use the configuration file shown here to set up your credentials. Name this file credentials.cfg and put it somewhere easily identified:

```
AWSAccessKeyID=MyAccessKey
AWSSecretKey=MySecretKey
```

You can make this the active credential file by setting an environment variable `AWS_CREDENTIAL_FILE` and pointing it to the full location of this file. On bash-based shells, this can be done with the following:

```
export AWS_CREDENTIAL_FILE=/full/path/to/credentials.cfg
```

You can also add this to your shell's RC file, such as .bashrc or .zshrc, or add the following to your .tcshrc if you use T-Shell instead:

```
setenv AWS_CREDENTIAL_FILE=/full/path/to/credentials.cfg
```

For boto, create a boto.cfg that enables you to configure some of the more boto-specific aspects of you systems. Just like in the previous example, you need to make this file and then set an environment variable, this time `BOTO_CONFIG`, to point to the full path of that file. Although this configuration file isn't completely necessary, some things can be useful for debugging purposes, so go ahead and make your boto.cfg:

```
# File: boto.cfg
# Imitate some EC2 configs
[Instance]
local-ipv4 = 127.0.0.1
local-hostname = localhost
security-groups = default
public-ipv4 = 127.0.0.1
public-hostname = my-public-hostname.local
```

```
hostname = localhost
instance-type = m1.small
instance-id = i-00000000

# Set the default SDB domain
[DB]
db_name = default

# Set up base logging
[loggers]
keys=root,boto

[handlers]
keys=hand01

[formatters]
keys=form01

[logger_boto]
level=INFO
handlers=hand01

[logger_root]
level=INFO
handlers=hand01

[handler_hand01]
class=StreamHandler
level=INFO
formatter=form01
args=(sys.stdout,)

[formatter_form01]
format=%(asctime)s [%(name)s] %(levelname)s %(message)s
datefmt=
class=logging.Formatter
```

The first thing to do here is set up an [Instance] section that makes your local environment act like an EC2 instance. This section is automatically added when you launch a boto-based EC2 instance by the startup scripts that run there. These configuration options may be referenced by your scripts later, so adding this section means you can test those locally before launching an EC2 instance.

Next, set the default SimpleDB domain to "default," which will be used in your Object Relational Mappings you'll experiment with later in this chapter. For now, all you need to know is that this will store all your examples and tests in a domain called "default," and that you'll create this domain in the following testing section.

Finally, you set up a few configuration options for the Python logging module, which specifies that all logging should go to standard output, so you'll see it when running from a console. These configuration options can be custom configured to output the logging to a file, and any other format you may want, but for the basics here just dump it to your screen and show only log messages above the INFO level. If you encounter any issues, you can drop this down to DEBUG to see the raw queries being sent to AWS.

Testing It All

If you installed and configured boto as provided in the previous steps, you should be able to launch a Python instance and run the following sequence of commands:

```
>>> import boto
>>> sdb = boto.connect_sdb()
>>> sdb.create_domain("default")
```

The preceding code can test your connectivity to SimpleDB and create the default domain referenced in the previous configuration section. This can be useful in later sections in this chapter, so make sure you don't get any errors. If you get an error message indicating you haven't signed up for the service, you need to go to the AWS portal and make sure to sign up for SimpleDB. If you get another error, you may have configured something incorrectly, so just check with that error to see what the problem may have been. If you're having issues, you can always head over to the boto home page: http://github.com/boto/boto or ask for help in the boto users group: http://groups.google.com/group/boto-users.

What Does Your Application Need?

After you have the basic requirements for your application and decide what you need to implement, you can then begin to describe what you need to implement this application. Typically this is not a question that you think about when creating smaller scale applications because you have everything you need in a single box. Instead of looking at everything together as one complete unit or "box," you need to split out what you actually need and identify what cloud services you can use to fit these requirements. Typical applications need the following:

- Compute power
- Fast temporary storage
- Large long-term storage
- Small queryable long-term storage
- Communication between components or modules

Think about this application as a typical nonstatic website that requires some sort of execution environment or web server, such as an e-commerce site or web blog. When a request comes in, you need to return an HTML page, or perhaps an XML or JSON representation of just the data, that may be either static or dynamically created. To determine this, you need to process the actual request using your compute power. This process also requires fast temporary storage to store the request and build the response. It may also require you to pull information about the users out of a queryable long-term storage location. After you look up the users' information, you may need to pull out some larger long-term storage information, such as a picture that they may have requested or a specific blog entry that is too large to store in a smaller queryable storage engine. If the users request to upload a picture, you may have to store that image in your larger long-term storage engine and then request that the image be resized to multiple sizes, so it may be used for a thumbnail image. Each of these requirements your application has on the backend may be solved by using services offered by your cloud provider.

If you expand this simple website to include any service, you can realize that all your applications need the same exact thing. If you split apart this application into multiple layers, you can begin to understand what it truly means to build SaaS, instead of just the typical desktop application. One major advantage of SaaS is that it lends itself to subscription-based software, which doesn't require complex licensing or distribution points, which not only cuts cost, but also ensures that you won't have to worry about pirating. Because you're actually providing a service, you're locking your clients into paying you every time that they want to use the service. Clients also prefer this method because, just like with a cloud-hosting provider, they don't have to pay as much upfront, and they can typically buy in a small trial account to see if it will work for them. They also don't have to invest in any local hardware and can access their information and services from any Internet access. This type of application moves away from the requirements of having big applications on your client's systems to processing everything on your servers, which means clients need less money to get into your application.

Taking a look back at your website, you can see that there are three main layers of this application. This is commonly referred to as a three-tier application pattern and has been used for years to develop SaaS. The three layers include the data layer to store all your long-term needs, the application layer to process your data, and the client or presentation layer to present the data and the processes you can perform for your client.

Data Layer

The data layer is the base of your entire application, storing all the dynamic information for your application. In most applications, this is actually split into two parts. One part is the large, slow storage used to store any file-like objects or any data that is too large to store in a smaller storage system. This is typically provided for you by a network-attached-storage type of system provided by your cloud hosting solution. In Amazon Web Services, this is called **Simple Storage Service** or **S3**.

Another large part of this layer is the small, fast, and queryable information. In most typical systems, this is handled by a database. This is no different in cloud-based applications, except for how you host this database.

Introducing the AWS Databases

In Amazon Web Services, you actually have two different ways to host this database. One option is a nonrelational database, known as SimpleDB or SDB, which can be confusing initially to grasp but in general is much cheaper to run and scales automatically. This non-relational database is currently the cheapest and easiest to scale database provided by Amazon Web Services because you don't have to pay anything except for what you actually use. As such, it can be considered a true cloud service, instead of just an adaptation on top of existing cloud services. Additionally, this database scales up to one billion key-value pairs per domain automatically, and you don't have to worry about over-using it because it's built using the same architecture as S3. This database is quite efficient at storing and retrieving data if you build your application to use with it, but if you're looking at doing complex queries, it doesn't handle that well. If you can think of your application in simple terms relating directly to objects, you can most likely use this database. If, however, you need something more complex, you need to use a Relational DB (RDB).

RDB is Amazon's solution for applications that cannot be built using SDB for systems with complex requirements of their databases, such as complex reporting, transactions, or stored procedures. If you need your application to do server-based reports that use complex select queries joining between multiple objects, or you need transactions or stored procedures, you probably need to use

RDB. This new service is Amazon's solution to running your own MySQL database in the cloud and is actually nothing more than an Amazon-managed solution. You can use this solution if you're comfortable with using MySQL because it enables you to have Amazon manage your database for you, so you don't have to worry about any of the IT-level details. It has support for cloning, backing up, and restoring based on snapshots or points-in-time. In the near future, Amazon will be releasing support for more database engines and expanding its solutions to support high availability (write clustering) and read-only clustering.

If you can't figure out which solution you need to use, you can always use both. If you need the flexibility and power of SDB, use that for creating your objects, and then run scripts to push that data to MySQL for reporting purposes. In general, if you can use SDB, you probably should because it is generally a lot easier to use. SDB is split into a simple three-level hierarchy of domain, item, and key-value pairs. A domain is almost identical to a "database" in a typical relational DB; an Item can be thought of as a table that doesn't require any schema, and each item may have multiple key-value pairs below it that can be thought of as the columns and values in each item. Because SDB is schema-less, it doesn't require you to predefine the possible keys that can be under each item, so you can push multiple item types under the same domain. Figure 2.1 illustrates the relation between the three levels.

In Figure 2.1, the connection between item to key-value pairs is a many-to-one relation, so you can have multiple key-value pairs for each item. Additionally, the keys are not unique, so you can have multiple key-value pairs with the same value, which is essentially the same thing as a key having multiple values.

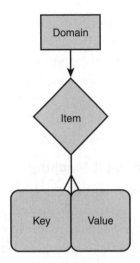

Figure 2.1   The SDB hierarchy.

Connecting to SDB

Connecting to SDB is quite easy using the boto communication library. Assuming you already have your boto configuration environment set up, all you need to do is use the proper connection methods:

```
>>> import boto
>>> sdb = boto.connect_sdb()
>>> db = sdb.get_domain("my_domain_name")
>>> db.get_item("item_name")
```

This returns a single item by its name, which is logically equivalent to selecting all attributes by an ID from a standard database. You can also perform simple queries on the database, as shown here:

```
>>> db.select("SELECT * FROM `my_domain_name` WHERE `name`
➥LIKE '%foo%' ORDER BY `name` DESC")
```

The preceding example works exactly like a standard relational DB query does, returning all attributes of any item that contains a key name that has foo in any location of any result, sorting by name in descending order. SDB sorts and operates by lexicographical comparison and handles only string values, so it doesn't understand that [nd]2 is less than [nd]1. The SDB documentation provides more details on this query language for more complex requests.

Using an Object Relational Mapping

boto also provides a simple persistence layer to translate all values so that they can be lexicographically sorted and searched for properly. This persistence layer operates much like the DB layer of Django, which it's based on. Designing an object is quite simple; you can read more about it in the boto documentation, but the basics can be seen here:

```
from boto.sdb.db.model import Model
from boto.sdb.db.property import StringProperty, IntegerProperty,
    ReferenceProperty, ListProperty

class SimpleObject(Model):
    """A simple object to show how SDB
    Persistence works in boto"""
    name = StringProperty()
    some_number = IntegerProperty()
    multi_value_property = ListProperty(str)

class AnotherObject(Model):
    """A second SDB object used to show how references work"""
    name = StringProperty()
    object_link = ReferenceProperty(SimpleObject,
        collection_name="other_objects")
```

This code creates two classes (which can be thought of like tables) and a SimpleObject, which contains a name, number, and multi-valued property of strings. The number is automatically converted by adding the proper value to the value set and properly loaded back by subtracting this number. This conversion ensures that the number stored in SDB is always positive, so lexicographical sorting and comparison always works. The multivalue property acts just like a standard python list, enabling you to store multiple values in it and even removing values. Each time you save the object, everything that was in there is overridden. Each object also has an `id` property by default that is actually the name of the item because that is a unique ID. It uses Python's UUID module to generate this ID automatically if you don't manually set it. This UUID module generates completely random and unique strings, so you don't rely on a single point of failure to generate sequential numbers. The `collection_name` attribute on the `object_link` property of `AnotherObject` is optional but enables you to specify the property name that is automatically created on the `SimpleObject`. This reverse reference is generated for you automatically when you import the second object.

boto enables you to create and query on these objects in the database in another simple manor. It provides a few unique methods that use the values available in the SDB connection objects of boto for you so that you don't have to worry about building your query. To create an object, you can use the following code:

```
>>> my_obj = SimpleObject("object_id")
>>> my_obj.name = "My Object Name"
>>> my_obj.some_number = 1234
>>> my_obj.multi_value_property = ["foo", "bar"]
>>> my_obj.put()
>>> my_second_obj = AnotherObject()
>>> my_second_obj = "Second Object"
>>> my_second_obj.object_link = my_obj
>>> my_second_obj.put()
```

To create the link to the second object, you have to actually save the first object unless you specify the ID manually. If you don't specify an ID, it will be set automatically for you when you call the put method. In this example, the ID of the first object is set but not for the second object.

To select an object given an ID, you can use the following code:

```
>>> my_obj = SimpleObject.get_by_id("object_id")
```

This call returns an instance of the object and enables you to retrieve any of the attributes contained in it. There is also a "lazy" reference to the second object, which is not actually fetched until you specifically request it:

```
>>> my_obj.name
u'My Object Name'
>>> my_obj.some_number
1234
>>> my_obj.multi_value_property
[u'foo', u'bar']
>>> my_obj.other_objects.next().name
u'Second Object'
```

You call `next()` on the `other_objects` property because what's returned is actually a `Query` object. This object operates exactly like a generator and only performs the SDB query if you actually iterate over it. Because of this, you can't do something like this:

```
>>> my_obj.other_objects[0]
```

This feature is implemented for performance reasons because the query could actually be a list of thousands of records, and performing a SDB request would consume a lot of unnecessary resources unless you're actually looking for that property. Additionally, because it is a query, you can filter on it just like any other query:

```
>>> query = my_obj.other_objects
>>> query.filter("name like", "%Other")
>>> query.order("-name")
>>> for obj in query:
...
```

In the preceding code, you would then be looping over each object that has a name ending with `Other`, sorting in descending order on the name. After returning all matching results, a `StopIteration` exception is raised, which results in the loop terminating.

Application Layer

The application layer is where you'll probably spend most of your time because it is the heart and soul of any SaaS system. This is where your code translates data and requests into actions, changing, manipulating, and returning data based on inputs from users, or other systems. This is the only layer that you have to actually maintain and scale, and even then, some cloud providers offer you unique solutions to handle that automatically for you. In Google AppEngine, this is handled automatically for you. In Amazon Web Services, this can be handled semi-automatically for you by using Auto-Scaling Groups, for which you can set rules on when to start and stop instances based on load averages or other metrics.

Your application layer is built on top of a base image that you created and may also contain scripts that tell it to update or add more code to that running instance. It should be designed to be as modular as possible and enable you to launch new modules without impacting the old ones. This layer should be behind a proxy system that hides how many actual modules are in existence. Amazon enables you to do this by providing a simple service known as Elastic Load Balancing, or ELB.

Using Elastic Load Balancing

Amazon's **Elastic Load Balancing**, or **ELB**, can be used simply and cheaply to proxy all requests to your modules based on their Instance ID. **ELB** is even smart enough to proxy only to systems that are actually live and processing, so you don't have to worry about server failures causing long-term service disruptions. **ELB** can be set up to proxy HTTP or standard TCP ports. This is simple to accomplish using code and can even be done on the actual instance as it starts, so it can register itself when it's ready to accept connections. This, combined with **Auto-Scaling Groups**, can quickly and easily scale your applications seamlessly in a matter of minutes without any human interaction. If, however, you want more control over your applications, you can just use **ELB** without **Auto-Scaling Groups** and launch new modules manually.

Creating and managing ELBs is quite easy to accomplish using boto and the `elbadmin` command-line tool that I created, which comes with boto. Detailed usage of this tool can be found by running it on the command line with no arguments:

```
% elbadmin
Usage: elbadmin [options] [command]
Commands:
    list|ls                        List all Elastic Load Balancers
    delete    <name>               Delete ELB <name>
    get       <name>               Get all instances associated
                                   with <name>
    create    <name>               Create an ELB
    add       <name> <instance>    Add <instance> in ELB <name>
    remove|rm <name> <instance>    Remove <instance> from ELB
                                   <name>
    enable|en <name> <zone>        Enable Zone <zone> for ELB
                                   <name>
    disable   <name> <zone>        Disable Zone <zone> for ELB
                                   <name>


Options:
  --version                 show program's version number and exit
  -h, --help                show this help message and exit
  -z ZONES, --zone=ZONES
                            Operate on zone
  -l LISTENERS, --listener=LISTENERS
                            Specify Listener in,out,proto
```

The first thing to do when starting out is to create a new ELB. This can be done simply as shown here:

```
% elbadmin -l 80,80,http -z us-east-1a create test
Name: test
DNS Name: test-68924542.us-east-1.elb.amazonaws.com

Listeners
---------
IN     OUT     PROTO
80     80      HTTP
```

```
Zones
----------
us-east-1a

Instances
----------
```

You must pass at least one listener and one zone as arguments to create the instance. Each zone takes the same distribution of requests, so if you don't have the same amount of servers in each zone, the requests will be distributed unevenly. For anything other than just standard HTTP, use the `tcp` protocol instead of `http`. Note the DNS Name returned by this command, which can also be retrieved by using the `elbadmin get` command. This command can also be used at a later time to retrieve all the zones and instances being proxied to by this specific ELB. The DNS Name can be pointed to by a CNAME in your own domain name. This *must* be a CNAME and not a standard A record because the domain name may point to multiple IP addresses, and those IP addresses may change over time.

Recently, Amazon also released support for adding SSL termination to an ELB by means of the HTTPS protocol. You can find instructions for how to do this on Amazon's web page. At the time of this writing, boto does not support this, so you need to use the command-line tools provided by Amazon to set this up. The most typical use for this will be to proxy port 80 to port 443 using HTTPS. Check with the boto home page for updates on how to do this using the `elbadmin` command-line script.

Adding Servers to the Load Balancer

After you have your ELB created, it's easy to add a new instance to route your incoming requests to. This can be done using the `elbadmin add` command:

```
% elbadmin add test i-2308974
```

This instance must be in an enabled zone for requests to be proxied. You can add instances that are not in an enabled zone, but requests are not proxied until you enable it. This can be used for debugging purposes because you can disable a whole zone of instances if you suspect a problem in that zone. Amazon does offer a service level agreement (SLA), ensuring that it will have 99% availability, but this is not limited to a single zone, thus at any given time, three of the four zones may be down. (Although this has never happened.)

It's generally considered a good idea to use at least two different zones in the event one of them fails. This enables you the greatest flexibility because you can balance out your requests and even take down a single instance at a time without effecting the service. From a developer's perspective, this is the most ideal situation you could ever have because you can literally do upgrades in a matter of minutes without having almost any impact to your customers by upgrading a single server at a time, taking it out of the load balancer while you perform the upgrade.

Although ELB can usually detect and stop proxying requests quickly when an instance fails, it's generally a good idea to remove an instance from the balancer before stopping it. If you're intentionally replacing an instance, you should first verify that the new instance is up and ready, add it to the load balancer, remove the old instance, and then kill it. This can be done with the following three commands provided in boto package:

```
% elbadmin add test i-2308974
% elbadmin rm test i-0983123
% kill_instance i-0983123
```

The last command actually terminates the instance, so be sure there's nothing on there you need to save, such as log files, before running this command. After each of these elbadmin commands, the full status of that load balancer is printed, so be sure before running the next command that the previous command succeeded. If a failure is reported, it's most likely because of an invalid instance ID, so be sure you're copying the instance IDs exactly. One useful tool for this process is the `list_instances` command, also provided in the boto package:

```
% list_instances
ID              Zone            Groups          Hostname
------------------------------------------------------------------
i-69c3e401      us-east-1a      Wordpress       ..compute-1.amazonaws.com
i-e4675a8c      us-east-1c      default         ..compute-1.amazonaws.com
i-e6675a8e      us-east-1d      default         ..compute-1.amazonaws.com
i-1a665b72      us-east-1a      default         ..compute-1.amazonaws.com
```

This command prints out the instance IDs, Zone, Security Groups, and public hostname of all instances currently running in your account, sorted ascending by start date. The last instances launched will be at the bottom of this list, so be sure to get the right instance when you're adding the newest one to your ELB. The combination of these powerful yet simple tools makes it easy to manage your instances and ELB by hand.

Although the load balancer is cheap (about 2.5 cents per hour plus bandwidth usage), it's not free. After you finish with your load balancer, remove it with the following command:

```
% elbadmin delete test
```

Automatically Registering an Instance with a Load Balancer

If you use a boto pyami instance, you can easily tell when an instance is finished loading by checking for the email sent to the address you specify in the `Notification` section of the configuration metadata passed in at startup. An example of a configuration section using gmail as the smtp server is shown here:

```
[Notification]
smtp_host = smtp.gmail.com
smtp_port = 587
```

```
smtp_tls = True
smtp_user = my-sending-user@gmail.com
smtp_pass = MY_PASSWORD
smtp_from = my-sending-user@gmail.com
smtp_to = my-recipient@gmail.com
```

Assuming there were no error messages, your instance should be up and fully functional. If you want the instance to automatically register itself when it's finished loading, add an installer to your queue at the end of your other installers. Ensure that this is done after all your other installers finish so that you add only the instance if it's safe. A simple installer can be created like the one here for ubuntu:

```
from boto.pyami.installers.ubuntu.installer import Installer
import boto
class ELBRegister(Installer):
    """Register this instance with a specific ELB"""
    def install(self):
        """Register with the ELB"""
        # code here to verify that you're
        # successfully installed and running
        elb_name = boto.config.get("ELB", "name")
        elb = boto.connect_elb()
        b = ebl.get_all_load_balancers(elb_name)
        if len(b) <1:
            raise Exception, "No Load balancer found"
        b = b[0]

        b.register_instances([boto.config.get_instance
        ➥("instance_id")])
        def main(self):
        self.install()
```

This requires you to set your configuration file on boot to contain a section called ELB with one value name that contains the name of the balancer to register to. You could also easily adapt this installer to use multiple balancers if that's what you need. Although this installer will be called only if all the other installers before it suc-ceed, it's still a good idea to test anything important before actually registering yourself with your balancer.

HTTP and REST

Now that you have your instances proxied and ready to accept requests, it's time to think about how to accept requests. In general, it's a bad practice to reinvent the wheel when you can just use another protocol that's already been established and well tested. There are entire books on using HTTP and REST to build your own SaaS, but this section provides the basic details.

Although you can use HTTP in many ways, including SOAP, the simplest of all these is Representational State Transfer (REST), which was officially defined in 2000 by Roy Fielding in a doctoral dissertation "Architectural Styles and the Design of Network-based Software Architectures" (http://www.ics.uci.edu/~fielding/pubs/dissertation/top.htm). It uses HTTP as a communication medium and is designed around the fundamental idea that HTTP already defines how to handle method names, authentication, and many other things needed when working with these types of communications. HTTP is split into two different sections: the header and the body (not to be confused with the HTML `<head>` and `<body>` tags), each of which is fully used by REST.

This book uses REST and XML for most of the examples, but this is not the only option and may not even suite your specific needs. For example, SOAP is still quite popular for many people because of how well it integrates with Java. It also makes it easy for other developers to integrate with your APIs if you provide them with a Web Service Definition Language (WSDL) that describes exactly how a system should use your API. The important point here is that the HTTP protocol is highly supported across systems and is one of the easiest to use in many applications because much of the lower-level details, such as authentication, are already taken care of.

The Header

The HTTP header describes exactly who the message is designed for, and what method the user is instantiating on the recipient end. REST uses this header for multiple purposes. HTTP method

names can be used to define the method called and the arguments
(path) which is sent to that method. The HTTP header also
includes a name, which can be used to differentiate between applications running on the same port. This shouldn't be used for anything other than differentiating between applications because it's
actually the DNS name and shouldn't be used for anything other
than a representation of the server's address.

The method name and path are both passed into the application. Typically you want to use the path to define the module,
package, or object to use to call your function. The method name
is typically used to determine what function to call on that module, package, or object. Lastly, the path also contains additional
arguments after the question mark (?) that usually are passed in as
arguments to your function. Now take a look at a typical HTTP
request:

```
GET /module_name/id_argument?param1=value1&param2=value2
```

In this example, most applications would call `module_name.`
`get(id_argument,param1=value1,param2=value2)` or
`module_name.get(id_argument,{param1=value1,param2=value2})`.
By using this simple mapping mechanism, you're decoupling your
interface (the web API) from your actual code, and you won't
actually need to call your methods from the website. This helps
greatly when writing unit tests.

Many libraries out there can handle mapping a URI path to
this code, so you should try to find something that matches your
needs instead of creating your own. Although REST and RESTful
interfaces are defined as using only four methods, most proxies
and other systems, including every modern web browser, support
adding your own custom methods. Although many REST developers may frown on it, in general it does work, and when a simple
CRUD interface isn't enough, it's much better than overloading
an existing function to suit multiple needs. The following sections
reference some of the most common HTTP headers and how
you can use them in a REST API.

If-Match

The most interesting header that you can provide for is the If-Match header. This header can be used on any method to indicate that the request should be performed only if the conditions in the header represent the current object. This header can be exceptionally useful when you operate with databases that are eventually consistent, but in general, because your requests can be made in rapid succession, it's a good idea to allow for this so that they don't overwrite each other. One possible solution to this is to provide for a version number or memento on each object or resource that can then be used to ensure that the user knows what the value was before it replaces it.

In some situations, it may be good to require this field and not accept the special * case for anyone other than an administrative user. If you require this field to be sent and you receive a request that doesn't have it, you should respond with an error code of 412 (Precondition Failed) and give the users all they need to know to fill in this header properly. If the conditions in this header do not match, you *must* send back a 412 (Precondition Failed) response. This header is typically most used when performing PUT operations because those operations override what's in the database with new values, and you don't know if someone else may have already overridden what you thought was there.

If-Modified-Since

The If-Modified-Since header is exceptionally useful when you want the client to contain copies of the data so that they can query locally. In general, this is part of a caching system used by most browsers or other clients to ensure that you don't have to send back all the data if it hasn't been changed. The If-Modified-Since header takes an HTTP-date, which must be in GMT, and should return a 304 (Not Modified) response with no content.

If-Unmodified-Since

If you don't have an easy way to generate a memento or version ID for your objects, you can also allow for an If-Unmodified-Since header. This header takes a simple HTTP date, formatted in GMT, which is the date the resource was last retrieved by the client. This puts a lot of trust in the client, however, to indicate the proper date. It's generally best to use the If-Modified header instead, unless you have no other choice.

Accept

The Accept header is perhaps the most underestimated header in the entire arsenal. It can be used not only to handle what type of response to give (JSON, XML, and so on), but also to handle what API version you're dealing with. If you need to support multiple versions of your API, you can support this by attaching it to the content type. This can be done by extending the standard content types to include the API version number:

```
Accept: text/xml+app-1.0
```

This enables you to specify not only a revision number (in this case, 1.0) and content type, but also the name of the application so that you can ensure the request came from a client that knew who it was talking to. Traditionally, this header will be used to send either HTML, XML, JSON, or some other format representing the resource or collection being returned.

Authorization

The Authorization header can be used just like a standard HTTP authentication request, encoding both the password and the username in a base64 encoded string, or it can optionally be used to pass in an authentication token that eventually expires. Authentication types vary greatly, so it's up to you to pick the right version for your application. The easiest method is by using the basic HTTP authentication, but then you are sending the username and password in every single request, so you *must* ensure that you're using SSL if you're concerned about security.

In contrast, if you choose to use a token or signing-based authentication method, the user has to sign the request based on some predetermined key shared between the client and server. In this event, you can hash the entire request in a short string that validates that the request did indeed come from the client. You also need to make sure to send the username or some other unique identifier in this header, but because it's not sending a reversible hash of the password, it's *relatively* safe to send over standard HTTP. We won't go into too much depth here about methods of hashing because there are a wide variety of hashing methods all well-documented online.

The Body

The body of any REST call is typically either XML or JSON. In some situations, it's also possible to send both, depending on the Accept header. This process is fairly well documented and can be used to not only define what type of response to return, but also what version of the protocol the client is using. The body of any request to the system should be in the same format as the response body.

In my applications, I typically use XML only because there are some powerful tools, such as XSLT, that can be used as middleware for authorization purposes. Many clients, however, like the idea of using JSON because most languages serialize and deserialize this quite well. REST doesn't specifically require one form of representation over the other and even enables for the clients to choose which type they want, so this is up to you as the application developer to decide what to support.

Methods

REST has two distinct, important definitions that you need to understand before continuing. A **collection** is a group of objects; in your case this usually is synonymous with either a class in object terms, or a table in database terms. A **resource** is a specific instantiation of a collection, which can be thought of as an instance in object terms or a row in a table in database terms. This book also uses the term **property** to define a single property or attribute on an instance in object terms, or a cell in database terms. Although you can indeed create your own methods, in general you can probably fit most of your needs into one of the method calls listed next.

GET

The GET method is the center of all requests for information. Just like a standard webpage, applications can use the URL in two parts; everything before the first question mark (?) is used as the resource to access, and everything after that is used as query parameters on that resource. The URL pattern can be seen here:

```
/collection_name/resource_id/property_name?query
```

The `resource_id` `property_name` and `query` in the preceding example are all optional, and the query can be applied to any level of the tree. Additionally, this tree could expand exponentially downward if the property is considered a reference. Now take a simple example of a request on a web blog to get all the comments of a post specified by POST-ID submitted in 2010. This query could look like this:

```
/posts/POST-ID/comments?submitted=2010%
```

The preceding example queries for the `posts` collection for a specific post identified as POST-ID. It then asks for just the property named `comments` and filters specifically for items with the property `submitted` that matches `2010%`.

Responses to this method call can result in a redirection if the resource is actually located at a different path. This can be achieved by sending a proper redirect response code and a `Location` header that points to the actual resource.

A GET on the root of the collection should return a list of all resources under that path. It can also have the optional ?query on the end to limit these results. It's also a good idea to implement some sort of paging system so that you can return all the results instead of having to limit because of HTTP timeouts. In general, it's never a good idea to have a request that takes longer then a few seconds to return on average because most clients will assume this is an error. In general, most proxy systems will time out any connection after a few minutes, so if your result takes longer than a minute, it's time to implement paging.

If you use XML as your communication medium, think about implementing some sort of ATOM style next links. These simple tags give you a cursor to the next page of results, so you can store a memento or token of your query and allow your application to pick up where it left off. This token can then be passed in via a query parameter to the same URL that was used in the original request. In general, your next link should be the *full* URL to the next page of results. By doing this, you leave yourself open to the largest range of possibilities for implementing your paging system, including having the ability to perform caching on the next page of results, so you can actually start building it before the client even asks for it.

If you use Amazon Web Services and SimpleDB, it's generally a good idea to use the next_token provided by a SimpleDB query as your memento. You also need to provide enough information in the next link to build the entire original query, so just using the URL that was originally passed and adding the next_token to the end of the query is generally a good idea. Of course if this is a continuation, you have to replace the original next_token with the new one.

Performing a GET operation on the root path (/) should return a simple index that states all the available resource types and the URLs to those resource types. This machine-readable code should be simple enough that documentation is not required for new developers to build a client to your system. This methodology enables you to change around the URLs of the base resources without modifying your client code, and it enables you build a highly adaptable client that may adapt to new resources easily without making any modifications.

PUT

The HTTP definition of a PUT is *replace*, so if you use this on the base URL of a resource collection, you're actually requesting that everything you don't pass in is deleted, anything new is created, and any existing resources passed in are modified. Because PUT is logically equivalent to a SET operation, this is typically not allowed on a collection.

A PUT on a resource should update or create the record with a specific ID. The section after the collection name is considered the ID of the resource, and if a GET is performed after the PUT, it should return the resource that was just created or updated. PUT is intended as an entire replacement, but in general, if you don't pass in an attribute, that is assumed to be "don't change," whereas if you pass in an empty value for the attribute, you are actually requesting it to be removed or set to blank.

A PUT on a property should change just that specific property for the specified resource. This can be incredibly useful when you're putting files to a resource because those typically won't serialize very well into XML without lots of base64 conversions.

Most PUT requests should return either a 201 `Created` with the object that was just created, which may have been modified due to server application logic, or a 204 `No Content` if there are no changes to the original object request. If you operate with a database that has eventual consistency, it may also be a good idea to instead return a 202 `Accepted` request to indicate that the client should try to fetch the resource at a later time. You should also return an estimate of how long it will be before this object is created.

POST

A POST operation on a collection is defined as a *creation request*. This is the user requesting to add a new resource to the collection without specifying a specific ID. In general, you want to either return a redirection code and a Location header, or at the least the ID of the object you just created (if not the whole object serialized in your representation).

A POST operation on a resource should actually create a sub-object of that resource; although, this is often not used. Traditionally, browsers don't handle changing form actions to PUT, so a POST is typically treated as a special form of a PUT that takes form-encoded values.

A POST operation on a property is typically used only for uploading files but could also be used as appending a value to a list. In general, this could be considered an append operation, but if your property is a single value, it's probably safe to assume that the client wanted this to be a PUT, not a POST.

DELETE

A DELETE operation on a collection is used to drop the entire collection, so you probably don't want to allow this. If you do allow it, this request should be treated as a request to remove every single resource in the collection.

A DELETE operation on a specific resource is simply a request to remove that specific resource. If there are errors in this request, the client should be presented with a message explaining why the request failed. The resulting error code should explain if the request can be issued again, or if the user is required to perform another operation before reissuing the request. The most typical error message back from this request is a 409 Conflict, which indicates that another resource is referencing this resource, and the server is refusing to cascade the delete request. A DELETE may also return a 202 Accepted response if the database has eventual consistency.

A DELETE operation on a specific property is identical to a PUT with an empty value for that property. It can be used to delete just a single property from a resource instead of having to send a PUT request. This can also be used as a differentiation between setting a value to blank and removing the value entirely. In programming terms, this the difference between an empty string and None or Null.

HEAD

A HEAD request on any URL should return the exact same headers as a standard GET request but shouldn't send back the body. This is typically used to get a count of the number of results in a response without retrieving the actual results. In my applications, I use this to send an additional header X-Results, which contains the number of results that would have been retrieved.

OPTIONS

An OPTIONS request on any URL returns the methods allowed to be performed on this URL. This can return just the headers with the additional Accept header, but it can also return a serialized version of them in the body of the results that describes what each method actually does. This response should be customized for the specific user that made the request, so if the user is not allowed to perform DELETE operations on the given resource for any reason, that option should not be returned. This allows the client to specifically hide options that the users aren't allowed to perform so that they don't get error responses.

Authorization Layer

The authorization layer sits just above your application layer but is still on the sever. In most application systems, this is actually integrated directly with your application layer. Although this is generally accepted, it doesn't provide for as much flexibility, and it's a lot harder to code application logic and authorization in the same location. Additionally, if you go to change your authentication, you now have to worry about breaking your application layer and your authentication layer. If you build this as a separate layer, you can most likely pull all authorization directly out of a database, so you don't have to worry about changing your code just for a minor change in business logic.

If you use XML for your object representation, you can use XSLT for your authorization layer, and use some custom tags to pull out this authorization logic directly from your database. If you use an application framework such as Django or Ruby Rails, chances are you already have this layer built for you, either directly or in a third-party module. Check your specific language for how to build your own extensions for XSLT. When you can build your own extensions into your XSLT processor, not only can your filters

be retrieved from a shared filesystem so that you can update them
without redistributing them to each of your servers, but you can
also pull the exact details about authorization from there. These
XSLT filters can be used to specifically hide elements of the
response XML that the user shouldn't see. The following example
code assumes you've already built a function called `hasAuth` that
takes three arguments, authorization type (read, write, delete),
object type, and property name:

```
<xsl:stylesheet version="1.0"
   xmlns:xsl="http://www.w3.org/1999/XSL/Transform"
   xmlns:app="url/to/app">
  <!-- By default pass through all XML elements -->
  <xsl:template match="@*|node()" priority="-10">
    <xsl:copy>
      <xsl:apply-templates select="@*|node()"/>
    </xsl:copy>
  </xsl:template>

  <!-- Object-level permissions -->
  <xsl:template match="/node()">
    <xsl:if test="app:hasAuth('read', current())">
      <xsl:copy>
        <xsl:apply-templates select="@*|node()" mode="property"/>
      </xsl:copy>
    </xsl:if>
  </xsl:template>

  <!-- Property-level permissions -->
  <xsl:template match="node()" mode="property">
    <xsl:if test="app:hasAuth('read', .., current() )">
      <xsl:copy>
        <xsl:apply-templates select="@*|node()" />
      </xsl:copy>
    </xsl:if>
  </xsl:template>

</xsl:stylesheet>
```

The preceding example is for output from your server, but you
could easily adapt this to any method you need by changing the

first argument to each `hasAuth` call to whatever method this is filtering on. You could also easily use this as a base template and pass in the method name to the filter. This example assumes you have an input XML that looks something like the following example:

```
<User id="DEAD-BEAF">
    <name>Foo</name>
    <username>foo</username>
    <email>someone@example.com</email>
</User>
```

Using this example as a base, you could also build filters to operate with JSON or any other representation, but XSLT still seems to be the simplest because you can also use it to create more complex authorization systems, including a complicated group-based authentication, and it can be used to include filters within other filters. If you do need to support sending and receiving information in other formats, you can always use another filter layer on top of your application to translate between them.

Client Layer

After you build your complex application server, you need to focus on making that simple WebAPI usable to your clients. Although developers may be fine with talking XML or JSON to your service, the average user probably won't be, so you need to build a client layer. The biggest concept to understand about this layer is that *you cannot trust anything it sends*. To do so means you're authenticating the client, and no matter what kind of protection you try to do, it's impossible to ensure that the information you get from any client is *your* client.

You must assume that everything you send to your client is viewable by the user. Don't assume the client will hide things that the user shouldn't see. Almost every web service-based vulnerability comes from just blindly trusting data coming from a client, which can often be formed specifically for the purpose of making your application do something you didn't intend. This is the entire basis behind the SQL injection issues many websites still suffer from. Because of these types of security concerns, you have to ensure that all authentication and authorization happens *outside* of this layer.

You can develop this layer in several different ways, the easiest of which is to expose the API and allow other third-party companies to build their own clients. This is the way that companies such as Twitter handled creating its clients. You can also make your own clients, but by having a well-documented and public-facing API, you expose yourself to having other people and companies developing their own clients. In general, you have to be ready for this event, so it's always a good idea to ensure that the client layer has only the access you want it to have. You can never tell for sure that the client you're talking to is one that you've developed.

Browser-Based Clients

With the release of the HTML5 specifications and local database storage, it's become increasingly easier to make rich HTML and JavaScript-based clients. Although not all browsers support HTML5, and even less support local databases, it's still possible to create a rich experience for the user with just a browser.

Although some browsers do support cross-site Ajax requests, it's generally not a good idea to rely on that. Instead, use something such as Apache or NginX to proxy a sub-URL that can be used by your JavaScript client. Don't be afraid to use Ajax requests for loading data. It's also a good idea to build up a good base set of functions or use an existing library to handle all your serializing and deserializing of your objects, and making Ajax requests and handling caching of objects. You don't want to hit your server more often than absolutely required because HTTP requests are relatively expensive. So it's a good idea to keep a local cache if your browser supports it, but don't forget to either keep the memento provided, or the time when it was retrieved so that you can send an If-Modified-Since header with each request.

If you use a JavaScript-based client layer, it's strongly recommended that you use something such as jQuery to handle all your cross-browser issues. Even if you hate using JavaScript, jQuery can make creating this client layer simple. This, however, can be tricky because it relies a lot on the browsers feature support, which can be entirely out of your own control. Additionally, this generally doesn't work well for mobile devices because those browsers have much less JavaScript support, and they typically don't have much memory at all.

If you don't want to use JavaScript, Flash is another option. Flash has several libraries for communicating over HTTP using XML, so you should use something that already exists there if you want to support this. If you don't like the representations that these libraries supply, you can also use the `Accept` header and a different version number to allow your system to support multiple different representations. Flash has the advantage of being easy to code in, in addition to providing a much more unified interface. It's also quite heavy and can be easy to forget that this is an untrusted layer. Most mobile devices don't support Flash, so if that's important to you, you need to stick to JavaScript and HTML.

Another option if you don't want to use either HTML/ JavaScript or Flash is using a Java Applet. Although there's a lot of possibilities that you can do with these little applets, they're also heavy weight, and if you're trying to get it to work on mobile browsers, this just won't work. Additionally, few mobile devices support either Flash or Java Applets, so if you're going for the most support, you probably want to stick with HTML and JavaScript. Still, if you need more features than Flash or HTML can support, this might be a good option for you.

Native Applications

If you've ever used Twitter, chances are you know that not only is there a web interface, but there are also dozens of native client applications that work on a wide variety of platforms. In your system, you can make as many different client applications as you want to, so eventually you may want to branch out and make some native applications for your users. If you're building that wonderful new electronic filing cabinet to organize your entire world online, it might be a good idea to also provide some native apps, such as an iPhone application that also communicates to the same API as every other client to bring you the same content wherever you are in the world.

Even if you're not the one building native applications, it may still be a good idea to let other third parties have this option. If you make your API public and let third-party companies make money from creating client layers, you not only provide businesses with a reason to buy into your app, but you also don't need to do any of the development work yourself to increase your growth. Although this may not seem intuitive because people are making a profit off your system, every penny they earn is also bringing you business, and chances are they're marketing as well. Not only does this give your users more options for clients, but it also gives your system more exposure and potential clients.

Summary

Just like cloud providers give you *hardware as a service*, developing your applications as *Software as a Service* gives you another level of benefit, expanding your applications beyond the standard services. By expanding your application to be a service instead of just software, you're giving yourself a huge advantage over any competition. Services are always growing and have infinite potential to keep customers. SaaS gives your customers the same advantage that the cloud gives to you, low initial cost and a reason to keep paying. Everything from business-level applications to the newest games are being transformed from standard single-person applications into services. Don't let your development time go to waste by developing something that will be out of date by the time it's released.

3

Cloud Service Providers

Many of the patterns and concepts in this book pertain to cloud computing in general, and you can usually apply the examples to one of many different providers. This chapter covers the many different services offered by some of these cloud providers. Although most cloud providers offer many common services, some providers offer unique services. If you're looking for something specific, check around before settling on one specific offering.

Although many cloud provider solutions are available, there are actually only two different types of solutions. The traditional infrastructure services provided by companies such as Rackspace and Amazon offer you the most flexibility, but you also have to build your entire platform to work with these systems. The platform services offered by Google handle a lot of that for you, but then you are severely limited by what you can do.

Amazon Web Services

Of all the cloud providers, Amazon Web Services by far offers the most services and support. Amazon was the original pioneer into the field and has been the largest driving force in the area. It started with just a few services and has grown to now hosting almost everything you could want. The API behind these services is constantly evolving and adapting to new requirements. Amazon provides a simple REST interface and a more complicated SOAP interface for all services.

Amazon's best asset by far is the large developer community. This community has been growing and developing new concepts for the ever-changing cloud computing world. Amazon sponsored numerous events worldwide and has a team devoted to the open source community. Most of the development libraries and support code have been created and maintained by open source developers. This method of developing the API and simply giving the developers a nudge in the right direction often leads to surprising new results and often helps Amazon design each new cloud service. Unlike many companies that try to tell their developers how to design their applications, this solution enables developers to decide what they want, and then Amazon can add solutions based on what the community needs.

All Amazons services are broken into **regions**. A region is a single geographic location where the servers are stored; however, they might not necessarily be stored at the same data center. Several regions exist, including two in the United States and one in Europe. Most services are available in all regions, although some actually supersede regions entirely (such as CloudFront). Regions can be further broken into **zones**, which are actual data centers within a region. Some services supersede zones because you're not guaranteed anything other than at least one zone will be available at all times. All services charge you data usage between regions, and some will also charge you for transfers between zones. Because these zones are physically separated, the latency between zones will also be higher than to services within the same zone. If the service you use doesn't have a zone specification, it automatically communicates using the closest zone without any manual intervention.

The biggest concern that users have with diving in deep with Amazon Web Services is that they are afraid of having their systems rely on a third party to operate. Fortunately, Amazon built its web services using *the same infrastructure it uses for its own applications.* It relies entirely on its systems and brings in millions of dollars an hour, so when Amazon Web Services breaks down, its systems are also offline.

Simple Storage Service (S3)

One of the first services Amazon introduced was Simple Storage Service (S3), a distributed file storage system. Unlike a traditional network attached storage (NAS), this system simply offers a way to store and retrieve file-like objects. Although you can store some basic metadata about the objects, it's not a traditional filesystem and does not support locking, linking, or even directories.

Perhaps the most confusing aspect of this storage system is that it's also only eventually consistent, meaning that your writes are done asynchronously in the background, and the object you wrote is not guaranteed to be there immediately after you fire off a write. Typically there is almost no lag time between posting a file and when it becomes available, but there's no guarantee. The only guarantee provided is that your object will *eventually* be there.

As you can see in Figure 3.1, S3 is broken into buckets and keys, with no subbuckets or folders. Bucket names are globally unique across all accounts. They also must be Domain Name System (DNS) safe, meaning they cannot contain any characters other then lowercase characters, numbers, and dashes. This enables you to access your bucket directly from the web with a hostname such as `bucket-name.s3.amazonaws.com`.

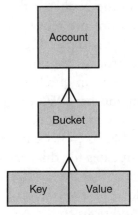

Figure 3.1   The S3 hierarchy.

Buckets can be shared giving read and/or write access to other accounts and can even be made public. This complex access control system also enables access to be granted on the bucket or key level, so you can share only a specific key if you don't want to share the whole bucket.

There are also many ways to provide access to these buckets. Because all services use a simple URL signing method, you can also create a signed URL that is safely distributable to your end users without giving them any secret keys, and you can even attach a time limit for how long the URL is active. Additionally, S3 has the capability to create URLs to POST data to, enabling you to let your users store files directly in S3 without going through a proxy server.

S3 is also the only AWS cloud service that comes with a service level agreement (SLA). This ensures that the service remains up at least 99.9% of the time. Amazon also promises that no keys will be lost. So far, it has completely lived up to this agreement. It has never had a single confirmed report of a lost key in the several years it has been in operation (http://aws.amazon.com/s3-sla/).

The billing for usage within S3 is split into three separate pieces. The first piece is storage per month, which is actually calculated throughout the entire month, so you pay for the total storage-months, not just what's in the bucket at the end of the month. Next, you pay a small amount per request you make to S3, although this is insignificant compared to the rest of your bill. The last thing you are charged for is data transfer in and out of Amazon's data centers. This is unique because it means you don't pay for transferring from another AWS service such as EC2, as long as they're both in the same region.

One of the first uses of S3 is to back up existing systems. As such, one of the recent updates for this service introduced two important features. The first feature enables versioning within S3. This enables you to upload new versions of a single key while still retaining the originals. Additions to the API now enable you to specify a version to retrieve or defaults to the latest if you don't specify one. The second feature enables you to prevent deletions of keys without specifying an authentication token. Even if your API keys are compromised, your data will still be there because your keys alone cannot remove anything. With these two features combined, you can create a read-only bucket that contains every version of any file you send to it.

A recent modification of this service is **Reduced Redundancy Storage** (RRS). This is exactly the same as S3, except your data is stored on less partitions, which reduces the overall data redundancy and stability for a reduction in cost. For files that you are less concerned about, you may elect to use this service instead.

After you install and configure boto, it's easy to connect and start using S3. You begin by creating a connection to S3 using the `connect_s3` method of the boto module:

```
>>> import boto
>>> s3 = boto.connect_s3()
```

After you connect, you need to create a new bucket to start storing files. Do this using the `create_bucket` method of the connection you just created:

```
>>> bucket = s3.create_bucket("my-test-bucket")
```

Note that because S3 buckets are *globally unique*, you cannot create a bucket with the same name that anyone else using S3 has used. If you copy the previous code directly, you'll most likely end up with an error that looks like the following:

```
Traceback (most recent call last):
  File "<stdin>", line 1, in ?
  File "boto/connection.py", line 285, in create_bucket
    raise S3CreateError(response.status, response.reason)
boto.exception.S3CreateError: S3Error[409]: Conflict
```

You need to choose a new bucket name. It's generally accepted to prefix your bucket names with your company name, or even your own username to ensure uniqueness. Of course, you can also use your public key, which is your access key id, available in the `aws_access_key_id` property of the S3 connection object:

```
>>> bucket = s3.create_bucket("%s-my-test-bucket" %
➥as3.aws_access_key_id)
```

This is the only way to be absolutely ensure you're not going to get a conflict error because there's almost no reason anyone else would create a bucket using your access key id as a prefix. This naming convention is used by some libraries in boto (such as the SDB Blob property) to generate unique bucket names with suffixes.

After you have your bucket, you can create new keys within this bucket. Although S3 doesn't support directories, it does support splitting up keys by a delimiter to emulate a typical directory structure. You can search only by prefixes; you can't do any sort of full-text searching within S3, so you need to name your keys so that you can easily identify them. For example, assume you're storing a video about how to use this S3 interface. You could say this is a tutorial, about aws, about boto, and specifically about s3:

```
>>> key = bucket.new_key("tutorials/aws/boto/s3.m4v")
```

You could then upload the contents of this video from a file in your current directory called "s3.m4v" by using the set_contents_from_filename function:

```
>>> key.set_contents_from_filename("s3.m4v")
```

Alternatively, you could use the set_contents_from_file function and pass in the file object:

```
>>> key.set_contents_from_file(open("s3.m4v", "r"))
```

This file object must be seekable because boto first computes an MD5 sum of the file to send along with the file contents. This ensures that the file contents remain intact as they're pushed to S3.

You can also set the contents of the file from a simple string:

```
>>> key.set_contents_from_string("My Content")
```

This is fundamentally equivalent to using the StringIO class to wrap your string before sending it to set_contents_from_file:

```
>>> from StringIO import StringIO
>>> key.set_contents_from_file(StringIO("My Content"))
```

If you need to send a file directly to S3 without having boto calculate any of the md5 or length headers, you need to set those fields manually in your file and just call `send_file` directly:

```
>>> key.md5 = my_md5_sum
>>> key.base64md5 = my_b64_md5
>>> key.size = my_file_size
>>> key.send_file(open("s3.m4v", "r"))
```

Using the `send_file` will bypass everything that seeks the file object, so you don't need to worry about the file being hit more then once there. This can greatly help to improve performance if you need to send large files that aren't easily seekable.

After you have a file in S3, you can access it by using the `lookup` method on the bucket:

```
>>> key = bucket.lookup("tutorials/aws/boto/s3.m4v")
```

If you want to list all your keys within a bucket, you can do that using the `list` function:

```
>>> for key in bucket.list():
...     print key.name
tutorials/aws/boto/s3.m4v
```

Of course, if you have a lot of files in this bucket, it may not be feasible to look through every file—for example, if you just want to list all the base prefixes in this bucket. As discussed before, S3 doesn't have directories but does let you list through keys selectively by offering a prefix and a delimiter:

```
>>> for key in bucket.list(prefix="", delimiter="/"):
...     print key.name
tutorials/
```

Only the base directories will be listed, not everything. This doesn't even give you your keys, just all the prefixes you can use. The key returned isn't actually a key, but simply a placeholder for that prefix. You can determine this to be true by noting the trailing delimiter (in this case a "/"), or you can also check to see that the size of the key was indeed zero:

```
>>> print key.size
0
```

Next, drill down and list everything under the prefix
"tutorials/":

```
>>> for key in bucket.list(prefix="tutorials/", delimiter="/"):
...     print key.name
tutorials/aws/
```

Now you see there's a prefix under "tutorials/" called
"tutorials/aws/"; you can continue listing everything under the
"tutorials/aws/" prefix:

```
>>> for key in bucket.list(prefix="tutorials/aws/", delimiter="/"):
...     print key.name
tutorials/aws/boto/
```

And finally, down to your boto prefix:

```
>>> for key in bucket.list(prefix="tutorials/aws/boto/",
delimiter="/"):
...     print key.name
tutorials/aws/boto/s3.m4v
```

Of course, printing out the name is probably not all you want to
do, so now explore some of the other things you can do with the
key object. Because S3 is web-accessible, one cool feature you can
use is to create signed URLs to pass along to clients. This can be
done by calling the generate_url function with the length of time
this URL should be active for in seconds. For example, do the following to generate a URL that can be accessed for the next 30
seconds:

```
>>> print key.generate_url(30)
https://...s3.amazonaws.com/tutorials/aws/boto/s3.m4v?...
```

You can make the file publicly visible without requiring a signa-
ture by using the make_public function:

```
>>> key.make_public()
```

You can also fetch the contents of the key directly to a file:

```
>>> key.get_contents_to_filename("s3.m4v")
```

Or use a file object directly, including a temporary file:

```
>>> from tempfile import TemporaryFile
>>> f = TemporaryFile()
>>> key.get_contents_to_file(f)
```

You can also get the contents directly as a string:

```
>>> key_string = key.get_contents_as_string()
```

After you finish with the key, you can remove it using the `delete` function:

```
>>> key.delete()
```

You can also remove the bucket when you finish using it with the same `delete` function, this time on the bucket object:

```
>>> bucket.delete()
```

CloudFront

CloudFront is built on top of S3 and requires a bucket to copy files to. Instead of simply hosting files out of S3 to your end users, you may elect to put this on top and have your files served from Amazon's **Content Distribution Network**. This network has edge locations all over the globe and provides you with a single DNS name that automatically chooses the closest point to host files from (see Figure 3.2). This system also enables you two provide your own custom CNAME so that the files appear under your own domain.

The first adaptation of this service was the addition of streaming video sources. This enables you to provide an **RTMP** stream to your clients so that you can dynamically stream videos directly from CloudFront. This method of serving up videos not only helps to protect your videos from being downloaded directly, but it also enables you to provide the ability for your users to "scrub" to a specific part of your video and skip over parts without having to download the video first. This can become extremely useful when dealing with large videos and mobile devices.

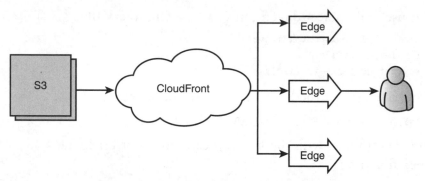

Figure 3.2   The CloudFront hierarchy.

The second addition to this service was enabling you to provide private distributions. This provides you with the ability to still secure your data and require signed URLs while tapping into the vast CDN provided by CloudFront. Just like with S3, you can create secure expiring URLs for distributing your content without opening it up to the whole world. Recently, this was also provided to streaming distributions, meaning you can now also provide secure video content to your users.

CloudFront also enables you to gather statistics on usage similar to any other analytics agent. This enables you to monitor usage so that you can see what's going on and who is viewing your content. These logs are available by accessing one of the standard APIs.

The biggest disadvantage of CloudFront is that updates may take up to 24 hours to reach all endpoints. This is only true of changed files, not newly added files, so a good workaround is to use a version number in your URL scheme for static content. However, if you need to ensure that an item is removed from public access immediately, this can be troublesome because deletes also may not propagate for up to 24 hours. If you store sensitive material such as this, it's a good idea to use the private distribution option and provide a middle-man URL signing system to enable access.

Accessing CloudFront from boto is simple; just like with S3, you start by connecting to the CloudFront interface:

```
>>> import boto
>>> cf = boto.connect_cloudfront()
```

You can use CloudFront to create streaming and static HTTP distributions:

```
>>> d = cf.create_distribution(
...     origin="my-bucket-name.s3.amazonaws.com",
...     enabled=True,
...     caller_reference="MyStaticDistribution",
...     cnames=["my-cname.example.org"]
...     )
>>> d = cf.create_streaming_distribution(
...     origin="my-bucket-name.s3.amazonaws.com",
...     enabled=True,
...     caller_reference="MyStaticDistribution",
...     cnames=["my-cname.example.org"]
...     )
```

Here the `cnames` and `caller_reference` are both optional, and you can always add a CNAME to your distribution later:

```
>>> d.update(cnames=["my-cname.example.org"])
```

You can also disable a distribution if you need to stop anyone from accessing files on that distribution temporarily:

```
>>> d.disable()
```

When you're ready to resume distributing, you can reenable the distribution again:

```
>>> d.enable()
```

CloudFront will serve files only out of the origin if those files are made public. To help with this, there's a nice convenience method on distributions to add files and make them public for you:

```
>>> d.add_object("my_video.m4v", open("my_video.m4v"))
```

One of the newer features of CloudFront is to invalidate specific file caches to force CloudFront to repull the file from the origin, or remove it entirely if it no longer exists in the origin. This can be incredibly useful if you're ever given a DMCA Takedown request, or in general if you need to forcibly push updates without having to wait the expire time you set on your original objects:

```
>>> cf.create_invalidation_request(d.id, [
...    "my_video.m4v",
...    "my_second_video.m4v"
... ])
```

This sends off your requests to CloudFront to have it invalidate the cached files, which may take a few minutes to hit all the edge locations in the network.

When you finish using your CloudFront distribution, you can remove it using the delete method:

```
>>> cf.delete()
```

Simple Queue Service (SQS)

SQS is a central service used to store and receive messages. You can use it to send communications between processes asynchronously. Queues promise no order but generally follow first-in-last-out (FIFO). Messages submitted to queues can be read by any AWS account that you grant access to. These messages are limited in size but, in general, can store enough information to trigger an event. They can be thought of as an **asynchronous procedure call**.

Messages also have a built in method to handle errors. At the time the message is read from the queue, it's hidden, or locked, from anyone else trying to read it for a set period of time. You also receive a message handle that must be used to delete the message, which can also be used to prolong the lock you acquired. This makes SQS the ideal system for processing tasks asynchronously.

As with all Amazon services, SQS is started by making a connection:

```
>>> import boto
>>> sqs = boto.connect_sqs()
```

The basic object in SQS is the queue, which can be created using the create_queue function:

```
>>> q = sqs.create_queue("myqueue")
```

Unlike S3, SQS queues are *not* globally unique but are shared only with your own account, so you don't need to worry about prefixing your queues with something unique to your account. Queues have a default timeout of 30 seconds for each new message, which can be set on creation. Following, you override this default time with 60 seconds:

```
>>> q = sqs.create_queue("myqueue", 60)
```

The preceding queue would have a default timeout of 60 seconds. You can see the default timeout on a queue by calling the get_timeout method:

```
>>> print q.get_timeout()
60
```

Of course, if you already have the queue created, you can just use the lookup function:

```
>>> q = sqs.lookup("myqueue")
```

Next, you want to create a new message in your Queue. By default, you can send any message string as plain text to the queue:

```
>>> from boto.sqs.message import Message
>>> m = Message()
>>> m.set_body("Hello SQS!")
>>> q.write(m)
```

Although this is useful if you're sending basic messages, you may want to set a custom message class to handle the data you're sending. boto comes with a few Message classes, and you can also make your own by extending the boto.sqs.message.Message class. One useful message class is the JSONMessage class, which enables you to specify almost any basic Python object to serialize in the JSON format. You can write this message to your queue the same way you wrote the standard one:

```
>>> from boto.sqs.jsonmessage import JSONMessage
>>> m = JSONMessage()
>>> m["my_string"] = "Hello"
>>> m["my_list"] = ["a", "list", "of", "items"]
>>> m["my_dict"] = {"key": "value"}
>>> q.write(m)
```

If you want to know how many messages are in a queue, you can use the count function to gather an approximate number of messages remaining to be read:

```
>>> print q.count()
1
```

You can treat the JSONMessage as any standard dictionary, with key-value pairs, and you can set any standard Python data types (nonobjects) as values. This includes strings, integers, lists, and dictionaries. These types are automatically encoded to JSON format as long as you're running at least Python 2.6 or have the simplejson module installed.

Reading from the queue can be done using the read function. Before you call this function, however, you should ensure that your queue uses the same message class that you're writing to this queue by default. This example uses the JSONMessage class, so you need to set that as the message handler by using the set_message_class function:

```
>>> q.set_message_class(JSONMessage)
>>> msg = q.read()
>>> print msg["my_string"]
"Hello"
```

A good rule to follow when using SQS is to not delete your message until you've dealt with what the message wanted you to do. Messages are marked as invisible for the specified visibility timeout after your read them, which means you have that amount of time to either handle what you need to do and delete the message, or update the invisibility timeout again to keep the message hidden for another bit of time. This can be done by calling the change_visibility function:

```
>>> msg.change_visibility(60)
```

You have the message hidden for *an additional* 60 seconds from the time you submit this call. This gives you some additional time to process your instructions, and then when you're ready, you can delete the message:

```
>>> msg.delete()
```

After you finish with your queue, you can delete it, too:

```
>>> q.delete()
```

Elastic Compute Cloud (EC2)

When Amazon jumped into the area of virtualized servers, it started with a simple service built off of Xen and took it a level further by adding APIs around common tasks. Unlike traditional virtual servers, these instances launch based on an image. This image is read-only, so the instance makes a copy of the image at the initial boot. After the instance is terminated, the modified local copy is lost. This introduces the concept of **disposable instances**. Instead of wasting lots of time dissecting how to fix a broken instance, all you need to do is terminate the troubled instance and launch a new one. No matter how much damage is done to your running instance, the image you started from will never be modified.

Anything that needs to be stored long term needs to be pulled out of another service, such as S3. Instances are also given some configuration data, and there's also an API to pass in custom configuration data that is available to the instance after it's launched. Some images use this instance data to enable you to pass in a custom script to be run at boot, which can bootstrap your instance and install your custom services from a basic image. Others use this instance data to simply configure how the instance is used, specifying things such as your AWS credentials and which SQS queue to listen on.

Although Amazon does have a few images it controls and maintains, the large majority of the images used by developers are actually based on community-supplied images. The easiest way to create your own custom image is by starting up an existing image and then bundling it up to a new image after you have everything set up the way you want. There are hundreds of prebuilt images already in the community that are free to use and hosted out of Amazon's reliable S3 service. These images can be up to 10GB and are essentially just a root partition. Another drive is also provided to your instance that is a large temporary disk that can be used to store instance-level data for use in your processing.

By default, all instances are provided with a random internal IP address within the Amazon network, and a random external IP address within Amazon's block of available IPs. Amazon also offers a service called **Elastic IP** in which you may reserve an IP address that you can then attach to any instance you have running. As long as the IP is attached to an instance, you pay nothing additional for it, but if you reserve an IP without having it attached, you pay a small fee to continue to have it reserved for you.

Amazon now offers Windows-based images that can be used to run your standard windows virtual systems. These instances are created with an administrator account you specify at boot and let you log in via Remote Desktop to manage your instance.

Just like all Amazon services, the first step to using EC2 with boto is to create your connection object:

```
>>> import boto
>>> ec2 = boto.connect_ec2()
```

By default, EC2 operates in the us-east-1 region, but you can see all available regions by calling the get_all_regions function:

```
>>> for region in ec2.get_all_regions():
...     print region
RegionInfo:us-east-1
RegionInfo:us-west-1
RegionInfo:eu-west-1
```

Given one of these regions, you can initiate a new connection using the connect method:

```
>>> ec2 = region.connect()
```

Next, you need to create your security group in which you'll launch your instances:

```
>>> group = ec2.create_security_group("development", "Dev Servers")
```

Because this is your development group, just SSH to everyone:

```
>>> group.authorize(ip_protocol="TCP",
...     from_port=22,
...     to_port=22,
...     cidr_ip="0.0.0.0/0"
... )
```

You can also open up ports to other security groups, including security groups in other users AWS accounts by passing in another group object into the src_group parameter:

```
>>> from boto.sqs.securitygroup import SecurityGroup
>>> other_group = SecurityGroup()
>>> other_group.name = "OtherGroupName"
>>> other_group.owner_id = "123456"
>>> group.add_rule(ip_protocol="TCP",
...     from_port=22,
...     to_port=22,
...     src_group=other_group
... )
```

If you want to later remove these rules, you can do so using the remove_rule function:

```
>>> group.revoke(ip_protocol="TCP",
...     from_port=22,
...     to_port=22,
...     cidr_ip="0.0.0.0/0"
... )
>>> group.revoke(ip_protocol="TCP",
...     from_port=22,
...     to_port=22,
...     src_group=other_group
... )
```

Next, you need to create an SSH key-pair so that you can log into any instances you want to launch:

```
>>> key = ec2.create_key_pair("test")
>>> key.save(".ssh")
```

The preceding code will create a key-pair "test", and save it to ".ssh/test.pem". For security reasons, you can never get the contents of your key back again, so you need to save this ssh key in a safe place where you can access it. It's often suggested that you back up your key-pairs on external devices, such as a hard drive or other secure locations, to prevent losing them and locking you out of your instances.

Of course, you can't do much without an image to start with, so now look at how to get some images:

```
>>> for img in ec2.get_all_images():
...     print img.root_device_type, img.location
ebs i386 137112412989/amzn-ami-0.9.9-beta.i386-ebs
ebs x86_64 137112412989/amzn-ami-0.9.7-beta.x86_64-ebs
ebs x86_64 137112412989/amzn-ami-0.9.9-beta.x86_64-ebs
ebs i386 137112412989/amzn-ami-0.9.7-beta.i386-ebs
ebs x86_64 137112412989/amzn-ami-0.9.8-beta.x86_64-ebs
ebs i386 137112412989/amzn-ami-0.9.8-beta.i386-ebs
instance-store x86_64 amzn-ami-us-east-1/
➥amzn-ami-0.9.9-beta.x86_64.manifest.xml
instance-store x86_64 amzn-ami-us-east-1/
➥amzn-ami-0.9.8-beta.x86_64.manifest.xml
instance-store i386 amzn-ami-us-east-1/
➥amzn-ami-0.9.8-beta.i386.manifest.xml
instance-store i386 amzn-ami-us-east-1/
➥amzn-ami-0.9.9-beta.i386.manifest.xml
.... More Images ....
```

This list can be quite large, so you often need to filter by what you're looking for. You can filter on architecture (i386 or x86_64), owner, root device type (ebs or instance-store), name, manifest id, and many other filters. For a complete list of filters, see the Amazon Describe Instances API (http://docs.amazonwebservices.com/AWSEC2/latest/APIReference/).

Amazon also offers a web-based portal to search Amazon machine images (http://aws.amazon.com/amis). It recently also announced the availability of a few machine images being maintained by Amazon. Using the web-based portal, you can see the full list of AWS supported AMIs (http://aws.amazon.com/amis/AWS). The cheapest instance type you can run is a t1.micro instance, which requires an EBS-backed image, so start with Amazon's 64-bit EBS-backed AMI (http://aws.amazon.com/amis/AWS/4158). You can get this image by using the get_image function on our connection:

```
>>> img = ec2.get_image("ami-38c33651")
```

You can now run this image using the run function, making sure to pass in your instance_type to override the default m1.small. Also make sure to pass in your security group and your key-pair name:

```
>>> r = img.run(instance_type="t1.micro"
...    security_groups = [group],
...    key_name="test"
... )
```

Although you may expect the return value here to be an Instance object, instead you get back a Reservation object, which is a collection of instances. This is because you are allowed to request a minimum and maximum amount of instances to be run with a single command, and they all come back as a single reservation. This enables you to quickly launch several instances of the same type.

Getting to the instances in the reservation can be done by accessing the instances attribute on the reservation:

```
>>> for instance in r.instances:
...    print instance.id, instance.state, instance.public_dns_name
...
i-c10c171 pending
```

Your instance starts in the state "pending" with no public DNS name. The instance object won't change until you call the update function, which also returns the current status. You can poll this function to determine when the instance changes state:

```
>>> import time
>>> while instance.update() == "pending":
...     time.sleep(1)
...
>>> print instance.status
running
```

This loop continues to run until the instance is no longer pending, so you can just sit back and wait for it to finish. When it comes back, you can check your `public_dns_name` again:

```
>>> print instance.public_dns_name
ec2-XXX-XXX-XXX-XXX.compute-1.amazonaws.com
```

You can now SSH into your instance with the key-pair you created:

```
$ ssh -i .ssh/test.pem ec2-user@ec2-...
```

Of course, you're charged for every hour that your server runs, and with EBS-backed instances, you're also charged for the time that your EBS volumes are alive. You can shut down your instance by simply powering off the instance using the `halt` command, but if you want to terminate the EBS volume as well, you need to call the `terminate` function on your instance:

```
>>> instance.terminate()
```

Elastic Block Storage (EBS)

One of the first major complaints about EC2 was that they had no way to keep data between instance shutdowns. This meant that if you lost an instance, you couldn't look through the log files to see what happened, and worse yet if you had temporary data stored on there that you needed, you would lose it all. This was extremely horrible if you were running a database that used the local filesystem. Even if you did back up into S3, you could still lose everything since the last backup.

Amazon's response was to develop a new service known as Elastic Block Storage (EBS). This storage offers developers a way to create a virtual disk within the cloud that can be attached to any running instance. If your instance is terminated, you can simply launch a new one and attach the EBS volume that contains all your important data. Coupled with the ability to take snapshots and restore from snapshots, this system provides a flexible way to store persistent data across terminated instances.

Amazon also provides a way to create instances based on these EBS volumes as a root partition. This enables you to stop and start instances like traditional servers instead of as disposable traditional EC2 instances. This voids the disposable property of EC2 instances, but it opens up a wide range of possibilities for systems that must have a consistent local filesystem.

Because EBS is an extension of the EC2 interface, connect to EC2 to begin using it:

```
>>> import boto
>>> ec2 = boto.connect_ec2()
```

Creating EBS volumes can be done either from scratch or from an existing "snapshot." Some public snapshots are available, and you can also use your private snapshots. Start by simply creating a blank EBS volume, which won't have a filesystem installed on it:

```
>>> volume = ec2.create_volume(
...     size=10, # Size is in GB
...     zone="us-east-1a",
... )
```

Volumes, just like EC2 instances, have statuses. When first created, your volume will be in the creating status:

```
>>> print volume.status
creating
```

Also like EC2 instances, you can update this status by calling the update function, which also returns the status. The following loop waits until the volume is no longer creating:

```
>>> import time
>>> while volume.update() == "pending":
...     time.sleep(1)
...
>>> print volume.status
available
```

You can then attach your volume to an instance using the attach function:

```
>>> volume.attach("i-c10c171", "/dev/sdh")
```

You can then log into your instance and do whatever you want with /dev/sdh, which first involves creating the filesystem and mounting it:

```
$ mkfs -t ext3 /dev/sdh
/dev/sdh is entire device, not just one partition!
Proceed anyway? (y,n) y
...
$ mkdir /mnt/ebs
$ mount /dev/sdh /mnt/ebs
```

You now have a fully functional EBS volume available at /mnt/ebs, where you can create, read, modify, and delete files. This volume interacts exactly like a native device, but there are some noticeable differences in speed because it's actually a network-attached device. Still, these devices are fast enough to use as root-partitions, so it's not a huge concern.

After you finish with your volume, you should unmount it from within your instance:

```
$ unmount /mnt/ebs
```

Then you can detach it from the instance, leaving it open to be attached elsewhere or deleted:

```
>>> vol.detach()
```

You can quickly create snapshots at the block-level for volumes, which is extremely efficient and easy to do:

```
>>> snap = vol.create_snapshot()
```

Just like volumes and instances, snapshots have statuses, and you can update them using the `update` function:

```
>>> while snap.update() == "pending":
...    time.sleep(1)
...
>>> print snap.update()
100%
```

You can use the snapshot id to create a new volume based off of this snapshot:

```
>>> vol2 = ec2.create_volume(size=10,
...    zone="us-east-1a",
...    snapshot=snap
... )
```

You cannot remove a snapshot until all volumes that use that snapshot have been deleted. When you finish with a snapshot or volume, you can delete it with the `delete` function:

```
>>> vol2.delete()
>>> vol.delete()
>>> snap.delete()
```

Elastic Load Balancing (ELB)

For small applications, you often don't need more then one or two servers with elastic IP addresses backed behind round robin DNS. However, using Elastic IPs causes problems when you want to scale your services to beyond just a few servers because you're limited to how many of them you are allowed per account. When you need to provide a single endpoint powered by multiple different servers, balancing out the load equally, you want an ELB.

ELB enables you to create your own load balancers, which cost a fraction of the amount as regular EC2 instances and also scale much better and are more reliable because they span zones. These balancers pass through traffic via standard protocols and enable you to map input ports to instances. They also enable you to dynamically add instances to your balancer on-the-fly as they come up.

Instances in the balancer are monitored to make sure they're working and are automatically disabled if they go offline. These balancers provide a DNS name that can be mapped to with a CNAME to use your own domain name.

boto provides access to ELB through a standard connection interface:

```
>>> import boto
>>> elb = boto.connect_elb()
```

You can create load balancers by calling the `create_load_balancer` function. This function takes a name, the availability zones to start serving, and a list of ports to listen to and map to. The listeners are a tuple of input port, output port, and protocol (TCP, HTTP, or HTTPS). As of the 2010-07-01 API, you can now create HTTPS-based listeners, which enable you to accept requests in HTTPS and pass through to a standard HTTP port on your instance. Create a simple load balancer that proxies port 80 to port 80 on your instances:

```
>>> balancer = elb.create_load_balancer(
...    name="my-balancer",
...    zones=['us-east-1a'],
...    listeners= [ (80,80,"HTTP") ]
... )
```

From the balancer object, you can see the DNS name that you need to point any CNAMEs to, or just access directly:

```
>>> print balancer.dns_name
my-balancer-1234567.us-east-1.elb.amazonaws.com
```

Of course, this balancer isn't actually doing anything until after you register some instances for it to proxy data to:

```
>>> balancer.register_instances(['i-c10c171'])
```

If you need to upgrade your instance, or remove it from your balancer for any reason, you can deregister it using the `deregister_instances` function:

```
>>> balancer.deregister_instances(['i-c10c171'])
```

You can enable and disable zones easily after a balancer is launched as well:

```
>>> balancer.enable_zones(['us-east-1b'])
>>> balancer.disable_zones(['us-east-1a'])
```

From a connection, you can get a list of all load balancers you have created:

```
>>> for balancer in elb.get_all_load_balancers():
...     print balancer.dns_name
my-balancer-1234567.us-east-1.elb.amazonaws.com
```

After you finish with a load balancer, you can delete it:

```
>>> balancer.delete()
```

SimpleDB

One major problem with S3 is that it's not designed for quick access and searchability. Amazon's reaction to this was to create a special type of database that is nonrelational and schema-less, known as SimpleDB. This system originally used a special query language but now has been modified to use a SELECT style query language. This, however, is only for aesthetic appeal because it does not support joins, subselects, or any functions other than count.

SimpleDB uses a simple hierarchy for storing metadata (see Figure 3.3). It can be used to fetch an item by its name or query on values by key name. It can also search for patterns, sort, and compare lexicographically. It doesn't support any types, so all values need to be stored in a lexicographically sortable string. Everything in SimpleDB is automatically indexed, but it can take time before the items are added to the indexes.

SimpleDB also enables two different modes. In any system, you can either have consistency or high-availability. Originally, SimpleDB only had a high-partitioning mode but has recently been updated to support a consistent mode for systems that require immediate reactions instead of perfect availability. This is handled by enabling you to send a list of expected values on a write, and request the most updated version on a read or query. The high-availability mode enables you to perform more of a "fire and forget" request where you know only that your data will *eventually* be saved.

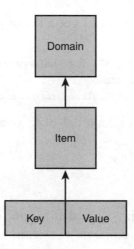

Figure 3.3   The SimpleDB hierarchy.

Like EC2 and S3, SDB connections begin with a simple method call:

```
>>> import boto
>>> sdb = boto.connect_sdb()
```

From here, you need to create your domain:

```
>>> db = sdb.create_domain("test")
```

Again, these domains are not globally unique, so you can create a domain called test as directed without having to prefix it with your key id. You can also look up domains that already exist:

```
>>> db = sdb.lookup("test")
```

The basic object underneath a domain is an item, which you can create using the new_item function:

```
>>> item = db.new_item("test-item")
>>> item["key"] = "value"
>>> item["my-list"] = ["item1", "item2"]
>>> item.save()
```

This item can then be fetched by its name using the `get_item` function:

```
>>> item = db.get_item("test-item")
```

Of course, most of the time you will use SDB because of the queryable nature of it, so you'll probably want to use a query to get items:

```
>>> query = db.select("select * from `%s`" +
...    " where `key` = 'value'" % db.name)
>>> for item in query:
...     print item.name
test-item
```

You can use a lot of sql–like query functions, which are not all covered here. For a full list of how to use the select function, see "Using Select to Create Amazon SimpleDB Queries" (http://docs.amazonwebservices.com/AmazonSimpleDB/2009-04-15/DeveloperGuide/UsingSelect.html).

Of course, you can then delete items and domains when you finish with them:

```
>>> item.delete()
>>> db.delete()
True
```

Removing a domain removes all items under it automatically. As of the writing of this book, you're limited to one billion key-value pairs or 10GB per domain. You're also limited to 256 key-value pairs per item, so if you use all 256 key-value pairs for every item, you can get approximately 3.9 million items into a single domain. Domains also are much quicker to access data that has been recently accessed, so it may take longer to perform a query if you're looking for items that haven't been touched in a while.

Relational Database Service (RDS)

The biggest complaint of SimpleDB is that the nonrelational nature of it means that you can't do any complex queries. Many complicated systems don't work properly without this capability, and any system that requires complex reporting can't be done without using joins and other functions not available on SDB. Amazon's solution to this was to build off of EC2 and EBS to provide a *managed SQL service*, known as a Relational Database Service.

RDS currently supports only MySQL but has the option to choose a backend, so it will be possible for Amazon to scale this down the road to use other backends. It offers it in regular form and a high-availability cluster format. Updates are handled automatically by Amazon, and you can specify a time frame for when Amazon may shut down and restart your database.

One of the biggest advantages to using this system versus running your own MySQL servers on EC2 is that you can also perform backups similar to how EBS snapshots work. These backups automatically flush the tables to disk, so you are ensured to have reliable backups. These backups can be referenced by time, so you can automatically revert to a specific moment in time for your database.

Although RDS is built on EC2, it has its own connection interface that adds quite a bit of functionality:

```
>>> import boto
>>> rds = boto.connect_rds()
```

RDS doesn't share anything with EC2, which means the security groups, auto scaling groups, and other management features you may have already created for your EC2 instances don't translate over directly. Before you can start creating RDS instances, you need to set up a security group that provides the same functionality for RDS as it does for EC2; it enables you to set your firewall rules to decide who can access your instances. You can authorize an IP range, or a security group, which can be your own EC2 security group or another user's EC2 security group. Start by creating a development security group for your RDS instances:

```
>>> sg = rds.create_dbsecurity_group("development",
...     "Development Security Group")
>>> sg.authorize("0.0.0.0/0")
```

The last line here authorizes every IP address to access this RDS security group, which is probably okay for a nonproduction instance, but if you want to limit the access down even tighter, you probably want to authorize only a specific EC2 security group. Before you can do this, you need to connect to EC2 and grab your security group:

```
>>> ec2 = boto.connect_ec2()
>>> egrp = ec2.get_all_security_groups(['default'])[0]
>>> sg.authorize(ec2_group=egrp)
```

Of course, if you did authorize everyone previously, you probably want to revoke that access now that you've limited it down to just your EC2 instances in the default security group:

```
>>> sg.revoke("0.0.0.0/0")
```

Next you need to create a Parameter Group, which defines how all instances in that parameter group will be run. It contains all the settings you need to launch new instances, similar to how auto-scaling groups work. To create this group, you need to call the `create_parameter_group` function:

```
>>> pg = rds.create_parameter_group("developer",
...     description="Developer Parameter Group")
```

The `create_parameter_group` function also enables you to pass in the name of the engine to use, but for now there is only one supported engine, so you can use the default. The Parameter Group is nonspecific and more like a dictionary of configuration options that you can update than a defined list. To get a full list of all the parameters, you can fetch all available parameters from RDS and then list them out:

```
>>> pg.get_params()
>>> param_keys = pg.keys()
>>> param_keys.sort()
>>> for param_name in param_keys:
...     print param_name
...
allow-suspicious-udfs
auto_increment_increment
```

```
auto_increment_offset
automatic_sp_privileges
back_log
basedir
binlog_cache_size
binlog_format
bulk_insert_buffer_size
character-set-client-handshake
character_set_client
character_set_connection
character_set_database
character_set_filesystem
character_set_results
character_set_server
collation_connection
collation_server
completion_type
concurrent_insert
connect_timeout
datadir
default_storage_engine
default_time_zone
default_week_format
delay_key_write
delayed_insert_limit
delayed_insert_timeout
delayed_queue_size
div_precision_increment
event_scheduler
flush
flush_time
ft_boolean_syntax
ft_max_word_len
ft_min_word_len
ft_query_expansion_limit
general_log
group_concat_max_len
init_connect
innodb_adaptive_hash_index
innodb_additional_mem_pool_size
innodb_autoextend_increment
innodb_autoinc_lock_mode
```

```
innodb_buffer_pool_size
innodb_commit_concurrency
innodb_concurrency_tickets
innodb_data_home_dir
innodb_file_per_table
innodb_flush_log_at_trx_commit
innodb_flush_method
innodb_lock_wait_timeout
innodb_locks_unsafe_for_binlog
innodb_log_buffer_size
innodb_log_file_size
innodb_log_group_home_dir
innodb_max_dirty_pages_pct
innodb_max_purge_lag
innodb_open_files
innodb_rollback_on_timeout
innodb_stats_on_metadata
innodb_support_xa
innodb_sync_spin_loops
innodb_table_locks
innodb_thread_concurrency
innodb_thread_sleep_delay
innodb_use_legacy_cardinality_algorithm
interactive_timeout
join_buffer_size
keep_files_on_create
key_buffer_size
key_cache_age_threshold
key_cache_block_size
key_cache_division_limit
language
lc_time_names
local_infile
log-bin
log_bin_trust_function_creators
log_error
log_output
log_warnings
long_query_time
low_priority_updates
```

Given an individual parameter name, you can fetch the full
parameter and print out a few useful details about it:

```
>>> param = pg['connect_timeout']
>>> print param.name
connect_timeout
>>> print param.description
The number of seconds that the MySQLd server waits for a
connect packet before responding with Bad handshake.
>>> print param.value
None
>>> print param.source
engine-default
>>> print param.allowed_values
2-31536000
>>> print param.is_modifiable
True
>>> print param.apply_method
None
```

You can modify only parameters if the `is_modifiable` returns
`True`; otherwise, it's just informative and not something to be configured. Here you can see that the current value for this parameter
is actually not even set, but you can make this anywhere between
2 and 31,536,000 seconds, enabling you to have quite a bit of flexibility on how long your server will wait before timing out a connection. You can update this value by simply setting the `value`
attribute and then calling the `update` method:

```
>>> param.value = 15
>>> param.update()
```

Now that your parameter group is set up, it's time to make your
first DB instance. There are quite a few parameters here that you
can configure on initial creation, and most of them can also be
changed later, so don't worry about missing something. DB
instances are created using the `create_dbinstance` function on the
RDS connection object:

```
>>> inst = rds.create_dbinstance("my-db-instance",
...     allocated_storage=10,
...     instance_class="db.m1.small",
```

```
...      master_username="root",
...      master_password="my-secret-password",
...      param_grop=pg.name,
...      security_groups=[sg],
...      availability_zone="us-east-1a",
...      preferred_maintenance_window="Sun:05:00-Sun:09:00",
...      backup_retention_period=30,
...      preferred_backup_window="05:00-06:00",
...      multi_az=False)
```

The first parameter here is actually an ID, which must be DNS-safe. You now have a brand new RDS instance available to you in the inst variable, which you can use to discover the status and endpoint:

```
>>> print inst.status
creating
>>> print inst.update()
creating
>>> print inst.update()
available
>>> print inst.endpoint
(u'my-db-instance.a03461dfb.us-east-1.rds.amazonaws.com', 3306)
```

Your endpoint begins with your instance's ID, which is why that field must be DNS-safe. You can now connect using any MySQL client to your instance using the domain name and port provided by the endpoint property. You can go back in and modify the instance with the modify function:

```
>>> instance.modify(master_password="a-new-password",
... apply_immediately=True)
```

You can always force a snapshot of the instance using the snapshot function:

```
>>> snap = instance.snapshot("my-first-snapshot")
```

You can use this snapshot to launch a new DB instance from this snapshot using the restore_dbinstance_from_dbsnapshot function passing in the snapshot id:

```
>>> re_inst = rds.restore_dbinstance_from_dbsnapshot(
... "restored-instance", "my-first-snapshot")
```

If you don't know a specific snapshot ID, you can also create an instance based on a point-in-time, which restores using the closest snapshot to that point:

```
>>> re_inst = restore_dbinstance_from_point_in_time(
...     source_instance_id="my-db-instance",
...     target_instance_id="my-restored-instance",
...     restore_time=datetime(YYYY,MM,DD))
```

After you finish with your instance, don't forget to stop it using the stop function:

```
>>> inst.stop(skip_final_snapshot=True)
```

Simple Notification Service (SNS)

Many users of cloud-based systems need to send out emails on a subscription basis to end users. Unfortunately, the Internet is also full of spammers, so most email servers outright reject emails sent from servers that don't have proper SPF configurations. Most email servers also block the ip ranges for all the EC2 instances because anyone could launch spam servers there.

To solve this problem, Amazon released a special service known as Simple Notification Service (SNS), designed for notification delivery. The primary use of this system is to enable you to send emails out to your subscribers. In compliance with the CANN SPAM act, your subscribers can also easily remove themselves from this list by clicking a link in any email you send to them.

As you can see from Figure 3.4, SNS enables you to create topics to which you can add subscribers. You can then post messages that will be delivered to each subscriber under your topic. These messages can be delivered by emails, SQS, or even delivered directly to an HTTP server via JSON. This enables you to not only provide a useful subscription service for regular email delivery, but it also enables you to create a robust event-driven system. This can be most useful when working with an observer pattern, where you need to add subscribers dynamically to track events.

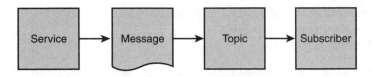

Figure 3.4   The SNS hierarchy.

Like many other Amazon Services, using SNS from boto begins with creating a connection:

```
>>> import boto
>>> sns = boto.connect_sns()
```

Because all points in SNS begin with topics, the next step is to create a topic:

```
>>> topic = sns.create_topic("BookTopic")
>>> print topic
{u'CreateTopicResponse': {u'ResponseMetadata':
{u'RequestId': u'b6584da7-ef70-11df-b60d-f317956a1877'},
u'CreateTopicResult': {u'TopicArn':
u'arn:aws:sns:us-east-1:111111111111:BookTopic'
}}}
>>> arn = topic['CreateTopicResponse']
➡['CreateTopicResult']['TopicArn']
>>> print arn
arn:aws:sns:us-east-1:111111111111:BookTopic
```

boto provides a lot of information, and this is the first boto module that was released that uses a JSON module, so you either need Python 2.5+ or the simplejson module installed to use it. The responses come directly from the SNS API, so there's no auto-mated handling there for you, which is why you need to access three levels deep to get what you're looking for, which is the TopicArn. This field acts as the unique identifier for this topic, which is what you need to pass into all your other functions.

Now subscribe to this topic, which can be done using the sub-scribe function on the SNS connection:

```
>>> sns.subscribe(arn, "email", "myemail@example.com")
{u'SubscribeResponse': {u'SubscribeResult':
```

```
{u'SubscriptionArn': u'pending confirmation'},
u'ResponseMetadata': {u'RequestId':
u'111111-111-1111-1111-111111111'}}}
```

Next, check your email; you should get something from SNS that asks you to confirm this subscription. After you do, you can see your subscription has been confirmed by using the `get_all_subscriptions_by_topic` function:

```
>>> subs = sns.get_all_subscriptions_by_topic(arn)
>>> subs = subs["ListSubscriptionsResponse"]
➡️["ListSubscriptionsResult"]["Subscriptions"]
>>> for sub in subs:
...     print sub
...
{u'Owner': u'111111111111',
u'Endpoint': u'myemail@example.com',
u'Protocol': u'email', u'TopicArn':
u'arn:aws:sns:us-east-1:111111111:BookTopic',
u'SubscriptionArn': u'...111111111-1111-1111-1111'}
```

The response requires you to drill down a bit to see anything useful, but when there, you get a fully functional subscription object that includes the owner (you), the endpoint, the protocol, and the topic id and the subscription id. This `SubscriptionArn` is the ID you use to represent this specific subscription, which is what you need to pass to the unsubscribe function:

```
>>> sns.unsubscribe(subs[0]["SubscriptionArn"])
```

To send messages to the topic, use the `publish` function:

```
>>> sns.publish(arn, "Test Message Body", "My Subject")
{u'PublishResponse': {
u'PublishResult':
{u'MessageId': u'1111-1111-1111-...'},
u'ResponseMetadata':
{u'RequestId': u'11111-1111-1111-....'}}}
```

Again, you need to drill down a little bit to see anything useful, but here you can see the confirmations and message IDs that relate to your specific message you posted. If you check back in on your email, you can see the message you just published.

Another useful endpoint for SNS is the HTTP endpoint. This can be extremely useful to add the "webhook" functionality to your applications, and you need to confirm your subscription without human interaction because it's not over email. You can create a simple HTTP subscription by using the `subscribe` command again, this time using a full URL as the endpoint:

```
>>> sns.subscribe(arn, "http", "http://my-host.com")
```

Next, take a look at your web server, and you should see something like the following appear on your server:

```
POST / HTTP/1.1
Content-Length: 1219
Content-Type: text/plain; charset=ISO-8859-1
Host: cmoyer.homeip.net:9080
Connection: Keep-Alive
User-Agent: Amazon Simple Notification Service Agent

{
  "Type" : "SubscriptionConfirmation",
  "MessageId" : ".....",
  "Token" : "....",
  "TopicArn" : "arn:aws:sns:us-east-1:11111:BookTopic",
  "Message" : "You have chosen to subscribe to the topic.....\n
To confirm the subscription, visit the SubscribeURL
included in this message.",
  "SubscribeURL" : "https://....,
  "Timestamp" : "2010-11-13T22:48:21.175Z",
  "SignatureVersion" : "1",
  "Signature" : "......."
}
```

As the message suggests, you simply need to do a GET request on the URL provided to subscribe. Alternatively, you could use the `confirm_subscription` function on the SNS module:

```
>>> sns.confirm_subscription(arn,token="....")
```

When you finish, you need to clean up your topic using the `delete_topic` function:

```
>>> sns.delete_topic(arn)
```

Virtual Private Cloud (VPC)

In an ideal world, you need only the resources provided by the cloud to power your entire system. However, if you work with an existing infrastructure, it's often more desirable to simply use EC2 and other Amazon services as a way to expand and handle periods of high load. Many enterprise customers often complained that there was no way to simply merge their existing network with Amazon servers.

To solve this issue, Amazon released Virtual Private Cloud, a service that enables you to extend your existing network to be used with AWS. This service enables you to assign internal ip addresses to your servers, and use your existing servers such as LDAP and Active Directory. This can be especially useful when running windows servers to allow for overflow within your existing network.

As you can see from Figure 3.5, the VPC service enables you to extend your existing network into the cloud using a virtual network connection. This acts just like a normal VPN, enabling you to connect a given security group directly into your internal network.

This means you can also use your existing firewall services and even host your servers from your own IP instead of giving it an Amazon IP.

Similar to many other Amazon services, the first step to connecting to VPC with boto is to create a VPC connection:

```
>>> import boto
>>> conn = boto.connect_vpc()
```

After you have a connection, it's time to create your VPC:

```
>>> vpc = c.create_vpc('10.0.0.0/24')
>>> print vpc.id
vpc-11111111
>>> print vpc.state
pending
>>> print vpc.cidr_block
10.0.0.0/24
>>> print vpc.dhcp_options_id
default
```

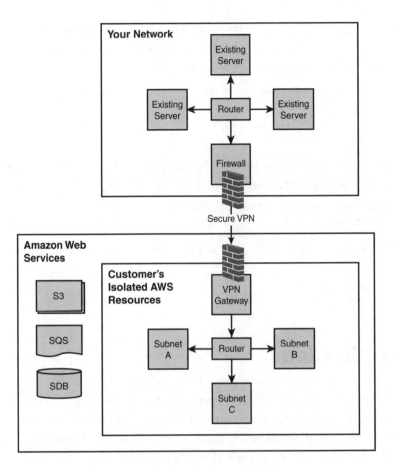

Figure 3.5   Overview of VPC.

You can see a new VPC that will operate in the IP range
10.0.0.x, enabling you to provision that part of your network to
EC2 instances. From here, you can create a subnet to be associated
with this VPC, enabling you to launch EC2 instances within a
specific part of this connection:

```
>>> s = c.create_subnet(vpc.id, '10.0.0.0/25')
>>> print s.cidr_block
10.0.0.0/25
>>> print subnet.available_ip_address_count
123
>>> print subnet.availability_zone
us-east-1a
```

There are 123 available IP addresses within this subnet that you can allocate to EC2 instances. The next step is to create a customer gateway, connecting to your local router:

```
>>> cg = c.create_customer_gateway(
...     type='ipsec.1',
...     ip_address='12.1.2.3',
...     bgp_asn=55555)
```

You then need to create a VPN gateway and attach it to your VPC, completing the connection:

```
>>> vpn = c.create_vpn_gateway("ipsec.1")
>>> vpn.attach(vpc.id)
```

When you finish with your connections, you can delete them:

```
>>> vpn.delete()
>>> cg.delete()
>>> vpc.delete()
```

Google Cloud

Although late to the game, Google has always been a large supporter of cluster computing. It recently has been diving further into the field of cloud computing, offering some new interesting services. Whereas Amazon focused on the individual pieces of an application and what individual needs it had, Google focused on the application as a whole, introducing the concept of **Platform as a Service (PaaS)** in which it controls the scaling and distribution, and you simply write the application. This new concept gives you no control over the actual architecture but enables you to focus solely on the web application.

AppEngine

Google's first cloud service was Google AppEngine. This service is not a true compute service offering, nor does it let you run background services or split your system apart properly. It builds off existing frameworks, such as Django, and enables you to quickly and rapidly deploy a web application. You are much more limited in what you can develop, but it also makes it much quicker and easier to develop if your application fits within the constraints of the platform. To use AppEngine, you have to use Google's framework. It does not give you raw access to the underlying virtual systems, thus limiting you quite a bit.

Unlike EC2, AppEngine doesn't charge you for standby time, just for actual processing or CPU usage time. The completely different billing system makes it ideal for applications with low usage but overall is more expensive and less powerful if you need a large-scale application. The initial "free" tier of pricing for AppEngine makes it a preferred platform for start-up companies because they can actually test-drive applications before they start paying for them. This offering from Google gives developers a limited amount of usage per day before charging occurs, so you don't pay for your application until you start getting a lot of traffic.

Initially AppEngine supported only Python, but it has now been expanded to also support Java. In both cases, you use a provided set of libraries that gives you a WSGI-like interface. They also provide you with the ability to store data in a unique database similar to SimpleDB but enables you to specify custom indexes. It also comes with some other unique features such as a built-in versioning system, along with the ability to preview versions before promoting one to the production version.

AppEngine also integrates directly with many other Google services. For example, you can use Google Authentication instead of providing your own authentication mechanism (or integrating with another third-party service), to give your users a simple single sign-on system. You can also integrate directly with Google Mail to send emails to your users, and even use Google's Instant Message (XMPP) system to interact directly with your users in real-time.

Google also offers a unique Task Queue system that enables you to create Cron-like jobs that execute on specific intervals. This eliminates your need to create this system to ensure that specific tasks occur only once and enables you to spend more time developing the specifics of your application and less time developing the framework.

The biggest disadvantage of using Google AppEngine is that it's literally the only one of its kind out there. Although there are emulators out there to run an AppEngine-like environment on regular servers (or even other cloud provider platforms), these systems are often behind the curve and don't provide identical interfaces. Using AppEngine locks you into using Google as your vendor and gives you little choice if it changes its offering or you need to move for any reason.

This risk, however, may be acceptable for most small start-up companies. Although Google is now making a push to provide AppEngine in the Google Apps marketplace for Enterprise, many companies still won't switch to using Google Mail for their corporations, or trust everything to Google. For any small company, however, Google AppEngine provides a small start-up cost both in terms of Google's charges and in terms of development hours. It's simple to develop applications for Google AppEngine, whereas developing an application for either Amazon Web Services or any other cloud provider stake a skilled developer who is familiar with the system to provide a scalable system. If you can afford to trust Google and want a simple start-up solution, Google AppEngine may be a solution for you. When you're ready to move to bigger and more robust applications, you can move to the more advanced topics in this book and build your own platform to suite your specific needs.

Because Google AppEngine is a fully featured framework, you must use its tools to build and upload your application. You need to create your custom application using its start-up guides (http://code.google.com/appengine/docs/), and then you use the configuration tool provided to update your application. Typically, this just means using the following command:

```
$ appcfg.py update .
```

You can use its web interface to set the currently active version, and you can demo a version before making it live. In general, this is a good idea because you should always make sure that everything uploaded and works correctly in its system because it's slightly different than your local running environment. After you're convinced the version works, simply use that interface to set the newly uploaded version to the active version.

Google Storage

One major issue developers had with AppEngine was that it lacked access to long-term file storage. To achieve long-term file storage, many developers turned to using boto in their application and connected directly to S3. Google saw this problem as an opportunity for growth and set forth to bring its file-like storage solution to the market.

Google Storage is similar, and almost identical, to Amazon S3. This was a huge advantage for Google because it could simply take advantage of the existing tools out there to manage S3 and enable you to change the endpoint and suddenly have your application communicate with Google Storage. They even made its primary storage utility gsutil, run directly off boto. The users who had previously been using S3 in their Google App Engine applications need to change one configuration line to switch over to Google Storage and never have to worry about multiple bills for the same application again.

The good news is that boto and Google Storage play nicely together, so you don't have to learn too much to use it. Before you begin, however, you need to make sure you have your Google credentials set up. You need to add the following lines to your boto.cfg:

```
[Credentials]
gs_access_key_id = MyGoogleAccessKey
gs_secret_access_key = GoogleSecretKey
```

Next, you can just connect to Google Storage directly using boto:

```
>>> import boto
>>> gs = boto.connect_gs()
```

From here you can use this gs connection exactly as you did with the s3 connection earlier, creating buckets and keys as you need.

Rackspace Cloud

Rackspace is slowly emerging into the cloud marketplace with a few Amazon-like products. Unlike Amazon, Rackspace immediately saw the need to not tie down developers to a single cloud provider and open sourced its entire infrastructure, so you can easily replicate its service offering on your own custom hardware. You are not locked into one cloud provider; even if you severed ties with Rackspace, you can transition your entire application to your private cloud and continue to operate.

Although Rackspace is still new to the game, it has been making a few waves with its fully open infrastructure. It has also created its own libraries to communicate with its API in Python, Java, and many other languages. This means you don't need to rely on open source libraries provided by people with other day jobs that don't have time to keep up with all the new features and services as they come out.

CloudFiles

The first cloud service offered by Rackspace was CloudFiles. This service is similar to S3 and has similar pricing. It offers a simple interface that enables you to store files and provide permissions on those files. Partnered with LimeLight CDN, it also offers the ability to push these files to edge locations, providing a CloudFront-like service on top. Currently, the LimeLight integration has more edge locations than CloudFront, but with CloudFront expanding rapidly, this is not a reason to choose one way or another.

Rackspaces also has a Python binding for accessing its storage engine, but unlike Google Storage, it has not merged this into boto. As such, it's slightly more complicated to use CloudFiles as a provider if you're also using Google Storage and/or AWS.

To start, go to https://github.com/rackspace/python-cloudfiles/ tree and download the latest copy of the cloudfiles binding. From there browse to the docs folder and follow the tutorial in index.html.

CloudServers

CloudServers is similar to EC2, offering users a compute platform to run their applications. Unlike EC2, CloudServers acts more like a traditional virtual machine, offering the ability to start and stop instances. CloudServers also has a tight integration with rPath, which offers the ability to build your images with exactly the packages and software you need, without any extra crust on top. This unique solution enables you to transition between virtualization and cloud services seamlessly.

CloudServers offers a much cheaper run cost than EC2. Starting at approximately $11 per month, CloudServers can be a cheap alternative to EC2. CloudServers can also be much easier for developers to start with because it is more like a virtual machine than a disposable system. It is more relatable to traditional servers than cloud servers.

CloudSites

CloudSites is Rackspace's only PaaS offering. This service is similar to Google AppEngine, except that it's much less limiting in terms of what you can actually use to run your code. It's more like traditional webhosts, where you are given a method of uploading your application written in PHP, .NET, Perl, or one of many other supported languages up to Rackspace's cloud servers, and then the rest is handled automatically for you. This includes scaling and monitoring and backups and redundancy for server failures. These backups, however, are not available to you as a customer, and are used only if an emergency occurs with Rackspace in which they need to recover everything. It's not possible to request a recovery of a single CloudSite.

CloudSites offers you either a Linux server running Apache or a Windows server running IIS. This gives you the flexibility to simply launch an existing LAMP application or develop applications just like you normally have in the past and not worry about the scaling. You can continue to develop just like you would with normal applications, without having to worry about how they scale or how to make it support more customers. This has its limitations, however, because the fundamental technology behind using a single central database, such as MySQL, means that you will eventually be limited by the capacity of that central database.

CloudSites is also one of the more expensive offerings because it starts at over twice the cost of a single EC2 instance. However, because it uses existing technologies most developers are already familiar with, you'll probably spend a lot less time learning and developing, saving you money in the short term. However, if you're reading this book, it means you're probably not looking for the "quick fix" that this service provides.

Summary

In the end, it comes down to what your requirements are. If you want to develop your own platform, or if you need something that doesn't exactly fit in another providers platform, you need to use an infrastructure service. There are also quite a few platforms built on top of the infrastructure services, most which can enable you to migrate from one infrastructure cloud to another. This enables you to have the most flexibility and not lock yourself into a single provider.

II

Patterns

4

Designing an Image

Although you may not think of patterns when you build an image for your instances to be based off of, it actually is the core of your entire application. These patterns determine how your OS and base system plays a role in your application. If you don't plan your core system properly, you can waste a lot of time updating or installing each individual system instead of your application as a whole. The last thing you want to do is suddenly increase your overall usage by 100 times and not have your application be scalable to it because you have to manually launch each new instance and make adjustments to it.

Usually if you're just starting out developing in the cloud, you can begin with a prepackaged image; but before long, you'll want to create your own. Most cloud service providers start you off with a set of base images, but this typically won't include everything you need for your custom application. In some environments, you can even get access to images created by others that may aid you in your development. Typically, it's easier to start with a base image close to what you need for your system; then start up that image as a single instance and rebundle from there. Building your image from another base image can help because they've already handled all the special requirements about your specific cloud provider including handling how you can log into it. For images based on Linux or UNIX, this includes setting up the SSH keys or administrator accounts, and for Windows or Apple-based instances, this includes setting up the login and any other base services required for remote access.

After you determine which instance to start your base image from, you need to add in any extra packages that you need for that particular instance to boot. This is a balancing process because you can make scripts to install things on boot as well, but the more you put into the base instance, the less you have to install later. You want to make sure that any manual installation processes are handled before you bundle the instance because you need to launch these images automatically to scale your application on-demand.

If you put too much into your image, updates will be harder to maintain, and it can also over-inflate the size of your image. Additionally, more software installed on your image will make your overall start-time for that image longer, although adding that software into it later, if you need it, will still be even longer. It's truly a balancing act to make sure you install just the basic requirements of your instance onto the image, and then install any configuration-level information *after* the instance is started. Although the perfect balance is hard to achieve, there are some guidelines to follow. In general, you can use the three patterns in this chapter to determine how to build that starting image that will also serve as the base for your application.

Note: Each pattern in this chapter begins on a new page.

Prepackaged Images

Prepackaging an instance provides you with a comprehensive image that includes everything you need for your application. It's the simplest method to install software because you can build it all by hand, but it also takes a lot more effort to maintain because everything is a manual process. If you're just starting out in the cloud, making a prepackaged image is the easiest way to go.

Overview

In Figure 4.1, you can see that the boot process for a prepackaged image requires you to pass in only a minor configuration file to start the instance. Each instance takes an image and configuration metadata to build it.

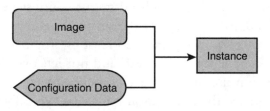

Figure 4.1   The Prepackaged image.

Reasons for Usage

You need to use this pattern if *any* of the following apply:

- You know *exactly* what you need to have installed on your image.
- You want to *quickly* launch application servers that don't change.
- You don't want to rely on *external services* to launch a new instance.

Description

In a prepackaged image, you start with some basic image that has the core of what you need, the OS, and any basic packages. You start this instance just like you would any other instance and then log in and install any application-specific software that you need. In this type of image, install everything including your application, not just the prerequisites. The only thing you pass into this instance is configuration information like the database connection strings and hostname configurations.

Use this pattern when you need to quickly launch new instances of the same type. It can either be useful when you first start developing instances or after you determine what you need for each instance. If you don't know what you need on each instance, or it may vary, this is not the pattern for you.

If you've already built an application but you just need to push it into the cloud, this is probably the simplest pattern for you to start with. If you're working from an existing instance, make sure it contains *only* the packages you need and not left over log files or other information used in the development process.

If you don't have the application built, you typically won't use this pattern because you'll be constantly adding and removing packages from your image. This instance type is designed for a single application, so if you want to build a single image to host multiple types of applications, choose a different pattern, such as the prototype image.

Implementation

Although the actual creation of each image varies greatly for each cloud provider, the overall pattern for creating this specific type of image is the same.

The first step to develop your image is to choose a base image. This is important because you want to choose an image that contains as much of what you need as possible, without having more than you need. You also need to make sure that this image was created by a trusted source because if there's a problem with the image (either because of a lack of understanding or because of malicious intent), it will be harder to fix. If the users who created your image put a back door into each image they made, it will span down into every image you make and in turn they will have full access to everything you have. Alternatively, if they don't know what they're doing and they unwittingly leave an insecurity in your image, anyone can break into it, and you're equally in trouble.

Many trusted sources provide images for the general public, including Ubuntu, Oracle, and even Amazon. Only recently has Amazon begun releasing its own images, but you can still use one of these trusted sources if you want. Before choosing a base image to build yours off of, consider looking around and asking other developers in the community for well-known image vendors.

The second step to develop your image is to start up an instance with your chosen base image, log into it, and start selecting the other packages you need for your application. In this stage, install your base application into this image and make sure everything runs appropriately. Make sure you test this instance before bundling it, but you also need to make sure you clean up everything (including your history) before bundling.

The third step to develop your image is to make sure to develop a proper location for your log files and, if possible, set up a system to store these log files in a central location. The most common problem with instances is running out of storage on your root partition; the reason that happens is because of logging. You may need to set up the logging level configuration as metadata so that you can change how much you log without having to rebundle the image. If you use a UNIX-based OS, you may want to look at using **logrotate** to clean up files and **syslog** to push these logs to some other location. Make sure you look at both system level logs and your own application logging to make sure everything is in-check. If your cloud provider offers an **ephemeral store** (a temporary storage device and only for that instance), consider moving all your log files over to this device and off your root partition.

The fourth step to develop your image is to enable any services and scripts that need to be launched at start time. This typically involves setting up services with proper prerequisites and making sure you have proper error checking to ensure each service is running and alerting if it fails. Consider writing a small script that runs at a given interval (in UNIX this is a **cron** command) and checks to make sure that all the required processes are running. This instance-level checking can be used to make sure you're not proxying to a partially alive system with your requests. It's also important to make sure that each of the services running uses proper permissions, and not running with administrative access unless absolutely necessary. On a UNIX-based OS, the root user is the only one that can typically break the system by filling up the entire root partition, causing a kernel panic. Most other users will be warned and blocked out of writing when the filesystem reaches a given capacity. If possible, avoid writing anything dynamic to the root partition. This partition should be written to only at the time you create your image, or when installing additional software.

The fifth step to develop your image is to verify and bundle your running instance into your actual image. This process varies greatly depending on your cloud provider, but it typically involves first cleaning up your trail on the instance, bundling it up into a file or files with some metadata, and then uploading that to a shared medium. You need to make sure that you permission this upload appropriately because it may contain sensitive data, such as your entire application on it. Make sure you share this image only with your own accounts.

The sixth and final step to develop your image is verification and validation. You now have an image ID that can be used to launch a new instance, so you need to test it to ensure that you don't need to log into it to start everything up. You should also make sure there's no manual process involved with going from an image to a fully launched instance other than the initial request.

Example

The best example of this pattern is when you work on converting an existing application to be used in the cloud. This type of pattern can be incredibly useful at this point because you already know exactly what kind of environment you need for your application to run. Now consider the simple example of a LAMP application, which is a typical web pattern that combines Linux, Apache, MySQL, and PHP.

The first step is to find an existing image that closely matches what you want to use in your final product. For this example application, the first thing you look for is a Linux-based image. Say you're more familiar with Ubuntu, so that would be the first thing you'd look for. After you narrow down your choices to only Ubuntu-based images, you need to make sure that you limit it down further to just the ones you trust. Because you trust the people at Ubuntu, if they have any images they have developed, that would be a good starting point. If you can find another instance that already has Apache, PHP, and MySQL installed, you would probably want to choose that because it already has everything you need. Ideally, you'll probably use a separate instance for MySQL and Apache, but for the sake of this example, say they're on the same machine.

After you choose your base image, start it up and wait for it to boot up. After it's fully booted, you would log into it via SSH and use the SSH key or root account that you provided to it on boot. After log in, you would first install all the base packages you need, in this case MySQL, Apache2, and PHP. In Ubuntu this is just one command:

```
$ apt-get install apache2 mysql-server-5.0 libapache2-mod-php5
➡php5-mysql
```

You're installing the php5 mysql bindings here so that you can connect to your database from your application. After you have your base packages installed, you can copy over your application to your root partition under /usr/local and set up any additional initialization scripts to launch on boot. In Ubuntu, this is done by adding an executable script in /etc/init.d, and running

```
$ update-rc.d <my_app> defaults
```

The `update-rc.d` command takes the name of the script, minus the /etc/init.d prefix, and the command "defaults," which tells it to start up after networking has been enabled. After you run this, your script will be passed the standard start option at boot, and stop on shutdown. This not only enables you to cleanly start your app at boot, but also enables you to cleanly stop it before your system terminates.

Now verify your installation by going to your external IP address and verifying that the server is indeed running on the external ports it should be running on, in this case port 80 for your web service. You also need to make sure that your trail is all cleaned up, cleaning your history by running `history -c` and removing any private SSH keys from `~/.ssh`.

Lastly, bundle your image and then make it available to all your accounts, or the world if it's public. This process is vastly different for each cloud provider, but it typically involves running something to bundle your image and then register it.

First, you need to copy your private and public x509 certificates and copy them up to the instance. Typically this is done on the ephemeral store (/mnt) because this partition is not bundled with the rest of the image. After this is done, run the following commands to bundle the image and store it in S3:

```
% ec2-bundle-vol -c <cert_file.crt> -k <key_file.key> -u <owner_id> -p
<prefix> -s <size> -d /mnt
```

You need to get your AWS user id, which is rather complicated to get, but can be done by some utilities out there already, so I won't go into much detail about that. The `prefix` is what you refer to for this image, so make sure it includes something unique. You also can include a date here so that you know when you created it.

After it's all bundled up, which can take a few minutes, you need to upload that bundle to an S3 bucket that you own. Do this by running another simple command:

```
% ec2-upload-bundle -m /mnt/<prefix>.manifest.xml -b <bucket_name>
➥-a <aws_access_key_id> -s <aws_access_key_id>
```

Now that your image is all bundled and uploaded, register it so that you can launch it as an instance. Do this on the client side through an API call, but if you use boto, you can call the `ec2.register_image` command with the `name` and `image_location` arguments. You can also allow other users to run this image if you have their AWS user IDs by calling `ec2.set_launch_permissions` with their user id or group name. See the boto documentation for more details.

Summary

Overall, the prepackaged image is a useful option when you know exactly how your instances should be built and what you need. If you've already planned out what should be on your instance and you're relatively confident that you won't have a lot of changes to that list, this solution can help you speedily launch instances when needed. The added advantage of not relying on any external sources also appeals to a lot of developers because even if your repository is down, you can still launch new instances.

Singleton Instances

Singletons are used when you need to ensure that only one copy of the instance is running at any given time. Although it's generally a bad idea to rely on this type of architecture, sometimes it's unavoidable when you need to ensure that you have a proper locking mechanism. This typically is done when you need to generate sequential numbers, support transactions, or process and delete files.

Overview

In Figure 4.2, you can see that the singleton instance, unlike the prepackaged instance, requires only one single input to run. This input contains all the metadata and all your packages required for your application. This type of instance is most similar to a standard server or virtual machine because all its data persists through shutdown on an Elastic Load Balancer Volume.

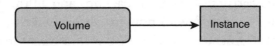

Figure 4.2   The singleton image.

Reasons for Usage

Use this pattern if *all* the following apply:

- You need to ensure that *only one copy* of your software is running.
- You care more about *consistency* than reliability, scalability, and performance.
- You have a known *low load* on your system that a single instance can handle.

Description

A singleton instance should be used only if you need to absolutely ensure that you have only one copy of an instance running at any given time, and you need to keep data around between relaunches. By definition, it is the most unscalable form of an instance that you can have and, if at all possible, it should be absolutely avoided. If you're worried about scalability, this is not the design for you. If, however, you need to ensure that you have only one copy of any given process running, this will be a necessary evil.

In a singleton instance, you build everything up like you would a typical standard computer. These instances aren't built using the standard method in which you have a regular image and metadata but are instead like a typical machine, backed by a persistent storage device on the root partition. This presents itself with many issues because you are retaining possibly bad information between launches. You can't kill and relaunch an instance if you're worried about it being corrupted. Rely on backups and all the standard problems that you would with nonvirtualized systems.

The singleton instance is the most typical type of instance to be launched if you're converting legacy systems over to cloud computing, but it doesn't do justice to what cloud computing has to offer.

Implementation

Each cloud computing provider has a different solution for a singleton-based instance, but the most common solution is a different type of instance that has a persistent storage device at its root partition. Start building this instance similarly to how you build the prepackaged image, but then the process can vary greatly depending on your specific cloud provider.

Example

The best example of how to use a singleton instance is a stand-alone MySQL instance. In this case, make sure that *only* the essentials to your database are installed on this instance, and that it's properly scaled to your demands. It's hard to change an instance like this after it's already launched, so be sure to keep it simple.

With Amazon Web Services, you use the **Elastic Block Storage backed instance**. This type of instance uses an Elastic Block Storage volume for its root partition instead of an Ephemeral disk copied out of S3. You can build your own EBS-backed image by creating a 10GB EBS volume, launching a standard base image, and attaching that EBS volume to the instance you just launched. Next, update your local install and perform a few simple tasks. If you use Ubuntu, you can run the following commands:

```
% apt-get update && apt-get upgrade
% apt-get install cpipe
% mkfs -t ext3 /dev/sdh
% mkdir /ebs
% mount -t ext3 /dev/sdh /ebs
% tar cpS / | cpipe -tv -b 1024 | gzip -c | tar xzpS -C /ebs
% umount -f /ebs
```

After running these commands, you've successfully copied your entire root partition over to that EBS volume. In a standard computer, this is how you would migrate your root disk over to another disk so that you can boot off of that other disk. Because that's essentially what you're doing here, you can now boot off of that EBS volume and get the instance that you just created. At this point, make a snapshot of the image you just created for use with your new image:

```
% ec2-create-snapshot <volume_id>
```

Now bundle the image up just like you did with the old prepackaged instance with a few new twists. You need to create an EBSBlockDevice and a BlockDeviceMapping. If you use boto, this can be done as follows:

```
>>> from boto.ec2.blockdevicemapping import EBSBlockDeviceType
>>> ebs = EBSBlockDeviceType()
>>> ebs.snapshot_id = 'my-snapshot-id'
>>> from boto.ec2.blockdevicemapping import BlockDeviceMapping
```

```
>>> block_map = BlockDeviceMapping()
>>> block_map['/dev/sda1'] = ebs
>>> c.register_image("my_image_name", "My Image Description",
...    root_device_name="/dev/sda1"
...    block_device_map=block_map)
```

Now that you have your image based on the EBS snapshot, you can launch a new instance and the instance data will persist even when it's shut down. Make frequent backups just in case things break, because it's much harder to revert. Given a volume v, you can easily grab a snapshot with the following code:

```
>>> v.create_snapshot(description="My Snapshot Description")
```

The Description field is optional and enables you to better identify multiple snapshots if you want to specify what you did at each point. Think of these like a commit message in a revision control system. Although they're optional, if you're doing something important, you'll want to note that for future reference.

Summary

The singleton image is typically not one you want to use a lot, and you must be careful not to overuse it. However, when you need to ensure that a server has exactly one copy running at any given time, it's important to make sure you do it correctly. Following the detailed design here can help ensure that your instance is running properly and only once. Be wary, though, because this type of instance is the most prone to failures and speed issues. This type of image provides you with consistency over performance, scalability, and availability.

Prototype Images

Use prototype images whenever possible. They are the most cloud-based types of images you can create, and they enable you to build a base image that you can maintain separately from your core code base. Instead of maintaining several instances, you have one of them with the basic requirements of all your systems, and a few extra pieces to enable you to install new code automatically at boot.

Overview

You can see in Figure 4.3 the prototype image starts by building off of the base image and then adds in configuration data that provides the package data to launch a single instance. Because each layer of this pattern builds off of the other, you need to determine where each piece goes.

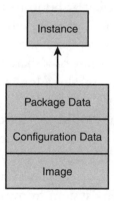

Figure 4.3   The prototype image.

Reasons for Usage

Use this pattern if *any* of the following apply:

- You are still in *development* and don't know what you need on your image.
- You want to maintain only a single copy of your image for *multiple purposes.*

- You want your system to *automatically update* whenever you launch a new instance.
- You want to provide *expandability* to your system.

Description

In the prototype image, you start with a basic image, add in some of the basic requirements for your applications, and then add in another system that enables you to put in a hook at boot that enables you to add in extra packages. This is typically done by putting something in your `rc.local` file if you use Linux, or a service if you use Windows.

When your instance first boots up, it checks the configuration data passed into it to determine if you need to install any packages. You can pass in package names and have them automatically passed to your local package installer at boot. To install packages of your own in a private distribution, you can either modify your local image to point to a private repository, or you can install some special scripts to pull packages out of a shared storage location. The shared storage solution is typically a lot easier and safer because you can control that more.

After you become an advanced user of cloud web services, you'll want to have to maintain only a single instance for updates. This enables you to maintain only a single copy of your base operating system and then upgrade and redeploy if necessary. In this case, you abstract your base operating system from the rest of your code.

Implementation

When you first start to develop this base image, add in everything you need for all your servers but not much more. If something takes a long time to install but doesn't take up a large footprint, you might also consider installing it even if you don't enable it at boot. It's quite safe usually to install something like Apache, but then just disable it instead of having to install it each time you launch a new instance.

The simplest implementation of a prototype instance is to use a basic Ubuntu image that reads from the configuration metadata passed into it and passes each line into `apt-get -y install`. Also make sure you reconfigure the base image to not prompt for any input by running `dpkg-reconfigure debconf` and selecting `Noninteractive`. This ensures that no questions are asked when you're installing, which would impact anything from automatically installing on your instance.

Example

With Amazon Web Services, you can set up two separate types of installation requests. If you pass in a MHMessage-based configuration file as the metadata, you can set a single value as the list of packages to be installed, passed directly into `apt-get`. Another alternative is to run what was passed into the configuration metadata file as if it were a shell script.

In boto-based images (also known as **pyami** images), it's more accepted to use custom installers made in a simple Python script instead of passing things directly onto the shell. This helps because you can then provide common methods for things done regularly, such as setting up cron jobs, installing init scripts, or copying files out of S3. Installers can be instantiated by passing in the following metadata into an instance at boot:

```
[Pyami]
packages = sqlalchemy, s3:my_bucket/my_installer.tar.gz
scripts = my_installer.InstallerClass
```

In the preceding example, the "packages" option shows where to grab the files from. The first package is just passed directly into `easy_install` because it's a standard package, but the second package is pulled out of `s3`, from `my_bucket`. After all the packages are installed, the scripts line is read, which contains a comma-separated value of installers to be run. Each of these is imported, and the `main` method is executed on the class. The strings here are passed directly to the `boto.utils.find_class` method and then executed. An example of such an installer to install Apache can be seen here:

```
from boto.pyami.installers.ubuntu.installer import Installer
from boto.utils import fetch_file
import boto
class ApacheInstaller(Installer):
    """A simple Apache Installer"
    def install(self):
        """Install Apache"""
        self.run("apt-get update")
        self.run("apt-get -y install apache2")
        self.run("a2enmod rewrite")
        self.run("a2enmod ssl")
        self.run("a2enmod proxy")
        self.run("a2enmod proxy_http")

        self.stop("apache2")
        myapp_zip = open("/mnt/myapp.tar.gz", "w")
        fetch_file(boto.config.get("MyApp", "package_url",
➥file=myapp_zip)
        myapp_zip.close()
        self.run("tar --directory=/mnt/myapp -xzf
➥/mnt/myapp.tar.gz")
        myapp_apacheconf = open("/etc/apache2/sites-
➥available/myapp")
        fetch_file(boto.config.get("MyApp", "conf_url",
➥file=myapp_apacheconf)
        myapp_apacheconf.close()
        self.run("a2ensite myapp")
        self.start("apache2")
    def run(self):
        import os, os.path
        if not os.path.exists("/etc/apache2/sites-available/myapp"):
            self.install()
```

This installer first checks to make sure that it hasn't already been installed and then updates the local package list. Next, install Apache 2 and enable a few Apache modules. Then stop Apache and pull in your package from S3 as determined by your metadata configuration file. Pull this into `/mnt` because that is typically where you store your ephemeral drive. Then extract your package and pull down your Apache configuration file into the site available. The last step is to enable that site and then restart Apache.

You may want to do several other things here, such as install cron scripts and other init scripts that will be used to start your specific application. You can also do extra things on reboot if you want, such as upgrading your code. This is especially helpful because your code is recalled (although not updated) after each reboot. This can be useful if you want to make upgrading your servers as simple as rebooting them.

Summary

The prototype image is the most powerful type of image you can build. It scales exceptionally well and can accommodate an ongoing development and a production system. It's the most expandable type of image in the fleet because you can add in new software on a whim without having to rebuild your image. Because rebuilding images is often time-consuming, using this type of image helps reduce overall development time and enables you to upgrade your systems by rebooting or relaunching them.

5

Designing an Architecture

Now that your images are built, it's time to focus on designing your architecture for your application. The most important part of any application is making it work with the rest of the world. It's great to have everything working internally, but you need to find an appropriate way to spread requests to your instances and properly delegate to them. Several patterns in this chapter can help you decide how to split any incoming request apart between your instances.

Requests can come in all sorts of packages, but typically they begin with some sort of user interaction. In a typical application, this would be from a web-based request. The simplest example of such a request is a user requesting a webpage. In this event, the user's browser connects to an instance over port 80 and communicates the desire to retrieve a specific page. Although this chapter doesn't go into details about how this interaction takes place, you do need to know how the user picks which instance to connect to. In the typical cloud-based environment, you have several instances each representing the same application, so you can use one of these patterns to delegate to the instance that can handle this request. If you work with these types of synchronous requests, you probably want to look at the **proxy** pattern.

Another type of request is one that happens asynchronously, such as a request to transcode a video. Because such a request typically cannot be completed within the typical HTTP browser timeout, it's important to have this request queued up and delegated to the next available processing instance as it becomes available. If you deal with this type of request, take a look at the **Facade** pattern.

Anytime you deal with requests, you need to realize that you're communicating with the legacy world; the noncloud world is much less scalable than the cloud-based world. If you query external servers, make sure that you don't hit them to hard or too often. In most corporate worlds, they also expect your requests to come from a single IP address, and often they firewall you off and authenticate you based on that. If you run your applications in the cloud, you realize that providing your clients with every IP where your requests will come from is incredibly hard to do because you either need to have them enable every IP address in your cloud provider's IP space or ensure that your IP address never changes. The first solution leaves them wide open to attack, and the second solution is incredibly unscalable.

Note: Each pattern in this chapter begins on a new page.

Adapters

When you need to communicate with multiple different systems, it's often impractical to adapt your specific application to handle each new system in its own language. A more modular approach to these types of problems is to instead use an adapter to modify the existing interface of that system and hit your interface instead. This can be often useful when you're given access to something that you can't hit often, but you need to query against it quite a lot.

Overview

As you can see in Figure 5.1, there are four basic parts of the adapter pattern: client, target, adapter, and adaptee. The client makes the request to your target application, which then queries your adapter. Your adapter then has the choice to query its local cache or forward the request along to the adaptee.

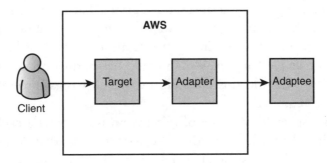

Figure 5.1   The adapter pattern.

A more likely scenario, however, is that your adapter will modify the request and add authentication if it's required. The advantage here is that you can give your clients access to act as you without giving them your credentials.

Reasons for Usage

Use this pattern if any of the following apply:

- You need to authenticate your requests to another endpoint.
- You need to provide a different interface to another endpoint.
- You need to provide more reliable access to a system you don't own.
- You want cheaper access to a system you don't own, by caching requests.

Description

In the most general sense, each request from the client goes directly to the target, which handles authentication and authorization, and then passes on that request directly to the adapter. The adapter then has to figure out how to dispatch this request to the adaptee, making a request and often signing that request. This can be particularly useful when you want to support authentication, but your adaptee also requires authentication. Instead of handing out the *keys to the kingdom*, which could be used to do anything, you can instead build this layer on top, which passes through only authorized requests.

Another specialized usage of this system is to insert a caching layer at the adapter level. In this case, each request that comes in to the adapter would first be checked against a cache system, and if a valid cache is available, it would return that response instead of hitting the adaptee directly. This can be incredibly useful when dealing with systems that limit how often you can hit them (such as the Twitter API), or ones that charge you per use.

Implementation

The actual implementation of this pattern is quite simple. Most applications use this pattern on a daily basis, but the key is where the adapter is stored. In Figure 5.1, notice that both the target and the adapter are inside of AWS. Do not allow your client to run the adapter program locally because that program has direct and total access to act as you on the adaptee. This is particularly bad if you give your users access to something like your database. Your client application may have use for information that comes out of SDB, but you obviously don't want your users accessing it directly.

A simple implementation of this pattern is used in almost every Gui-Over-Database application framework. A **Gui-Over-Database** application framework is where your application layer provides little more then the ability to Create, Read, Update, and Delete (CRUD) basic objects stored in your database, such as recipes and ingredients in a typical cookbook application. These frameworks typically include a specialized layer, an **Object Relational Mapping** or **ORM** layer. This ORM is simply an adapter that changes how you use the database API and instead gives your application a friendlier interface, hiding the authentication and connection frameworks and handling sessions and transactions automatically for you.

Example

The basic idea behind Twitter was to develop a simple web interface and an API so that third-party companies could create their own applications to use that data. Many companies have seized this idea and now use it to provide live news as it happens and updates that would previously never be spread so quickly. To protect their systems, Twitter has implemented **rate limiting**, which limits request against its API by IP address and user account. Additionally, it requires you to authenticate using **oAuth** if you want to see a user's **Friends Timeline**, or access any user's private timeline. oAuth is a proxy authentication system that enables you to authorize your application to read the Friends Timeline without having your username and password, and without having write access.

Start off by creating a Twitter user to use to follow people. Use this method to monitor exactly whose posts makes it into your system, and use the Twitter API to sign up new users as you see fit. You need to pull in your Friends Timeline and cache any statuses so that you don't continuously hit Twitter every time a user wants to see something.

After you create your Twitter User, you need to sign up your application to use oAuth by visiting http://twitter.com/oauth_clients and filling out the necessary information. This console enables you to register your application with Twitter so that your user can register with it directly. It then gives you a key and a secret key, often simply called a "secret," to sign up all your requests. Put these keys into your `boto.cfg` under a Twitter section, with the names `oauth_key` and `oauth_secret`.

The next step is to generate an authentication token for your application by using `oauth-python-twitter`. To install this, first install the prerequisite `oauth` by using `easy_install`:

```
$ easy_install oauth
```

Next, download `python-twitter`. You could grab this from http://code.google.com/p/python-twitter/ and then add in `oauth` from http://code.google.com/p/oauth-python-twitter, but you already did that and some other minor patching, so just copy it from http://bitbucket.org/cmoyer/python-twitter/. Then check this out and install it using the following commands:

```
$ hg clone https://bitbucket.org/cmoyer/python-twitter
$ cd python-twitter
$ python setup.py install
```

Of course, this assumes you already have **Mercurial** installed. Mercurial is a distributed version control system that enables you to check in code locally and also sync your repository with others. The basic command "clone" is similar to checking out a remote repository for the first time, but in reality it also copies down all change-sets locally, so you can view all the differences, logs, and even check in new changes without contacting the server again. Installation can be done using the following command:

```
$ easy_install mercurial
```

Mercurial has a few basic commands that you'll probably want to know about if you deal with these types of repositories, each which can be accessed using the mercurial command line tool hg (which is the scientific abbreviation for the element Mercury).

The clone command previously used can enable you to download and initialize an entire remote repository, and set the default push and pull targets. The pull command can enable you to update your local repository after it's been initialized. When triggered with the additional -u flag, it will also update your local checkout. The push command sends any local commits you've created to the target you initialized, or can also be called with a new target to send your entire repository to another location.

The commit command simply commits your changes to your local repository. Without doing the push command, these changes will not be merged into the repository you initially cloned from, and this typically means only you will have access to those changes. You can use this command to "stage" checkins without making them public yet.

Getting back to your application, you can now create a simple command-line application to generate your oAuth token. Store this token in SDB for use later so you don't have to authorize your application every time a user wants to make a request.

```python
#!/usr/bin/env python

#
# Author: Chris Moyer
# Description: Do the OAuth dance.
#
from twitter import OAuthApi
import boto

if __name__ == "__main__":
    sdb = boto.connect_sdb()
    try:
        db = sdb.get_domain("twitter")
    except:
        db = None
    if not db:
        db = sdb.create_domain("twitter")
    conf = db.get_item("twitter-config")
```

```
if not conf:
    conf = db.new_item("twitter-config")

oauth_key = boto.config.get("Twitter", "oauth_key")
oauth_secret = boto.config.get("Twitter", "oauth_secret")

twitter = OAuthApi(oauth_key, oauth_secret)
request_token = twitter.getRequestToken()

print twitter.getAuthorizationURL(request_token)
pin = raw_input("PIN: ")
twitter = OAuthApi(oauth_key, oauth_secret, request_token)

access_token = twitter.getAccessToken(pin=pin)
twitter = OAuthApi(oauth_key, oauth_secret, access_token)
print twitter.GetUserInfo()

conf['access_token'] = access_token.__str__()
conf.save()
print conf['access_token']
```

When you run this application, it first prints out a URL to the console that you'll go to in a browser, log in using your Twitter user account, and then authorize this application. Twitter then gives you a PIN to enter in back at your application. Then go back to your console, paste in your PIN, and press Enter. After this is done, your application prints out the access token and saves it to SDB under the `twitter` domain, in an item named `twitter-config`. You can use this later in your application to authenticate against Twitter.

Next, create your adapter program that enables you to have your users hit you instead of Twitter. This adapter can later be used to add in caching, but you see the basics here:

```
#!/usr/bin/env python
import boto
import time
from twitter import OAuthApi
from oauth import oauth
```

```
class TwitterConnection(object):
    """Twitter Connection Adapter"""

    def __init__(self):
        # Set up oAuth
        sdb = boto.connect_sdb()
        db = sdb.get_domain("twitter")
        conf = db.get_item("twitter-config")
        access_token = oauth.OAuthToken.from_string(
➥conf['access_token'])
        oauth_key = boto.config.get("Twitter", "oauth_key")
        oauth_secret = boto.config.get("Twitter", "oauth_secret")
        self.twitter = OAuthApi(oauth_key,
➥oauth_secret, access_token)

    def getFriendsTimeline(self, page=1):
        """Get the friends statuses"""
        attempt = 0
        backoff = 2
        while attempt < 10:
            try:
                return self.twitter.GetFriendsTimeline(page=page)
            except Exception, e:
                print "Twitter Exception: %s " % e
                backoff += backoff
                time.sleep(backoff)
                attempt += 1
        return None
```

When you create a new TwitterConnection, your application authenticates itself using the access_token you previously generated. You can then use this connection object to get your friends' timelines, and even access multiple pages for it. Because Twitter is a web application, it's prone to intermediate errors, so allow for some error recovery and attempt to access Twitter up to ten times, increasing your wait time each attempt.

Then plug this adapter directly into your web service and serve it up just like you do with any other API. To be fully flexible and modular, this API should be run on its own EC2 instance, so you can change it anytime you need to without taking down the rest of the system.

Summary

It's often more useful to adapt outside APIs to work with your existing system instead of making all sorts of adaptations on your entire system to handle their APIs. This becomes increasingly true when your application has to connect to multiple external end-points, each which may have their own method of authentication and data representation. In your example, you made a simple adapter on top of the Twitter API, so when it changes its authentication mechanism again in a year, you need to modify your adapter instead of your core system. Because you operate within a cloud architecture, this adapter lives on its own server, so changing it out is as easy as swapping out a hard drive in a RAID array.

Facades

A Facade pattern unifies multiple interfaces into a single interface. This type of interface is typically used in web-based applications because a browser does not typically like to connect to multiple endpoints for security reasons. Most Facades sit on top of multiple adapters providing their users with a single endpoint for easy access to multiple modules. This interface provides the basis for any modular application.

Overview

As you can see in Figure 5.2, the Facade sits on top of multiple APIs delegating requests coming in from the user.

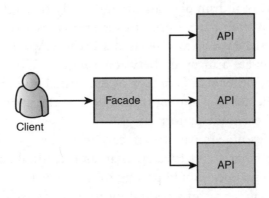

Figure 5.2   The Facade pattern.

Unlike an adapter, a Facade can take a single request and modify it to send out to multiple subsystems, sometimes waiting for responses from one subsystem before deciding what other systems to send to. For example, a few systems will upload a video to multiple different video hosting providers such as YouTube, Blip.tv, or Vimeo. A video upload system could attempt to use one of these services, and if it receives an error, manually upload to each of these separate APIs.

Reasons for Usage

You should use a Facade if any of the following apply:

- You have multiple APIs you want to grant access to via a single endpoint.
- You need to provide access to both static and dynamic content in a web browser.
- You need to adapt your system and add on modules after deployment.

Description

Unlike an adapter that modifies an existing API, Facades sit on top of multiple APIs and simply pass them directly through as-is to the client. In many web frameworks, this is known as a **mapper**. If you've ever used Apache, you've used a Facade. Apache's configuration files designate a mapping between a request URL, and what it should return, either static content or dynamic content if you use mod_proxy. The act of mapping the request to the appropriate handler itself is the Facade pattern.

Facades as a software pattern are easy to understand and simple in nature, but what about Facades as an architectural approach? Instead of the mapper simply passing off requests to another class, what if that mapper sat in a central location and passed off requests to other servers or **modules**? It's at this point where you can stop thinking about a Facade as a piece of software and start thinking about it as a central system in your overall architecture.

Implementation

The implementation of a Facade pattern is relatively simple. Almost every web application out there uses a Facade in some manor. Apache itself is an example implementation of a Facade. When creating modular applications, you often need to pull in data from multiple different systems and present them all in one location for the user.

Facades as an architectural approach, however, are less well known. One common usage for a Facade is to provide for authorization and authentication on top of several common, yet distinct modules. This enables you to combine multiple APIs under one location. This is important when dealing with web APIs because cross-site AJAX requests are not allowed in most modern browsers. Additionally, separating out each module enables you to take down a single part of the system without taking down the entire system.

The first step to building a proper mapper is making the mapping process as modular and expandable as possible. Wherever possible, try to have configuration options stored in a decentralized location or database. If you build your system correctly, a new route can be added without having to take down your mapper.

Separation of system is key when you're building a fault-tolerant system. If any single module returns an error, you have the option of retrying the request, or queuing it up for retry later if you don't need the response immediately.

Example

A few years ago, I was involved in a large identity management system for my college. We used a central system to map requests out to appropriate modules. Requests came into the central mapper (or Facade) and then modified them to the language that specific module required before sending it down to that module. The response was then reversely mapped back into the response and passed back in through the filter again to return the finalized response to the user.

Requests enter the mapper in the form of an XML document. This XML document contains actions directed to specific modules, and some actions may be directed to multiple modules. Each module registers itself with the mapper when it comes online and announces which actions it responds to.

In Figure 5.3, you see an example request for the system. The request from the user was to `ListComputers`, which translates into listing all computers that user owns. The first thing the mapper

does before processing through anything is to run the request
through the input filter. The resulting request is seen here:

```
<Request>
  <GetUser/>
  <ListComputers/>
</Request>
```

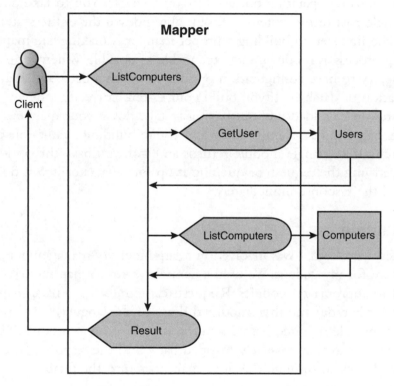

Figure 5.3   The mapper process.

The mapper next performs a GetUser on the Users module,
which returns the user object that is currently logged in. The
request sent to the mapper also included an HTTP cookie that
contained a token that identified this user so that's what's used to
fetch the user from the Users module. The user's module returns
the response back to the mapper, which is combined back to

formulate a request to the Computers module. As responses come back from modules, they translate the original request document forming a new request document. Although you started off with a simple one-line tag of <ListComputers/>, it has now become the more complicated document seen here:

```
<Request>
  <User id="34598712398712">
   <name>My User</name>
   <authGroups>
      <authGroup>Student</authGroup>
   </authGroups>
  </User>
  <ListComputers/>
</Request>
```

You see the request has been expanded and now includes the current user object. This request is then sent down to the Computers module that processes the request using both the original request for the Computers, and the User information provided. After the Computers module has received and processed the request, it calculates the Users' computers and then returns those results back to the mapper. The mapper then combines the results into the response document seen here:

```
<Request>
  <User id="34598712398712">
   <name>My User</name>
   <authGroups>
      <authGroup>Student</authGroup>
   </authGroups>
  </User>
  <ListComputers>
   <Computer id="2948712312312">
    <name>My Computer</name>
    <description>A computer</description>
    <mac>00:00:00:55:55:55</mac>
   </Computer>
   ...
  </ListComputers>
</Request>
```

The mapper now has all the modules' responses filled out, so the next thing it has to do is run the result through its output filter to produce the response. Because the only thing the user actually cares about is the <ListComputers> tag, strip out everything else and just return that as the response body:

```
<ListComputers>
  <Computer id="2948712312312">
   <name>My Computer</name>
   <description>A computer</description>
   <mac>00:00:00:55:55:55</mac>
  </Computer>
  ...
</ListComputers>
```

This response is forwarded along to the Client as the result and the process is completed.

Summary

If you need to provide multiple different services under a single endpoint, using a Facade is a perfect solution for you. Although you may be inclined to handle this by providing a software Facade, it can often be much more suitable to provide an architectural Facade. This method of mapping out requests to entirely separate systems helps to ease the burden of processing and enables you to provide a modular system that can be expanded at any time without shutting down the entire system.

Proxies and Balancers

Proxies and balancers are used in most major applications to hide the original application servers and to provide a single access point that can be answered by multiple recipients. Before starting to use proxy balancers, man developers instead split users apart manually onto different servers, directing users to contact different servers directly instead of seamlessly transitioning them to the most available server.

Overview

As you can see in Figure 5.4, the Proxy pattern here is actually used as a balancer and a proxy. This adaptation of the traditional Proxy pattern adds the ability to choose and balance incoming requests among multiple servers that can each handle the same request. The balancer chooses one of these endpoints to forward the request through untainted and returns the result.

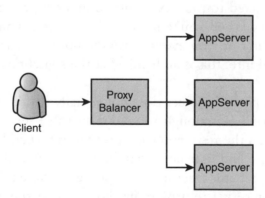

Figure 5.4   The Proxy balancer pattern.

Reasons for Usage

You should use a Proxy if any of the following apply:

- You need to provide reliable continuous access to your application server.

- Your application needs to run multiple copies for performance reasons.
- You need to seamlessly scale your application.

Description

Proxy balancers provide reliability and stability for your application
servers. In addition to splitting the load across multiple systems,
you also provide health checks for your servers that enable a single
server to fail without impacting your overall application. The proxy
balancer performs periodic checks against all of the application
servers registered to it and a validation of any response flowing
through it to ensure that users have seamless user experiences.

When you call technical support for a computer distributor, you
dial into one number. You don't have to dial one number and then,
if that number is busy, dial another, and you certainly don't have a
personal number that just you can dial. Instead, your call (or
request) is directed to the next available support person. You're
never informed when you're redirected away from your original
call-in point, nor do you ever receive the number that you're
actively dialed into; this is all handled at the switchboard, or proxy
balancer.

Similarly, a proxy balancer does not actually handle your request;
it simply dispatches it along to the next available server. This server
then formulates the response, which is then returned back through
your proxy. The end user never has direct contact with the application server, but it still receives the response unaltered. If, however,
the application server returns an invalid response, the proxy balancer may choose to forward the same request along to another
application server in its registry until it receives a valid response.

Implementation

For the most part, creating your own proxy balancer is not necessary. Apache has several modules for balancing the load between
application servers, and there are also several other prepackaged

proxy systems out there. Before you attempt to use any of these canned proxy systems, however, you should first check with your cloud provider to make sure they don't offer anything better.

Example

Amazon Web Services noticed that a majority of its users were struggling with how to properly build and deploy proxies. It released a service that provides cheaper and more reliable load balancing and proxying than what most users could build with just EC2 alone. It calls this service **Elastic Load Balancing** or **ELB**.

ELB enables you to proxy any generic TCP port, or HTTP. If you proxy HTTP, it actually provides some additional utilities that monitor the response and retries if a 500 level error occurs. If, however, you need to provide for HTTPS support, you have to use a generic TCP proxy because the encrypted traffic is not readable by the proxy.

Setting up an ELB is relatively easy and can be done using the basic commands provided by Amazon. To start first visit http://aws.amazon.com/elasticloadbalancing/ and sign up for ELB. You can then either use the tools provided by Amazon or use the `elbadmin` utility provided by boto. Because the Amazon tools are well documented, you can focus on how to use the `elbadmin` utility.

Most important, `elbadmin` provides its own help if you don't provide any arguments when calling it. This help can be seen here:

```
% elbadmin
Usage: elbadmin [options] [command]
Commands:
    list|ls                         List all Elastic Load Balancers
    delete     <name>               Delete ELB <name>
    get        <name>               Get all instances associated
                                      with <name>
    create     <name>               Create an ELB
    add        <name> <instance>    Add <instance> in ELB <name>
    remove|rm <name> <instance>    Remove <instance> from ELB <name>
    enable|en <name> <zone>        Enable Zone <zone> for ELB <name>
    disable    <name> <zone>        Disable Zone <zone> for ELB <name>
```

```
Options:
  --version               show program's version number and exit
  -h, --help              show this help message and exit
  -z ZONES, --zone=ZONES
                          Operate on zone
  -l LISTENERS, --listener=LISTENERS
                          Specify Listener in,out,proto
```

As you can see here, the `elbadmin` utility takes options and a command. When first starting out, you need to create a load balancer. This can be done using the `elbadmin create` command. You'll also need to specify at least one listener, which is the ELB term for the proxy port. The syntax for this listener is specified in the help page and requires you to specify the source port (in), the destination port (out), and the protocol that is to be used for communication. Currently this is limited to HTTP or TCP. Two listeners are specified for your proxy, 80 with HTTP, and 443 with TCP (because HTTPS is not proxyable over the HTTP protocol). Creating a new balancer using `elbadmin` can be done with the code here:

```
% elbadmin -l 80,80,http -l 443,443,tcp create www
Name: www
DNS Name: www-my-dns-name.elb.amazonaws.com

Listeners
---------
80        80        http
443       443       tcp

  Zones
  ---------

Instances
---------
```

Notice that only one of the three key sections is filled out here. The next important thing to do is to add in instances to the load balancer. ELB splits the load equally across all the zones that are enabled, so if you have two servers enabled in us-east-1a, and only

1 server enabled in us–east–1b, your two servers in us–east–1a receive the same number of requests *total* as that one server in us–east–1b. That is to say, each server in us–east–1a receives 50% of the request volume that the server in us–east–1b receives.

So now add a server to your balancer. This can be done using the simple `elbadmin add` command:

```
% elbadmin add www i-000111
Name: www
DNS Name: www-my-dns-name.elb.amazonaws.com


Listeners
---------
80        80        http
443       443       tcp


   Zones
---------


Instances
---------
i-000111
```

Now if you press your DNS name, you may expect to be directed to your server but still have one more step. To enable this server for traffic to be directed to it, you have to enable the zone it's running in. This can be done using the `elbadmin enable` command:

```
% elbadmin enable www us-east-1a
Name: www
DNS Name: www-my-dns-name.elb.amazonaws.com


Listeners
---------
80        80        http
443       443       tcp


   Zones
---------
us-east-1a
```

```
Instances
----------
i-000111
```

Notice now that traffic will flow directly to your server from this proxy. It's recommended that you use at least two different availability zones to maintain uptime because Amazon doesn't ensure availability of *every* zone at any given time. The EC2 SLA provides a limit to how long more than one zone in a single region will be down, meaning that at any given time, there should be at least three zones operating.

Although it may be tempting to enable every zone in your proxy balancer, it's important that you only enable zones that you have active running servers registered in. If you enable zones that have no registered active servers for that proxy, you will encounter timeout issues and random issues due to the proxy balancer attempting to proxy requests where it cannot. The proxy balancer does enable for health checks and validation that the servers are indeed working, but the more unhealthy servers in a proxy, the more time it can take to find a valid server.

Summary

Whenever you deal with a system that requires constant uptime, you absolutely have to use a proxy balancer to provide such a promise. You can not rely on a single point of failure if you need scalability and reliability. In the days before cloud computing, this was typically handled by using round robin DNS, but that relies too much on the client choosing which server to hit. Because you now have the option to handle the proxying and balancing behind the scenes, you can both mask and protect your application servers and, at the same time, ensure that the load is evenly distributed.

## 6

Executing Actions on Data

Building up your instance and communicating with the outside world has given you a lot of data that you can now use in your application, but what about operations on that data that take more than a small amount of time? What if that action could potentially fail and needs to be retried? This chapter doesn't focus on the objects themselves but instead focuses on the *interaction* between those objects.

This chapter covers several new patterns that help with executing actions on your data. Typically, your application has two forms of requests: synchronous and asynchronous. Most people can handle synchronous requests, but the cloud lends itself to be used in an asynchronous manor. Instead of returning results for a report instantly, it's typically more efficient to queue up a request and then notify the user when it is finished.

Note: Each pattern in this chapter begins on a new page.

Queuing

When you need to communicate with multiple, different systems, it's often impractical to have your systems communicate directly. Not only does this require you to inform every requesting system of the workers, but it also requires the requester to handle delegating the request directly, and managing whether the request failed.

Using a queue instead of direct communication enables you to perform these asynchronous requests automatically and enables new workers to come online without notifying anyone. Additionally, you provide for fault tolerance by updating your status in the queue and only deleting the message after you validate that you completed the task requested.

Overview

Figure 6.1 shows the highlights of the queuing pattern. In this figure, squares represent instances or physical machines. The diamond represents a service, which may be composed of multiple machines. The backward, rounded arrow represents data sent. The cylinder represents a database capable of including indexes and being queried quickly. Finally, the multiple layered box represents a distributed filesystem or file storage service.

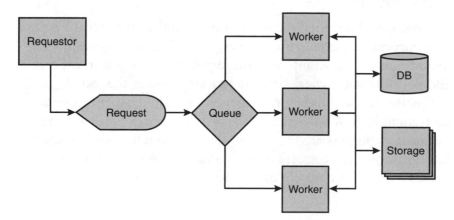

Figure 6.1   The queuing pattern.

In the queuing pattern, a requestor sends a request to a central queue service. This request is simply a bit of data that should not be language-specific and must be a standard format that can be understood by any worker listening to the queue. Any number of worker servers may be listening to this queue, and respond to any of these messages, where they may access a database and other distributed services. This is usually done because the requests are not intended to be large but simply a set of instructions to operate on data stored in these other distributed services such as a database or file storage system. For example, in a video-processing system, you wouldn't want to send the video through as a request but simply a pointer to the file in a distributed file system.

Reasons for Usage

Use this pattern if requests can be returned asynchronously and any of the following apply:

- You need fault tolerance for requests.
- You need to scale your worker pool in real-time.
- You want to hide the workers from your requestor.

Description

Queues have been used for years in many different systems. The sole purpose of a queue is to manage jobs. This management includes recording all information required for the job to process and periodic status checks on the process running the job.

Queues handle holding messages and enable those messages to be read, hidden, and deleted. Messages may or may not have the option of being updated and typically contain references to other locations for more data. It's often impractical to store all the data in a message, so you typically use a reference instead.

Implementation

A queue can be created using any central storage system accessible from all workers and requesters, which has some form of locking. Often, this means using a standard database, such as MySQL.

It is obviously important that the queuing system be accessible to all workers and requestors because you need to get your requests into and out of the system reliably from any system in the process. You need this central system to be as reliable and available as possible or your entire system will fall down. This central queuing system becomes your single point of failure, so it must be well designed. If possible, you should attempt to use something from your cloud provider, so you don't have to worry about managing your own queuing software and servers.

Queues hold this small amount of data and wait for a worker to request a message from them. The act of reading the message also triggers that message to be hidden for a period of time. The worker then spawns off two processes: one to process the task and another to monitor that process. As long as the task is processing, the monitor process continues to hide the message. After the task finishes, the monitor process deletes the message. This completes the cycle, as shown in Figure 6.2.

Example

Since the eruption of mobile devices in the marketplace, one common function of cloud computing has been to encode videos from one format to another. Most videos on the Internet today are available in **h.264**, an open video format made popular by Apple for use within mobile devices. This format is quite popular because there are a variety of hardware decoders available for it that reduces the battery and CPU utilization, which is incredibly important in mobile devices. If you want to provide videos to your clients, you need to convert your videos before sending them.

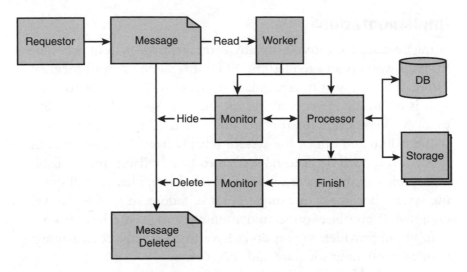

Figure 6.2   The worker processing a task.

Several resources exist that can convert videos to h.264, but you'll use a basic script that I've designed and have been using for conversion of almost any input type to h.264 for use on a mobile device. You'll use `ffmpeg` to handle your conversions because it has all the options you need, and it's easily scriptable. It's important to install `ffmpeg` with the `x264` encoder, so more than likely, you'll have to build it from source to enable all the proper functionality. Several good resources are available online for installing `ffmpeg` with this encoder using Ubuntu (including https://wiki.ubuntu.com/ffmpeg), so this chapter doesn't go into much detail about that.

After you have `ffmpeg` installed correctly, you need to script the actual encoding process. The following script works well to encode videos, taking almost any sort of input video file and producing a quality output video that can easily be streamed on either a 3G or WiFi connection:

```
#!/bin/sh
# File: encode_264.sh
# Usage: encode_264.sh <input_file> <output_file>
# Output: mp4
ffmpeg -i "$1" -pass 1 -an -vcodec libx264 \
```

```
-vpre fastfirstpass -vpre ipod640 -b 512k \
-bt 512k -s 640x480 -threads 0 -f rawvideo \
-y /dev/null && ffmpeg -i "$1" -pass 2 \
-acodec libfaac -ab 128k -ac 2 \
-vcodec libx264 -vpre hq -vpre ipod640 \
-b 512k -bt 512k -s 640x480 \
-threads 0 $2
```

This script takes two arguments: an input file and an output file. It does a two-pass encoding that produces a file named whatever you pass in as the second argument. Next, look at how to start this encoding process automatically. Because you use Amazon Web Services, you can use the queuing service Amazon created and maintains: Simple Queue Service (SQS). First, define your message format. You need the source, destination, and encoding for each encoding request.

Use a standard **MHMessage Format** that enables you to encode simple key-value pairs. Because it's impractical to actually pass the input file through in a message, use S3 to store the input file. You also store the output file in S3, so the destination is actually just an S3 bucket. The last requirement, encoding, is a key that tells your encoder what type of output you want. In this case, you support only one type of encoding, 264; however, you can still allow for this if you want to expand your processing later. This leaves you with a message that looks like the following:

```
Source: s3://input_bucket/input_file.flv
Destination: output_bucket
Encoding: 264
```

Next, start working on your message reader. To process the messages, you need to listen on the queue and fire off your processes as they come in. Start with the basic **sqs read loop**, which looks like this:

```
#!/usr/bin/env python

import boto
import sys
import time
```

```python
def process_request(m):
    """Process a single request"""

# Do the SQS Read-Loop Dance
if __name__ == "__main__":
    from boto.sqs.message import MHMessage
    sqs = boto.connect_sqs()
    q = sqs.get_queue(boto.config.get("video", "encode_queue",
"encode"))
    q.set_message_class(MHMessage)
    boto.log.info("Listening on Queue: %s" % q.name)
    while True:
        try:
            m = q.read()
            if m:
                # If we have a message, process it
                process_request(m)
            else:
                # If we don't, then just sleep for 60 seconds
                # before reading again
                time.sleep(60)
        except Exception, e:
            # If there was a problem, log it and continue
            boto.log.exception("EXCEPTION processing Video Encoding
➥Request")
            time.sleep(60) # Sleep 60 seconds before reading again
        except KeyboardInterrupt:
            boto.log.info("Terminated by user")
            sys.exit()
```

This simple shell sqs read loop can be used to process any
generic type of request, so it's a good starting point. Next, look at
what goes into the `process_request` function. This function can
handle all of the processing, including monitoring and deleting the
message if the task were successfully finished. First start with some
sanity checking and a bit of logging:

```python
def process_request(m):
    """Process a single request"""
    import re
    assert(m.has_key("Source"))
```

```
assert(m.has_key("Destination"))
assert(m.has_key("Encoding"))
assert(re.match("^[a-zA-Z0-9]*$", m['Encoding']))


boto.log.info("=================================")
boto.log.info("Encoding:     %s" % m['Encoding'])
boto.log.info("Source:       %s" % m['Source'])
boto.log.info("Destination:  %s" % m['Destination'])
boto.log.info("=================================")
```

Next, you need to identify the actual encoder to use. Because the user could have passed in anything that matches your regular expression of being a letter and number combination, you need to ensure that you know how to encode the requested video type. Find what command the user wanted to call and make sure it exists in one of your predetermined locations for these executables. You can use the following script to execute any available encoding script you may create at a later time as long as it follows the standard of encode_TYPE.py:

```
# Make sure the encoder exists
import os
command = "encode_%s.py" % m['Encoding']
has_command = False
for path in ['/usr/local/bin', '/usr/bin']:
   if os.path.isfile(os.path.join(path, command)):
      has_command = True
      command = os.path.join(path, command)
assert(has_command)
```

Because your encoder works with local files, not with files in S3, you need to pull down your file to your local filesystem. To make sure that this file is removed when the encoding has been completed, you can use Python's NamedTemporaryFile to temporarily store the video locally. This temporary file also has the capability to specify an optional suffix, which you can use to ensure that your temporary file has a similar name as the input file. This is required by ffmpeg because it uses the file extension to determine the type

of input video. You can use the following chunk of code to grab
the file from S3 into a temporary file locally so that you can
process it:

```
# Grab the input file
from tempfile import NamedTemporaryFile
from boto.utils import fetch_file
file_suffix = os.path.splitext(m['Source'])
if len(file_suffix) > 1:
    file_suffix = file_suffix[1]
else:
    file_suffix = ""
input_file = NamedTemporaryFile(suffix=file_suffix)
fetch_file(m['Source'], file=input_file)
input_file.flush()
```

The last step before encoding is to determine the output extension so that you can properly create your output's
NamedTemporaryFile. As you may recall from your encoder example, you added a comment that included this output extension.
Now use your Python script to read in the encoder and process
what the output extension should be:

```
# Find our output extension
output_ext = None
encoder_script = open(command, "r")
for line in encoder_script.readlines():
    match = re.match("#\s*Output:\s*([a-zA-Z0-9]*)", line)
    if match:
        output_ext =  match.group(1)
        break
if not output_ext:
    output_ext = "avi"
output_file = NamedTemporaryFile(suffix=output_ext)
```

Now it's time to start the actual encoding process. For this, use
the subprocess module introduced in Python version 2.4. This
module enables you to spawn an entirely new process and monitor
it via your script, so you don't have to worry about threading:

```
# Do the Encoding
import subprocess
```

```
process = subprocess.Popen('%s "%s" "%s"' %
 (command, input_file.name, output_file.name),
 shell=True,
 stdin=subprocess.PIPE,
 stdout=subprocess.PIPE,
 stderr=subprocess.PIPE)
start = time.time()
timeout = 0
while process.poll() == None:
    elapsed_time = int(time.time() - start)
    boto.log.info("elapsed time: %s" %
      int(time.time() - start))
    if elapsed_time >= timeout:
       timeout += 45
       m.change_visibility(60)
t = process.communicate()
boto.log.info("Output (%s)" % process.returncode)
boto.log.info(t[0])
boto.log.info(t[1])
```

The last two steps remaining are to upload the result and then clean up. Use the destination bucket and create your filename based on the input filename plus the extension you're now using. Then upload your resulting output file to that key, and delete our temporary files. Then remove your message to confirm that you succeeded in your encoding process. The following code enables you to upload the file, but times out after 10 minutes if the file doesn't upload successfully, enabling another process to attempt to do the encoding:

```
# Upload the results
# Allow 10 minutes to upload the file
m.change_visibility(600)
boto.log.info("====== Uploading Result ======")
output_file_name = "%s.%s" %
  (os.path.split(m['Source'])[-1], output_ext)
s3 = boto.connect_s3()
b = s3.get_bucket(m['Destination'])
key = b.new_key(output_file_name)
key.set_contents_from_filename(output_file.name)
```

```
# Cleanup
input_file.delete()
output_file.delete()
m.delete()
boto.log.info("====== Finished ========")
```

That's it! You can now run this processor on any encoding instance that has the `encode_264.sh` script, and it will automatically encode videos as requested. You can request a video to be encoded by simply sending a message to the queue you're listening on:

```
def submit_video(input, output, encoding="264"):
    """Submit a video to the encoding process"""
    import boto
    from boto.sqs.message import MHMessage
    sqs = boto.connect_sqs()
    q = sqs.get_queue(boto.config.get(
➥"video", "encode_queue", "encode"))

    m = MHMessage()
    m['Encoding'] = encoding
    m['Source'] = input
    m['Destination'] = output
    q.write(m)
    boto.log.info("Submitted video: %s" % input)
```

You can use this function to request that your video is encoded from your application. Of course, you don't have to make the request using this function, or even from a Python program. Any program may request a video to be encoded by simply submitting a message to the proper queue.

Summary

If you need to fire off requests asynchronously and have those jobs processed as quickly as possible, this is the solution for you. This type of request processing enables you to completely isolate your worker pool from your requesters and enables you to perform complex tasks without bogging down your primary servers. It gives you the advantage of scaling your workers separately from your other systems and enables you to isolate those workers to prevent them from being reached from the outside world. This modular approach and isolation of workers provides added security, scalability, and stability.

Command

The command (also known as the action, transaction, or job) pattern gives you the ability to encapsulate a request within an object. This allows for queuing, logging, and possible rollback operations. This method of packing up the request within a single object provides advanced flexibility for where the actual work is performed. It is often used with the queue pattern.

Overview

The command pattern encapsulates an entire request, input, output, status, and the actual execution to be processed. This data is then serialized between a database and other storage and can be sent along to another process for the actual work to be done using the queue pattern. Instead of dealing with how the data is transferred from one process to another, the command pattern simply deals with how the request itself is encapsulated. Figure 6.3 shows the basic overview of this pattern.

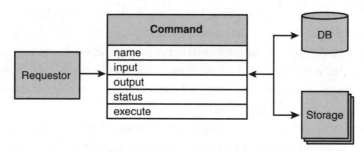

Figure 6.3   The command pattern.

Reasons for Usage

You should use this pattern if any of the following apply:

- You have multiple types of executable jobs to perform.
- You need to track detailed statistics about a job.
- You want to specifically define how a job is executed.

Description

Command objects encapsulate an entire processing instruction within an object. This object can then be serialized and transmitted along the network to be processed elsewhere. This helps to promote modular development and enables you to abstract your underlying framework from your application.

The architecture of the command pattern requires you to serialize the command object and recall it from any worker in your pool. These workers don't even know what the possible commands are. There needs to be a way to fully store every detail about the command including the entire environment required to execute and finish the task. Some commands also have the capability to rollback changes if something goes wrong in the processing of the command.

Implementation

Most queues don't enable more than 1MB to be in any single message, so the bulk of the command object must be serialized elsewhere. Most programming languages offer the capability to package all the related code for a given command, which can then be imported into the remote worker. Of course, each worker must contain the root class that all commands extend from, but using this package management system enables you to not have them know about every possible subclass to execute it.

There are many existing implementations of the command pattern as an architecture, the most famous of which is the Java-based **hadoop** cluster. This architecture enables the user to submit a job to the cluster that contains all the processing instructions within a jar file.

Of course, if you don't want to use Java, you can always develop your own command execution framework; all you need to do is serialize your entire request and send it to be processed. Typically, you'll use the queue pattern to fire off the request, and you'll store the command itself somewhere else.

Example

For AWS, store the bulk of your command data in S3, with the parameters in SDB. This enables you to reuse some of your commands by the abstraction of variables that can be changed. This example uses Python and setuptools to bundle your command into an egg, which can then be saved to S3. This, combined with a few utilities provided by boto, gives you almost all you need for your command class.

Because SQS handles only a limited amount of data, you can store most of your request data in SDB. The only things you need to send along via SQS is a reference to the configuration data stored in SDB. boto has a module known as `boto.sdb.db.model` that provides a link between Python objects and SDB/S3. You can set up properties on a given object that can be mapped to either SDB or S3 (depending on how much storage you need). Now look at creating a basic command object that can be serialized into these databases and then loaded onto a worker server:

```python
# File: command/__init__.py
# Author: Chris Moyer
# Description: The Command Pattern
import boto

from boto.sdb.db.model import Model
from boto.sdb.db.property import StringProperty,
➥DateTimeProperty, ReferenceProperty, BlobProperty
from botoweb.resources.user import User

class Command(Model):
    """Representation of an action that has
    been requested, When the Command is of status
    "queued" it is free to be run, otherwise
    it should not be run unless a specific
    re-process request has been received
    """
    name = StringProperty()
    # This is the URL to the package that
    # needs to be installed
    # in order for this Command to be even run
```

```
package_url = StringProperty()
package = StringProperty()

submitted_at = DateTimeProperty()
submitted_by = ReferenceProperty(User)
status = StringProperty(verbose_name="Status",
  choices=['standby',
           'active',
           'queued',
           'started',
           'finished',
           'error'],
  default="standby")
status_msg = BlobProperty()

processing_instance = StringProperty()
finished_at = DateTimeProperty()
```

Here, you define a few properties to determine how to serialize
this command and execute it. In addition to a few standard properties, you also have a special property to store the location of your
package required to execute this command. The `package_url` property is used to hold a URL to the egg to be installed. This URL
can either be an S3 URL (s3://bucket_name/package.egg) or any
other standard URL that can be passed in directly to `easy_install`.
Next, create a few functions to execute and install your command:

```
def exc(self, cmd):
    """Run a shell command"""
    import subprocess, time
    process = subprocess.Popen(self.command,
        shell=True, stdin=subprocess.PIPE,
        stdout=subprocess.PIPE,
        stderr=subprocess.PIPE)
    while process.poll() == None:
        time.sleep(5)
    t = process.communicate()
    return (process.returncode, t[0], t[1])

def install(self):
```

```
"""Install this command module so it
can be executed"""
if not self.package_url:
    return
if self.package_url.startswith("s3:"):
    package = fetch_file(self.package_url)
    package_url = package.name
else:
    package_url = self.package_url
self.exc("easy_install -Z %s" % self.package_url)
```

Here, you define two new functions: `exc` and `install`. You
abstracted out the shell command execution functionality because
that may be useful elsewhere in your script. The `install` function
is designed to ensure that the proper package is installed into the
local environment before the command is executed.

Setuptools has a unique functionality called **entry points**. This
enables you to define a hook into your egg that tells you what to
execute from this package. These hooks are added to the setup.py
file and then globally registered. This can be done like so:

```python
# File: setup.py
from setuptools import setup

setup(name = "examplecmd",
      version = "0.1",
      description = "Example Command",
      long_description="Example Commad pattern egg for Chapter 6
➡of my book",
      author = "Chris Moyer",
      author_email = "kopertop@gmail.com",
      url = "http://coredumped.org",
      packages = ["examplecmd"],
      license = 'MIT',
      platforms = 'Posix; MacOS X; Windows',
      classifiers = [ 'Development Status :: 3 - Alpha',
         'Intended Audience :: Developers',
         'License :: OSI Approved :: MIT License',
         'Operating System :: OS Independent',
         'Topic :: Internet',
      ],
```

```
entry_points = {
    "command.exc": [
        "example = examplecmd:main"
    ]
}
)
```

This creates a single entry point that points to your `examplecmd` module for a function called `main`. These entry points can then be pulled into your command object and executed. Now go back in and fill out your run method:

```
def run(self):
    """Run this Command"""
    from pkg_resources import get_entry_map
    entry_map = get_entry_map(self.package, "command.exc")
    output = {}
    for entry in entry_map:
        plugin = entry_map[entry].load()
        try:
            output[entry] = plugin(self)
        except Exception, e:
            boto.log.exception("Exception running: %s" % entry)
            output[entry] = e
    return output
```

The `get_entry_map` function returns a map of the entry points in the package you specified to be used in this command. Using these entry points enables you to map multiple functions to be run for each command. Next, define a function that calls this run command and wraps it in some notification and error recovery logs:

```
def start(self):
    """Start the Command, which wraps a
    few things before calling the run command"""
    from datetime import datetime
    boto.log.info("Starting Command: %s" % self.name)
    self.processing_instance =
     boto.config.get("Instance", "instance-id")
    self.status = "started"
    self.put()
    try:
```

```
        output = self.run()
        self.finished_at = datetime.utcnow()
        self.status = "finished"
        self.put()
        log = ""
        for entry in output:
            log += "<div>\n"
            log += "<h3>%s</h3>\n" % entry
            log += "<p>%s</p>\n" % output[entry]
            log += "</div>\n"
    except Exception, e:
        boto.log.exception("Exception running Command: %s" %
➡self.name)
        self.status = "error"
        self.status_msg = str(e)
        log = ""
        self.put()
    boto.log.info("Command Finished")
    if self.submitted_by:
        self.submitted_by.notify(
            subject="Command: %s" % self.name,
            body="<h2>%s</h2><div>%s</div>"
            % (self.status_msg, log))
```

The important parts here are that after the run command is executed, you generate a log string that returns the output that was returned by each of the entry points. This log is then emailed to the user that submitted the command.

This basic command object can also be extended if needed, but in general, this should enable you to submit basically anything via this command object.

Summary

You can use commands to serialize a single processing instruction for later use and handle information about what happened during the processing instruction. This, when combined with the queue pattern, enables you to create quite a functional request/worker pool and segregate your workers from your requests. It enables you to fully distribute everything in a cloud-like manner.

Iterator

Iterators provide access to a set of data without sending the entire set at once. This is often called **paging** and is most often associated with a **next token**, which provides a unique ID to get the next set of results.

Overview

As shown in Figure 6.4, iterators act as an intermediary between clients and the data sets produced by a system. As your requests come into your system, you can produce a result set and return it in increments using an iterator to prevent overloading the client and causing too much strain on your server.

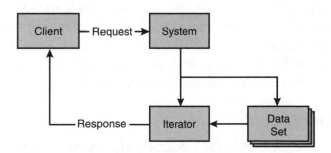

Figure 6.4   The iterator pattern.

As with any normal application, requests are sent from the client to the system. However, instead of the system responding directly with all the results, it responds with a reference to another system that handles iterating through all the results. This alternative response method was recently adopted by Twitter in its new streams API.

Reasons for Usage

You should use an iterator if any of the following apply:

- You have a large data set of results to return.
- You need to filter results being returned.
- You need to throttle how many results a client gets at once.

Description

You should use the iterator architecture if you need to provide a paging system to limit the number of results returned in a single request and allow the user to request the next page of results.

Iterators hold all their state internally and contain mementos to the next set of results. They must know from any given received token what to return. When the client requests another page of results, the iterator generates the results and can also apply filters (although must not modify any data set) before returning those results to the client. If the iterator receives the same token request twice, it needs to return the same results.

Each subsequent page request must return the results in chunks exactly as if they had all been queried for at the start; an iterator takes a snapshot of the results and returns them as they were at the initial time of the request. For example, if the client requests all documents created in the last 10 minutes, the results will be queried from the exact time of the request, not returning any new documents created after the request was issued.

Implementation

Iterators are used in ATOM feeds, providing a **next page** and **current page** link within the returned XML. These iterators provide you with the ability to control access to your data set and throttle usage to your clients. This becomes important when dealing with web browsers because the average HTTP request times out after only a few minutes. Additionally, most browsers cannot process large files at once.

When deciding on the size for your pages, you need to measure two things. The first is how long it takes you to generate those results, and the second is how large that resulting document can be. In some cases, you might need to allow this number to be modified by the client. This becomes increasingly useful when you deal with something such as a mobile client that has less resources available. Keep in mind that every roundtrip to the server adds overhead to the request, but you also can't have results returned back to the browser too late, or it will time out or overload the browser.

Example

For an example, look at how ATOM works. Recently, news feeds have become increasingly more available by being provided in RSS format, which is a standard built off of XML. Building on that, ATOM provides additional features that enable paging. First look at a typical ATOM feed:

```
<?xml version="1.0" encoding="utf-8"?>

<feed xmlns="http://www.w3.org/2005/Atom">
 <title>My Blog</title>
 <subtitle>A blog with paging</subtitle>
 <id>0000-0000-0000</id>
 <updated>2010-08-15T10:30:00Z</updated>
 <author>
  <name>Chris Moyer</name>
  <email>kopertop@gmail.com</email>
 </author>

 <entry>
  <id>1001-1010-1101</id>
  <title>Book Released!</title>
  <updated>2010-08-15T08:30:00Z</updated>
  <summary>I just released my book!</summary>
 </entry>

 <link href="http://blog.coredumped.org/rss
➥" rel="self" />
 <link href="http://blog.coredumped.org/rss
➥?token=23049" rel="next"/>
</feed>
```

Here, you see two links provided at the bottom of this XML document. They're differentiated by the rel tag, which tells you that one is a link to the current results, and the other is the link to the next page of results. Both links are provided as full links that contain a token that ensures that this link returns the same results regardless of when they're offered. The number of results returned may vary, and you could even receive no results, but if you receive a link with `rel="next"`, you do have more results.

Here you use a memento to determine the exact query to be sent for the next page of results. Because you use SDB as your backend, it's simple to generate this query because all you need to do is send the *exact same query* along with the provided **next_token**. Botoweb automatically handles this for you in the _get function, so now take a look at how that works:

```
# Add the count to the header
objs = self.search(params=request.GET.mixed(),
➥user=request.user)
response.headers['X-Result-Count'] =
➥str(objs.count())
objs = self.search(params=request.GET.mixed()
➥, user=request.user)
objs.limit = self.page_size
response.write("<%sList>" %
➥self.db_class.__name__)
for obj in objs:
   response.write(xmlize.dumps(obj))
params = request.GET.mixed()
if objs.next_token:
   if params.has_key("next_token"):
      del(params['next_token'])
   self_link = '%s%s%s?%s' %
➥(request.real_host_url, request.base_url,
➥request.script_name,
➥urllib.urlencode(params)
➥.replace("&", "&amp;"))
   params['next_token'] = objs.next_token
   next_link = '%s%s%s?%s' %
➥(request.real_host_url, request.base_url,
➥request.script_name,
➥urllib.urlencode(params)
➥.replace("&", "&amp;"))
   response.write('<link type="text/xml"
➥rel="next" href="%s"/>' % (next_link))
   response.write('<link type="text/xml"
➥rel="self" href="%s"/>' % (self_link))
response.write("</%sList>" % self.db_class.__name__)
```

First, determine the total number of results of the query and store that in the X-Result-Count header. Next, build out your list of results within your XML envelope. First build your self_link by building up the URL to this specific handler and then appending all the search parameters used. Your next_link is almost identical, except you also add a next_token, which is simply taken directly from SDB. To fetch the next page of results, the user simply needs to query the link provided in the href parameter. These links are provided *only* if there are more results left in the query, thus the client simply needs to check for the existence of those tags.

Summary

Whenever you deal with sending information over a network, you usually need to allow for some sort of paging. This allows you to keep the connectionless and stateless patterns while still allowing these connections to not overwhelm the client with a ton of data all at once. This method to provide an iterative access to a large data set allows you to grow and expand your data indefinitely without causing your system to break down.

Observer

Observers are systems that listen for events and then act on those events. Unlike the queue pattern, observers must modify the original event, or prevent other systems from reading the event. Observers are also often called listeners because they simply listen for specific things to happen but do not need to be explicitly notified.

Overview

As shown in Figure 6.5, there are two parts to this pattern. The first part is registration, to which the observer must identify itself and register which events it needs to be made aware of. This allows your system to handle part two of this pattern and trigger events for any given observer dynamically when they happen, allowing you to use the well-established queue pattern to handle the actual event handling.

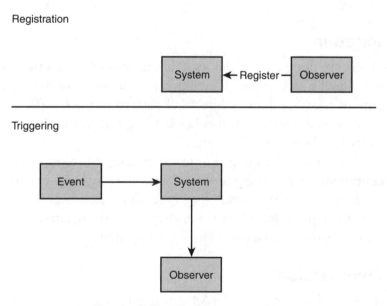

Figure 6.5   The observer pattern.

The observer pattern is common for when you don't care if a module succeeds or even exists in your original system. For example, when posting a message to Twitter, you don't care if everyone's desktop client receives the message, just that the message was successfully posted to Twitter. The individual desktop clients register themselves to Twitter as observers, and Twitter simply "fires and forgets" the messages to these desktop clients, not actually considering if they properly handle them.

Reasons for Usage

You should use an observer if any of the following apply:

- You need to add functionality after initial deployment.
- You need to develop a modular system that is not dependent on any given module.
- You provide access to third-party modules for your system that you don't control.

Description

Observers are designed for the specific purpose of abstracting out the individual modules and allowing you to loosely couple multiple systems together. This architectural pattern enables you to provide one central system that handles sending out notifications dynamically when events happen.

An observer has the obligation to verify that it is registered with the central server, notifying it whenever it starts up, and periodically ensuring the server hasn't forgotten about it. It also is required to respond to events when they're received; although, if it fails to do so, the central server is not concerned.

Implementation

Creating an observer is simple: All you need is to register yourself with the central system and then listen for events. When dealing with cloud-based systems, you typically use the queue pattern for the event listener and processor.

The second part of the observer pattern is the central server. This system is responsible for maintaining a list of events and systems to send those events to. Typically, this involves creating, deleting, and modifying objects, and an observer may register to as many events as it requires. When the observer registers, it sends along a pattern of events and the queue to send to.

Example

Now take a look at a simple mailing list application. Mailing lists are great examples because they contain external third-party observers that ask to listen on internal events. In a Mailing List application, individual subscribers are the observers, and they're subscribing to lists. Each message posted is an event to that list, which your observers are notified of. What happens after this event is fired off is entirely up to the user.

Amazon recently announced a new service: **Simple Notification Service (SNS)**. This service provides the full functionality for registering and deregistering event listeners and triggering events and sending them to the appropriate end points. Currently, SNS supports email, SQS, and HTTP delivery systems. SNS also enables for easy unsubscription, which is required by the **CAN-SPAM** act's **Unsubscribe Policy**. This policy requires that any bulk emails contain a simple link within the message that enables the user to unsubscribe easily, without any login.

To start, create some topics for users to subscribe to. Because you usually don't do this on-the-fly, just run this in the Python shell. Start off by importing boto, connecting to SNS, and then creating your topic:

```
>>> import boto
>>> sns = boto.connect_sns()
>>> sns.create_topic("test")
{u'CreateTopicResponse':
  {u'ResponseMetadata':
  {u'RequestId': u''},
```

```
u'CreateTopicResult':
 {u'TopicArn':
  u'arn:aws:sns:us-east-1:your-account-id:Test'}
 }
}
```

The important part here is the `TopicArn` response, which gives
you the unique ID for this topic. Specifically, this is a combination
of the region the topic was imported from, your unique account
ID, and the name of your topic. If you forget what topics you have
created, you can query them using the `get_all_topics` function:

```
>>> sns.get_all_topics()['ListTopicResult']['Topics']
[{u'TopicArn':
u'arn:aws:sns:us-east-1:your-account-id:Test'}]
```

The next step is subscribe users to your topic. You'll probably
want to set up a web form for this, but for now, just do it from the
command line:

```
>>> sns.subscribe("arn:aws:sns:us-east-1:
➥your-account-id:Test", "email", "your-email")
{u'SubscribeResponse':
 {u'SubscribeResult':
  {u'SubscriptionArn': u'pending confirmation'},
  u'ResponseMetadata': {u'RequestId': u'your-request-id'}
 }
}
```

After this is done, within a few minutes you should receive an
email to the address you provided. This email contains a link that
you can click to confirm your subscription. Until you click this
link, your email will not be signed up to the topic, and you will
not receive messages. You'll see the "pending confirmation" message until the user has accepted this request. You can check the
progress of this request and all others by using the following
method:

```
>>> sns.get_all_subscriptions_by_topic(
➥"arn:aws:sns:us-east-1:your-account-id:Test")
{u'ListSubscriptionsResponse':
 {u'ListSubscriptionsResult':
  {u'NextToken': None, u'Subscriptions':
```

```
[{u'Owner': u'your-account-id',
   u'Endpoint': u'your-email',
   u'Protocol': u'email',
   u'TopicArn': u'arn:aws:sns:us-east-1:your-account-id:Test',
   u'SubscriptionArn': u'arn:aws:sns:us-east-1:
➥your-account-id1:Test:subscription-id'}
   ]
 },
 u'ResponseMetadata':
 {u'RequestId': u'request-id'}}}
```

The only thing left to do now is to push a message to the queue. Assuming you've already clicked the link in your email that signed you up for this topic, you'll receive any message posted to this topic. Publishing a message to this queue is as simple as using the publish method:

```
>>> sns.publish("arn:aws:sns:us-east-1:
➥your-account-id:Test", "Test Message body",
➥"Test Message subject")
{u'PublishResponse':
  {u'PublishResult': {u'MessageId': u'message-id'},
  u'ResponseMetadata': {u'RequestId': u'request-id'}
}}
```

You can publish any message you want to this queue, and it will be sent out. Because Amazon has properly followed the CAN-SPAM act, and has properly set up all the SPF records for its mail servers, you can assume that your emails will not be blocked by most spam filters.

Summary

Observers are extremely useful in cloud-based systems and enable you to loosely couple modules to your central system. Using an observer-publisher architecture, such as the one presented here, furthers this abstraction and enables you to "fire and forget" any messages to clients. What happens to these messages after they're fired off doesn't matter to your system; even if the recipient doesn't receive the message, you're not affected.

7

Clustering

When dealing with cloud computing, the number one thing to remember is that clouds are tools, which provide easy access to utilities no different from electricity or water. Alone, these utilities are useless; but backed by the proper plumbing and design, they can achieve anything.

So far, this book discussed several unique methods to develop pieces of your architecture. This chapter covers some of the major parts of clustering, the most important part to create any scalable system. The overall architecture of major applications as a whole, not just the individual modules, is discussed.

All the patterns discussed here are general clustering patterns. There's nothing here that *requires* you to use a cloud service provider, but details of how to implement them inside of one is explained. The clustering patterns described here can help you develop your overall architecture, and most applications fit into one of them.

Note: Each pattern in this chapter begins on a new page.

The n-Tier Web Pattern

The n-tier web pattern is designed to help you extrapolate the major parts of your application and enable it to be more modular and scalable. This architecture is designed to provide a public-facing interface to your application as a whole. By splitting your application into multiple tiers, you can add middleware, secure each individual layer, and even offer up layers to untrusted third-party applications. You'll also have the ability to replace a layer to adapt to your needs.

Overview

The typical web application uses three layers: presentation, application, and database. When dealing with robust and modular web applications, however, you typically see the presentation layer split into two different layers: client and representation. Figure 7.1 shows the three-tier web pattern.

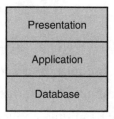

Figure 7.1   The three-tier web pattern.

In this pattern, the presentation layer defines what the clients see on their system. It's similar to a view in the model–view–control pattern. The application has both the model and the control bits, where all logic actually happens in this layer. Typically, the three-tier web-pattern has both presentation and application layers running within your servers removing the requirement for your clients' browsers to do much processing or rendering.

Figure 7.2 shows an alternative version of the tiered web pattern that splits the presentation layer into two layers. By splitting the presentation layer into a client and representation layer, you can offload the client layer to the actual client and simply provide one single representation for multiple different clients. This becomes increasingly important in today's world with mobile smart phones and devices that have less screen real estate and different interfaces, such as touch instead of a typical mouse.

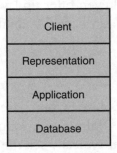

Figure 7.2   The four-tier web pattern.

Reasons for Usage

You want to use this pattern if any of the following apply:

- You need to build a modular web application.
- You need to provide multiple interfaces to you application.
- You need to integrate multiple applications with each other.

Description

The n-tier architecture was developed to separate layers that can be swapped out to provide more functionality. Just like the typical model-view-control pattern splits out application logic from how the data is stored, and how it's displayed, the n-tier architecture splits your database, representation, or display methodology and enables you to build your application from the bottom up. This method of layering enables you to interject authentication and authorization in between your client and your application code.

By doing so, you can provide for multiple methods of authentication and change them without modifying your application code. You can also add additional client layers on top of your existing system whenever a new platform becomes available, again without modifying your application code.

Implementation

Typical implementations of the n-tier architecture are built off of the four-tier architecture. Most important is *where* each layer goes. Figure 7.3 shows how you can distribute your layers across different services provided by your cloud service.

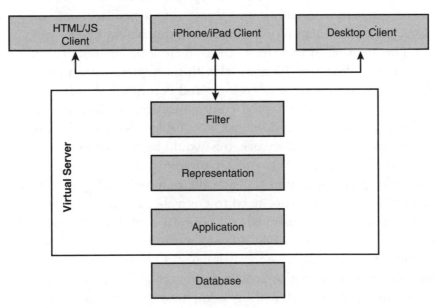

Figure 7.3   Deployment of the n-tier architecture.

In this method of the n-tier architecture, three different client layers are provided: one for basic HTML and JavaScript, another for iPhone and iPad clients, and a third for standard desktop clients. These three layers each can present the information to the user and sit directly on the client's machine. You cannot trust anything coming from any of these clients, so you must perform all authentication and authorization *below* this layer.

Directly under these client layers is the filter layer that enables you to abstract the authentication and authorization from the representation and application layers. It sits directly on top of the representation layer, modifying any input and output that flows through it. These two layers must both speak the same communication protocol.

The representation layer sits directly below the filter layer and typically is on the same system as the application layer. This layer modifies any output from the application layer into a usable format for the filter and client layers. This typically transforms your internal representation, usually a raw object, into a standard such as XML or JSON. In an MVC framework, this would be the view.

The application layer rests directly below the representation layer and is often actually merged with the representation layer. This layer contains all business logic and communicates directly with the database layer. Typical communication between this layer and the database layer is done using an Object Relational Mapping library. In an MVC framework, this would be the control.

The database layer rests outside of your primary servers. In some cloud platforms, this will actually be provided for you automatically, and you will not need to control it. Database layers come in two main flavors: relational and nonrelational. Typical relational database layers include MySQL and Oracle. Some newer databases, including SimpleDB, are nonrelational and do not support complex queries or joining to provide better scalability and stability. When using these databases, any complicated queries must be handled on the application layer.

Example

To make your example easy, use botoweb to create your application layer. This layer already has a built-in communication system for using SimpleDB as the database layer, so you don't have to worry about setting up anything complex. There are also many tools available for use for the client layer, so you don't have to spend a lot of time on repetitive tasks.

To start, set up your environment. botoweb takes a normal **Python egg** with a special bit of user data. These egg files are literally just compiled and zipped-up directories that include some special configuration files that tell the installer what to do with the egg. Egg distribution has been around since Java's jar files and is functionally equivalent. To start, you need to create a directory to host your application:

```
$ mkdir webapp
```

Next, you need a subdirectory for your configuration data. This is predefined by botoweb as `conf` and contains a few files that will be used to set up the URL mapping and other configuration data used by your app. You can also place any YAML file in this directory and have access to it through `botoweb.env.config.get("app-name", "file-name")`. There's also a few configuration files used by botoweb that you must provide.

The first required configuration file is your `handler.yaml` file. This file contains all the mappings between a URL and a handler. For your application, you need only a few entries. Start by taking a look at a single handler entry:

```
- url: /posts
  name: Post
  handler: webapp.handlers.post.PostHandler
  db_class: webapp.resources.post.Post
```

Here you see that you're defining the URL starting with `/posts` to be handled by this entry. You set a name for this entry (which you'll use later in your frontend) as `Post`. Then set this to be handled by the handler located at `botoweb.appserver.handlers.db.DBHandler`. This is a precreated handler that requires one additional configuration in this entry to serve up any DB object you provide and make it freely available to the API. Then pass in the configuration `db_class` to be set to your object you want to have this handler use. Point this to your `Post` object, which is defined next:

```
# File: webapp/resources/post.py
from botoweb.db.model import Model
from boto.sdb.db.property import *

class Post(Model):
  """Representation of a Blog Post"""
  title = StringProperty(verbose_name="Title")
  contents = BlobProperty(verbose_name="Contents")
```

Here, you're actually using the Model class from botoweb, not
just boto. This class provides some additional required properties
that can help your frontend with some accounting and logging
functionality. You also need to add an entry to your handler.yaml
file for users:

```
- url: /user
  name: User
  handler: botoweb.appserver.handlers.user.UserHandler
  db_class: botoweb.resources.user.User
```

The only difference here is that you use the UserHandler instead
of just the DB handler. This handler is actually a subclass of the DB
handler but enables users to edit only their own user, unless they're
an administrator.

Now that you have the application layer settled, look at the filter
and authentication layer. The authentication layer is handled
entirely using XSLT, with a few special functions. To have anything
run through these filters, you need to add an entry into webapp/
conf/filters.yaml:

```
- url: ^/$
  filters:
    output: python://webapp/filters/index.xsl
```

Here, the URL is provided as a regular expression, so this filter
applies only to the root path, which is an automatically generated
index required by the frontend. The filters section can contain
two entries: input and output. This enables you to pass both inputs
to the handler and outputs from the handler through a filter for
authorization purposes. You can also filter on custom handlers
directly like so:

```
- url: ^/posts
  filters:
    output: python://webapp/filters/post.xsl
```

This would filter all output from the Posts handler through the post.xsl filter. You can allow a few special functions within these filters, and you can even specify your own if necessary. The most interesting functions are the hasAuth and hasGroup functions. Each of these functions is specific to the session and calls the like-named function on the current users object. The index.xsl filter provided by boto follows:

```
<xsl:stylesheet version='1.0'
 xmlns:xsl='http://www.w3.org/1999/XSL/Transform'
 xmlns:bw='python://botoweb/xslt_functions'
 xmlns:boto='http://code.google.com/p/boto-web/wiki/FilterSchema'>
    <xsl:include href="base.xsl"/>

    <!-- By default we pull all the authentications out of the DB -->
    <xsl:template match="Index/api">
        <xsl:if test="bw:hasAuth('GET', @name)">
            <xsl:copy>
                <xsl:apply-templates select="@*|node()"/>
            </xsl:copy>
        </xsl:if>
    </xsl:template>
    <xsl:template match ="Index/api/methods/*">
        <xsl:if test="bw:hasAuth(local-name(), ../../@name)">
            <xsl:copy>
                <xsl:apply-templates select="@*|node()"/>
            </xsl:copy>
        </xsl:if>
    </xsl:template>
    <xsl:template match ="Index/api/properties/property">
        <xsl:choose>
            <xsl:when test="bw:hasAuth('', ../../@name, @name)">
                <xsl:copy>
                    <xsl:attribute name="perm">
➡<xsl:if test="bw:hasAuth('GET', ../../@name, @name)">read</xsl:if>
➡<xsl:if test="bw:hasAuth('PUT', ../../@name, @name)"> write</xsl:if>
➡</xsl:attribute>
```

```
                    <xsl:apply-templates select="@*|node()"/>
                </xsl:copy>
            </xsl:when>

            <!-- Some fields just simply must be readable -->
            <xsl:when test="@name='sys_modstamp'">
                <xsl:copy>
                    <xsl:attribute name="perm">read</xsl:attribute>
                    <xsl:apply-templates select="@*|node()"/>
                </xsl:copy>
            </xsl:when>
            <xsl:when test="@name='name'">
                <xsl:copy>
                    <xsl:attribute name="perm">read</xsl:attribute>
                    <xsl:apply-templates select="@*|node()"/>
                </xsl:copy>
            </xsl:when>
            <xsl:when test="@name='index'">
                <xsl:copy>
                    <xsl:attribute name="perm">read</xsl:attribute>
                    <xsl:apply-templates select="@*|node()"/>
                </xsl:copy>
            </xsl:when>
            <xsl:when test="@name='deleted'">
                <xsl:copy>
                    <xsl:attribute name="perm">read</xsl:attribute>
                    <xsl:apply-templates select="@*|node()"/>
                </xsl:copy>
            </xsl:when>

        </xsl:choose>
    </xsl:template>

    <!-- Mark all of these "auto" properties as read-only -->
    <xsl:template match="Index/api/properties/property[@name='created_by']
➥|Index/api/properties/property[@name='modified_by']
➥|Index/api/properties/property[@name='created_at']
➥|Index/api/properties/property[@name='modified_at']
➥|Index/api/properties/property[@name='sys_modstamp']"
➥ priority="5">
```

```
    <xsl:copy>
        <xsl:attribute name="perm">read</xsl:attribute>
        <xsl:apply-templates select="@*|node()"/>
    </xsl:copy>
    </xsl:template>

    <!-- Any properties of type query or calculated are read-only -->
    <xsl:template match="Index/api/properties/property[@type='query']
➡ |Index/api/properties/property[@calculated='true']"
➡ priority="5">
        <xsl:copy>
            <xsl:attribute name="perm">read</xsl:attribute>
            <xsl:apply-templates select="@*|node()"/>
        </xsl:copy>
    </xsl:template>
</xsl:stylesheet>
```

Here, you see the initial declaration of the **bw** xml prefix, which
loads in all the botoweb-specific XSLT functions. The first thing to
do is include the **base.xsl** filter. This filter includes a copy default,
which looks like this:

```
<xsl:stylesheet version='1.0'
 xmlns:xsl='http://www.w3.org/1999/XSL/Transform'
 xmlns:boto='http://code.google.com/p/boto-web/wiki/FilterSchema'>
    <xsl:template match="@*|node()">
        <xsl:copy>
            <xsl:apply-templates select="@*|node()"/>
        </xsl:copy>
    </xsl:template>
</xsl:stylesheet>
```

The **copy** function copies only the current XML node, and the
apply-template's function is run to also do the same thing to all
the other nodes and attributes. This means that if you do not
specifically match something, it will copy through directly.

Back at the **index.xsl** filter, you can look at the next important
line in the filter:

```
    <xsl:template match="Index/api">
        <xsl:if test="bw:hasAuth('GET', @name)">
            <xsl:copy>
```

```
            <xsl:apply-templates select="@*|node()"/>
        </xsl:copy>
    </xsl:if>
</xsl:template>
```

This filter maps to everything in the api. You copy nodes only if the user has the GET permission on the object itself. If not, the user will never even know about that object's existence in the system. Next, take a look at how to add authorizations to the individual properties of an object:

```
<xsl:template match ="Index/api/properties/property">
    <xsl:choose>
        <xsl:when test="bw:hasAuth('', ../../@name, @name)">
            <xsl:copy>
                <xsl:attribute name="perm">
➡<xsl:if test="bw:hasAuth('GET', ../../@name, @name)">read</xsl:if>
➡<xsl:if test="bw:hasAuth('PUT', ../../@name, @name)"> write
➡</xsl:if></xsl:attribute>
                <xsl:apply-templates select="@*|node()"/>
            </xsl:copy>
        </xsl:when>
    <xsl:choose>
    </xsl:template>
```

Here you see that for each property, you first check to see if the user has any authorization for that property, and then you add a perm attribute to the property. The next bit of XSLT code adds some overrides for specific properties that simply must be readable by the frontend if this object is to be usable.

The last bit of XSLT code uses the additional property attribute. Although you don't need to go over this too much, it enables you to override other matches and force the filter to run this one instead. This enables you to force that the special automatic properties are read-only no matter what the authorizations in the database are.

For your application, you don't require special permissions for the post handler, so you won't worry about that. For now, your entire authorization layer is now completed, so move to the client interface.

Luckily, botoweb provides a simple yet powerful template engine that is built using HTML5, JavaScript, and CSS. This enables you to create templates as easily as you would in a framework such as Django, without combining your presentation and application tiers. The actual communication out of your web server is raw XML but can enable you to quickly and rapidly build up a frontend that communicates back to that system.

The first thing to do is to check out **bwclient-js** from http://bitbucket.org/cmoyer/bwclient-js. This simple system is designed specifically for communicating via your botoweb application's standard XML API. You'll want to first start by creating a web root to host your static content in:

```
$ mkdir www
```

Next, you need to make sure your system proxies from a subroot path to your actual application. If you use Apache, this can be done by setting up a simple HTTP proxy in your `httpd.conf` or virtual host configuration file:

```
ProxyRequests Off

<Proxy *>
   AddDefaultCharset off
   Order deny,allow
   Allow from all
</Proxy>

<Proxy balancer://webapp>
   BalancerMember http://127.0.0.1:8080
</Proxy>

ProxyPass /api/ balancer://webapp/
ProxyPassReverse /api/ balancer://webapp/
```

Assuming you set up your document root to point to your applications www directory, your client can now access your application data by going to `/api/`. This is required because JavaScript security prevents cross-site ajax, so you must host both your client's static files and your dynamic data from the same system, although

both of them can be proxied. You normally would also want to
proxy static data to point to a CloudFront URL.

Now look at the `index.html` file in your web root:

```
<!DOCTYPE html>
<html lang="en">
 <head>
 <meta charset="utf-8"/>
 <title>bwclient-js example</title>
 <script src="/lib/jquery.min.js" type="text/javascript"></script>
 <script src="/lib/jquery.ajaxmanager.js" type="text/
➥javascript"></script>
 <script src="/src/botoweb.js" type="text/javascript">
➥ </script>
 <script src="/src/botoweb/util.js"
➥ type="text/javascript"></script>
 <script src="/src/botoweb/ajax.js"
➥ type="text/javascript"></script>
 <script src="/src/botoweb/model.js"
➥ type="text/javascript"></script>
 <script src="/src/botoweb/object.js"
➥ type="text/javascript"></script>
 <script src="/src/botoweb/property.js"
➥ type="text/javascript"></script>
 <script src="/src/botoweb/environment.js"
type="text/javascript"></script>
 <script src="/src/botoweb/ldb.js"
➥ type="text/javascript"></script>
 <script src="/src/botoweb/ldb/sync.js"
➥ type="text/javascript"></script>
 <script src="/src/botoweb/sql.js"
➥ type="text/javascript"></script>
 <script src="/src/botoweb/xml.js"
➥ type="text/javascript"></script>
 <script src="/src/botoweb/ui.js"
➥ type="text/javascript"></script>
 <script src="/src/botoweb/ui/markup.js"
➥ type="text/javascript"></script>
 <script src="/src/botoweb/ui/markup/parse.js"
➥ type="text/javascript"></script>
 <script src="/src/botoweb/ui/markup/block.js"
➥ type="text/javascript"></script>
```

```
<script src="/src/botoweb/ui/markup/block.js"
➥ type="text/javascript"></script>
<script src="/src/botoweb/ui/widget/search.js"
➥ type="text/javascript"></script>
<script src="/src/botoweb/ui/widget/search_results.js"
➥ type="text/javascript"></script>
<script src="/src/botoweb/ui/widget/data_table.js"
➥ type="text/javascript"></script>
<script src="/src/botoweb/ui/page.js"
➥ type="text/javascript"></script>
</head>
<body>
 <script type="text/javascript">
  $(document).ready(function() {
   botoweb.init('/api/',{
     templates: {
      home: 'pages/home.html',
      model: 'models/{{ name }}.html'
     }
    });
   });
  </script>

  <div id="botoweb_content"></div>
  <div id="loaded"></div>
 </body>
</html>
```

Here, you initiate botoweb by calling botoweb.init and providing it with the URL to your application server. There's also quite a bit more you can do with this client, specifically setting up the template's directory. The second argument to the initialization function is actually a JavaScript class, a mapping of key-value pairs. The only option you pass in here is templates, which is also a mapping. This templates option sets up two properties: home and model. The home property enables the client to set the first loaded page template, and the model property enables you to specify how to get to an individual model's page.

From here, you need at least two template files. Start off with the pages/home.html file:

```
<!-- File: pages/home.html -->
<section id="home">
 <header>
  <h1>WebApp</h1>
 </header>
 <div bwWidget="search" bwModel="Post" bwAttributes="name">
  <div class="col p20">
   <div class="block">
    <h2>Search Posts</h2>
    <ul bwWidget="editingTools"></ul>
   </div>
   <div class="block col p80">
    <h2>Posts</h2>
    <table>
     <thead>
      <tr>
        <th>Name</th>
        <th>Created By</th>
        <th>Created At</th>
      </tr>
     </thead>
     <tbody bwWidget="searchResults"
➥bwDefault="[['modified_at', 'sort', 'desc']]">
       <tr class="bwObject">
        <td><a bwLink="view" bwAttribute="name"></a></td>
        <td><span bwAttribute="created_by"></span></td>
        <td><span bwAttribute="created_at"></span></td>
       </tr>
     </tbody>
    </table>
   </div>
  </div>
</section>
```

There's a lot of stuff going on here. The first thing to note is that every page must be wrapped in a <section> tag and have a unique ID on it. This enables the bwclient paging system to cache preparsed versions of this page so that you don't have to reparse

this page every time the user requests it. Next, you see the
`<header>` tags, which set up the top menu that is blank.

The next thing you see is the search widget. This is instantiated
by setting the custom `bwWidget` attribute on a div tag. Technically, it
could be on any tag, but realistically, it works best on a div. This
widget also requires an additional `bwModel` attribute to define what
you're searching on. The name used here must correspond to the
name that you've used in your `handlers.yaml` config previously in
the application layer. The last attribute on the search widget you
use is `bwAttributes`. This defines the attributes that you want the
user to search on, in this case just name.

Under the search widget, you also set up a few other widgets.
The `editingTools` widget is set up within a side block so that you
can see the search tools beside your actual results. The next block is
the table where all your results will be displayed and contains the
important `searchResults` widget. This widget also contains the
important `bwDefault` attribute, which is actually a JSON array
that's passed into the server API. This specific request doesn't filter
but instead just sorts all the results by the `modified_at` parameter,
in descending order.

Under the `searchResults` widget, you need to have something
with a class `bwObject`. This acts as a template, telling `bwclient` how
to display your results. Under this template, you can use the
`bwAttribute` property to display a value for each object. You can
use the `bwLink` attribute to specify a value to use as a link to the
object page. This points to where you previously set up that model
in the `botoweb.init` section.

So how does all this pertain to the n-tier architecture? You saw
in the beginning how to make your application layer and then saw
how to add authentication and filtering on top of that; finally
you're now onto the client layer. The application happens on the
server side, where the client layer happens entirely within the user's
browser. To this end, ensure you don't assume that your client is
the one talking to your server. Handle all the authorization in the
XSLT so that if the user can't read an attribute, it's not even sent to

the client. This means that you can expose your API to the world and let anyone develop a client for your system.

Summary

Using the n-tier architecture enables you to develop a proper modular system that can be extended and expanded both vertically and horizontally. This enables you to open up your platform to many new possibilities. Interjecting layers in the middle of your architecture can also prove useful when you need to place additional logic into the system or allow for additional compatibility. Any time you develop a web application, you should consider using this architecture.

Semaphores and Locking

In a perfect world, you would never need to have any blocking code. In reality, there's always something that requires only one thread of a specific type to be run at the same time. Usually, this is done for things involving write operations where you simply can't have multiple threads writing to the same bit of data at the same time.

Overview

Figure 7.4 shows a basic overview of the locking pattern. The pattern is simple enough; it relies on one central lock that must run on a consistent system accessible by each process that will be required to use it. The lock can be something as simple as the existence of a file on a shared file system, but typically it also includes a timestamp.

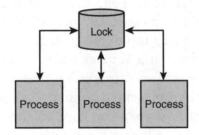

Figure 7.4   Semaphores and locking.

Reasons for Usage

Use this pattern if any of the following apply:

- You need to generate a sequence or counter.
- You need to have something run only once.
- You need to control changes for data consistency.

Description

You have dealt a lot with web patterns and discussed how the HTTP protocol is entirely stateless, but what about when you need to ensure that only one process is accessing a shared resource at any given time? How do you create a crontab that transcends the individual computer and spins off into the cloud? How about error checking and recovery if an instance dies while processing your cronjob?

The answer to all this is the same; you want to use the familiar semaphore, also known as a lock. This traditional pattern relies on a shared resource between processes that has consistency. In a cloud-based system, you cannot rely on any single instance to act as that lock. You must instead use the tools provided by your cloud provider that are accessible to every instance you run.

This shared resource holds a key that is unique to the process running your thread and contains a heartbeat timer, a simple time-stamp indicating when your application was last confirmed to be alive, which your thread must update periodically to prove that it's still running. Each other thread must look at that timer and may unfreeze the lock if the time is much older than a specified time-out period. In this way, if your processing thread dies, you can still reacquire the lock. This prevents a common problem, **resource deadlock**, which occurs when you have no way to recover a lock if the original thread dies before it can release it.

Implementation

For Amazon Web Services, you have a few options to store your lock. Previously, the only solution you had was to use MySQL or another consistent database because both S3 and SDB provided only eventual consistency. Recently, Amazon announced the availability of consistent read and conditional writes for SDB.

With this new service, you can easily create your own locking mechanism. You can also create counters and other single-thread operations. This service is both available to all services and will always retain the memory of what you put in it as long as you get a successful return message.

Acquiring a lock is simple. You first need to read the lock and make sure no one else has control over it. If the lock is used, you also need to check to make sure the heartbeat is recent; otherwise, it's time to free the lock and assume it's unused.

Example

One common example of needing a locking mechanism is when you need to send out an email and ensure it's sent only once per night. In a typical single-machine instance, you can do this by creating a cron entry, but in your multisystem distributed cloud, you can't rely on a single instance being up at all times. To solve this issue, create your cron within SDB, using a special domain and have processes watch and wait for jobs to process.

To properly handle these situations, you need to use SDB's new consistent feature, so create a special wrapper to act as a crontab. Start with a bit of initialization code to set up the database and get your instance id:

```
# File: sdbcron/__init__.py
class Cron(object):
    """SDB Representation of a Crontab"""

    def __init__(self, name, instance_id=
➥boto.config.get("Instance","instance-id")):
        """Initialize this cron, given a name, which
        corresponds to the SDB Domain Name"""
        sdb = boto.connect_sdb()
        try:
            self.db = sdb.get_domain(name)
        except:
            self.db = None
        if not self.db:
            self.db = sdb.create_domain(name)
        self.instance_id = instance_id
```

Next, add a function to add a new entry to the database. Follow the standard UNIX cron syntax and allow setting the minute, hour, day, month, and day of the week to run this command, and the user to run it as. Also allow the special * and */number patterns:

```python
def add(self, name, command, user="root", minute="*",
   hour="*", dom="*", mon="*", dow="*"):
    """Add a cron entry
    @param name: Name of this entry
    @param command: Command to run
    @param user: User to run as (default root)
    @param minute: Minute to be run (default *)
    @param hour: Hour to run (default *)
    @param dom: Day of month to run (default *)
    @param mon: Month to run (default *)
    @param dow: Day of week to run (default *),
            where Monday is 0, Sunday is 6
    """
    # Create the item
    item = self.db.new_item(name)
    item['created'] = time.time()

    # Add in our details
    item['command'] = command
    item['user'] = user
    item['minute'] = minute
    item['hour'] = hour
    item['dom'] = dom
    item['mon'] = mon
    item['dow'] = dow

    # Lock details
    item['lock'] = ""
    item['last_run'] = ""
    item['lock_time'] = ""

    # Save it
    item.put()
```

Here, you're also setting the created attribute to store the exact time when this cron entry was created, and you initialize the lock, last_run, and lock_time attributes to empty strings. Next, look at how to iterate over the results to find jobs to be run:

```python
def __iter__(self):
    """Iterate over a list of cron jobs
    to be run now, this is
    a locking call and it will add
    the lock to the item
    The process receiving this item
    MUST update "lock_time" every 5 minutes
    until it's finished, otherwise the
    lock will be considered released"""

    # We iterate over everything that
    # has no lock, or anything
    # with a lock time over 5 minutes old
    query = self.db.select(
        "SELECT * FROM %s WHERE lock = '' OR lock_time <= '%s'" %
        (self.db.name, time.time() - 300), consistent_read=True
    )
    for item in query:
        item = self.db.get_attributes(item.id, consistent_read=True)
        item.domain = self.db
        if self.check(item):
            try:
                self.lock(item)
                yield item
            except SDBResponseError, e:
                continue
            self.release(item)
```

Here, you select every entry in this domain that has either no lock or an expired lock. Before you run the check to be sure that this item should be run, refetch the item from SDB using consistent read mode. Then, run your check command, which checks to make sure that you should indeed run this item:

```python
def check(self, item):
    """Check to see if this item should be run"""
    # Make sure we're not run more then once every 60 seconds
    if not (int(time.time()) - int(item['last_run']) >= 60):
        return False
```

```
    if item['lock'] != '' and (time.time() - item['lock-time']) < 60:
        return False
now = datetime.utcnow()
if not self.match(now.minute, item['minute']):
    return False
if not self.match(now.hour, item['hour']):
    return False
if not self.match(now.month, item['mon']):
    return False
if not self.match(now.day, item['dom']):
    return False
if not self.match(now.weekday(), item['dow']):
    return False
return True
```

The first thing your check function does is to make sure that you haven't run this command in the last 60 seconds. Then check to ensure that the lock is either released or expired. (Because it may have been picked up since you started the query.) Next, check to make sure the minute matches, then the hour, month, day (0–31), and day of the week (0 representing Sunday, 6 representing Monday). All these checks use a common match function that runs a battery of tests that enables your complex pattern matching:

```
def match(self, val, p):
    """Returns true if "val" matches "p" cron pattern,
    patterns may be:
        single value
        "*" for any value
        "*/value" for any value evenly divisible by value
        CSV of any number of patterns
    """
    val = str(val)
    if (p == "*" or val == p):
        return True
    if "," in p:
        for s in p.split(","):
            if self.match(val, s):
                return True
        return False
    if p.startswith("*/"):
        return int(p[2:]) % int(val) == 0
    return False
```

The next thing to do in our check function is attempt to lock the item. Here, you must also use consistent mode, which for writing means you add preconditions by passing in what values you expect to be set to the `lock` and `release` functions:

```
def lock(self, item):
    """Lock this item to be run only by our instance"""
    new_val = {"lock": self.instance_id,
        "lock_time": time.time(),
        "last_run": time.time()}
    expected_values = {"lock": item['lock'],
        "lock_time": item['lock_time']}
    self.db.put_attributes(item.id,
        new_val,
        expected_values=expected_values)
    item = self.db.get_attributes(item.id, consistent_read=True)
    item.domain = self.db
    return item

def release(self, item):
    """Release a lock, assuming we have it"""
    self.db.put_attributes(item.id,
        {"lock": "", "lock_time": ""},
        expected_values={"lock": self.instance_id})
```

Here, you see both the lock and release functions that set up the expected values and the new values. You require that the values you currently have for `lock` and `lock_time` match what's in the actual DB. For the lock function, you're simply updating the `lock_time` to the current timestamp and the `lock` to your instance id.

You now have a complete object that can be used to generate and retrieve commands to be run in your cloud environment. All that's left is to poll for changes by running a script that checks for scripts to run. This can (ironically) be run from a cronjob every minute, or you could simply write a continuous polling class that waits a few seconds in between each check:

```
#!/usr/bin/env python
# File: pollCron.py
from sdbcron import Cron
import subprocess
```

```
import shlex
import time

if __name__ == "__main__":
    cron = Cron("sdbcron")
    for item in cron:
        cmd = item['command']
        args = shlex.split(cmd)
        p = subprocess.Popen(args, shell=True)

        # Wait for the process to finish,
        # keeping the lock for as long as it
        # takes
        while p.poll() == None:
            time.sleep(5)
            # Refresh the lock
            cron.lock(item)
```

This polling script should be run as often as possible and will use the functionality you created in the Cron object to grab and keep locks on any items that need to be run. The returned items include the command to be run. Use the shlex module to parse apart the arguments of this command into the array to be handled by the subprocess Popen module. While the process is running, run the poll function to check for when the process has finished. This function returns None until the process is finished, in which case it returns the status code of the executed process.

Summary

Although you prefer to never have to use locks, they are inevitably required in many systems. Using a proper locking pattern for use within the cloud helps to enable for the vast and ever-changing environment you'll be running in. This means that you don't have to rely on a single system to run your scripts, but you can instead use this pattern to store locks within a centralized database and prevent multiple scripts from performing the same task at the same time.

Map/Reduce

The map/reduce pattern is no different than the concept of divide and conquer. This simple pattern enables you to split large tasks into smaller tasks to make them more manageable. A common example of a task to use this pattern is encoding a large video file.

Overview

The map/reduce pattern states that you split the input data into manageable pieces and then combine them after processing. Figure 7.5 shows the basic structure of the two different pieces of this pattern.

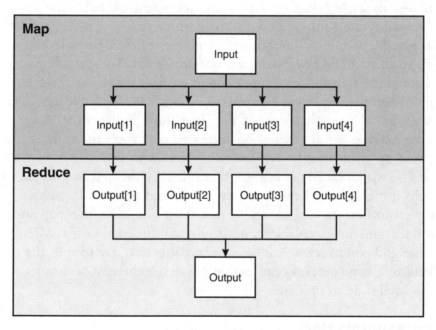

Figure 7.5   The map/reduce pattern.

In the figure, you can see that map/reduce is actually two patterns combined into one. The mapping pattern takes a single input and splits it into manageable chunks before being processed. The reducer takes the outputs from each processor and combines them into a single output.

Reasons for Usage

Use this pattern if all the following apply:

- You have a large input data set to process.
- Your data set can be split into multiple pieces.
- You need to process your data quickly.

Description

Before multiple cores, most programmers spent all their time decreasing the runtime of a given algorithm, making it run as fast as possible to churn through large amounts of data. Because of a realm of multiple processors, the amount of data you can churn through by splitting your input data into multiple streams to be processed has increased. When working with these vastly large data sets, you discover that some of the algorithms you spent all this time making fast are useless on large data sets. You instead must come up with entirely new ways to process this data.

The map/reduce pattern was first officially defined by Google to help it manage the large amounts of data and perform complex operations on those data sets. At its core, it combines the map and reduce functions available in most programming languages. Many large and complex systems use similar patterns today to split the load of a large process onto multiple systems, thereby decreasing the total time to process.

Implementation

Several implementations of map/reduce systems are available, but the overall concept is quite easy to implement on your own. The most common existing system is Apache Hadoop. Although Amazon also offers a Hadoop service, it's built on top of EC2 and doesn't actually leverage the full power of cloud computing.

Figure 7.6 shows the basic structure of a map/reduce system in the cloud. As input flows into the mapper, it splits it by storing data in the distributed DB and filesystems and sends off a message to the queue for each segment. The processors then read in each message from that queue and write their results to the DB and the output filesystem. The reducer listens to the DB for all the elements in the input to be processed and fires off once every piece has been processed. At this time, the reducer combines all the output pieces into the combined output and sends it off.

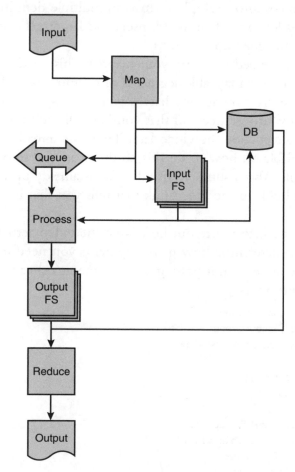

Figure 7.6   Map/reduce in the cloud.

Example

For the example application, you create a video encoder that specializes in large videos. In the simple case of videos only a few minutes long, your encoding could complete in just a few minutes, but when you extend that and look at videos of hours in duration (such as movies or long TV broadcasts), this could take a large amount of time. In the news industry, real-time is key, so a delay of a news broadcast of an hour is unacceptable. With the large surge of mobile devices on the rise, many companies are now transcoding their videos into multiple formats in multiple definitions, smaller ones for lower bandwidth users and larger HD versions for those on high-speed connections.

To start, you need to set up your mapper. This needs to split the video apart into manageable segments of no more than 15 minutes each. Assume that you already have a working copy of `ffmpeg` installed on your instance and that you have all the proper codecs you need to reencode the video later. There are already many great articles available on how to do this, so this won't go into much detail on that. Also assume your video file is already up in S3, so you have a URL to the video link that tells you that it needs to be encoded.

You first need to figure out how large the video actually is so that you can determine how many segments you need to create. This can be done by not passing any arguments other than the input file into `ffmpeg`:

```
# File: transcoder/video.py
import re, os, subprocess
from tempfile import NamedTemporaryFile

class Video(object):
    """Video object"""

    def __init__(self, input):
        """Initialize this video"""
        self._info = None
        self._input = input
```

```
    def get_info(self):
        """Get the info about this video file"""
        if not self._info:
            self._info = {
                "duration": None,
                "video": None,
                "audio": None
            }
            proc = subprocess.Popen(["ffmpeg", "-i", self._input.name]
➡, stdout=subprocess.PIPE, stderr=subprocess.STDOUT)
            info = proc.communicate()
            for line in info[0].split("\n"):
                matches = re.match("[ \t]*Duration:[ \t]*
➡([0-9]*\:[0-9]*:[0-9]*).[0-9]*,.*", line)
                if matches:
                    duration = matches.group(1).split(":")
                    self._info['duration'] = int(duration[0])*60*60
➡+int(duration[1])*60+int(duration[2])
                matches = re.match(".*Video:[ \t]*(.*)$", line)
                if matches:
                    self._info['video'] = matches.group(1)
                matches = re.match(".*Audio:[ \t]*(.*)$", line)
                if matches:
                    self._info['audio'] = matches.group(1)


        return self._info

    info = property(get_info)

    def get_duration(self):
        """Get the duration of this video file in seconds"""
        return self.info['duration']

    duration = property(get_duration)
```

Here, use the familiar subprocess module from Python to enable you to execute ffmpeg and get the info from the video file. Point STDERR to STDOUT because ffmpeg actually sends all this information as an error log rather than regular output. Then iterate over every line in your output and find your specific matches on duration, video, and audio to get those three bits of information into your cached information. Also add a convenient accessor to get just the duration of the video.

Now that you know how long the video is, you can split it and encode it in chunks. Also use ffmpeg to handle breaking the video apart, using a few special command-line arguments that you can pass into it. You can perform all the splitting at once or streamline the process and perform each split in a different process. Additionally, the ffmpeg process can combine the splitting and the encoding into one process, which is fundamentally the same as if you were operating on a single file, so there's no real need to split the file independently of the encoding operation. Because you already built an encoder in Chapter 6, "Executing Actions on Data," we won't go over the details of how to do that; all you need to do is add the ability to read a start and end parameter, and add in the -ss and -t flags appropriately. All that leaves is for you to figure out where to segment the video, so add a few new functions to your Video class. The first is a simple format_time function that will enables you to reformat a duration in seconds into the HH:MM:SS format. The second is the split function that can give you all the splits to perform. Both can be seen here:

```
def format_time(self, seconds):
    """Format a time in seconds as hh:mm:ss"""
    return "%02i:%02i:%02i" % (seconds/3600, (seconds%3600)/60,
➥seconds%60)

def split(self, seconds=900):
    """Split the video into multiple sections, by
    default we use 900 seconds (15 minutes)
    as the longest length for any given segment"""
    splits = []
    start = 0
    end = 0
    while end < self.duration:
        start = end
        end = min(self.duration, start + seconds)
        split = {"start": start, "end": end}
        splits.append(split)
    return splits
```

With these two new functions, you now have all you need to make your new mapper! All that's left is to combine the outputs after they have been properly encoded. The encoder process should also be modified to send a message to your output queue when it's finished. This enables you to perform the reduce operation.

Now all that's left to do is set up your reducer. Because it's mostly impossible to combine videos without re-encoding them again, create a playlist for your clients to view the video in 15-minute segments. In the mobile world, this is probably a better solution so clients don't have to worry about downloading the whole video at once to view just the small portion they want to see. Additionally, if you provided transcripts along with these segments in your encoding process, you could combine those transcripts into one, and they could choose which video "chapter," or segment, to start at. You *must* store all video files in S3 to allow those video files to be accessed from anywhere in your map/reduce application.

Reducing in this sense means taking all the input messages and creating a playlist XML that points to the output files. Given that you have a function that is called after all the input files are received, you can do something like the following:

```python
def reduce(inputs):
    """Return an XML playlist for all of these videos"""
    output = '<?xml version="1.0" encoding="UTF-8"?>'
    output += '<playlist version="1" xmlns="http://xspf.org/ns/0/">'
    output += '<tracklist>'
    for(x, input in enumerate(inputs)):
        output += '<track>'
        output += '<location>'
        output += input['url']
        output += '</location>'
        output += '<identifier>%s - Part %i</identifier>'
➥% (input['name'], x)
        output += '<meta rel="type">rtmp</meta>'
        output += '</track>'
    output += '</tracklist>'
    output += '</playlist>'
    return output
```

You've now developed a fully functional map/reduce system to run your input videos and produce a usable output system! All you need to do is make sure that `reduce` is called only when every video has been processed, so checking the encoder's status of each video every few minutes should do the trick. You can also wait for your output queue to send you your message saying the videos are finished and check the status of everything in your job to make sure they've all been processed before calling the reducer.

Summary

Whenever you work with large data sets, it's often more useful to figure out how to process tasks *in parallel* than to figure out how to process things *quicker*. When you need your input and output sources to be one combined data set, you need map/reduce. The example showed a simple case of a video file that can be split into multiples, but you could also be translating books, making graphs, or analyzing data in segments and then combine your results later. You can also combine map/reducers by splitting apart even further a second time if you need to. This makes the map/reduce pattern one of the most powerful in the cloud computing environment you could ever use. Combined with the utilities at your disposal by your cloud provider, this can be easy to develop and deploy.

III

Projects

## 8

A Simple Weblog

One of the simplest and most popular types of websites are blogs or forums. Although most people are happy with PHPBB, or other simple canned weblog systems, most of those systems don't scale well. As you remember from Chapter 2, "Making Software a Service," the best possible way to provide for maximum scalability and availability is to separate your database, application, and presentation layers. Most of the available canned systems don't actually split your database apart from your application layer, so if you want to scale, your only option is to run it on a bigger server. Although you could simply use one of these canned systems for your web blog, this chapter discusses how to start from scratch because most applications start in very much the same way.

Storage

Storage of your data is a major requirement of any weblog system. For your purposes, you use a database to store all your content so that you can quickly access and query this data when it's requested. It's also highly advantageous to insert a caching layer in between your DB and application layers to speed up frequently accessed pages.

Because there is a large generational shift to gathering information from online sources, such as blogs, for current up-to-date information, you need to make sure that you're ready if your user base drastically increases overnight. You don't need to worry about consistency as much as scalability, availability, and performance.

It's more important that users can see your blog posts, but if it takes a few minutes or even an hour from the time you post it until it's live, that's not as big of a deal. To facilitate this need, you can split up this application into three layers and monitor them equally to see where your load issues are. You also use a database that relies more on availability, performance, and scalability than consistency.

Figure 8.1 shows what your database needs to store. The first and most basic is the **Post**, which will contain the data of when you posted, when it was last updated, and several other fields pertaining to the post. You also need to store a **User** object that contains details of how to authenticate users and who they are. This usually contains a username, a password, a name, an email address, and permissions or authentication groups.

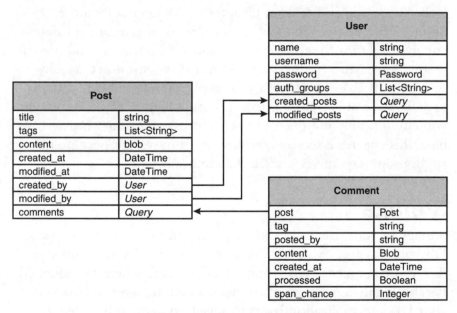

Figure 8.1   Weblog database schema.

For AWS, you have two choices for your database. The cheapest, most scalable and available option is SimpleDB without the consistency feature. This database option is hosted by Amazon and requires little to no setup or maintenance by you. This means that when your system load increases, you don't need to worry about your database.

If you don't like the schema-less nature of SimpleDB, you can also choose to use MySQL or another SQL-based database that offers read-based clustering. Amazon does offer a **Relational Data Service** that can be used for this type of high-availability system, but it means you're responsible for scaling.

Creating a Domain

For the purposes of this example, you choose SimpleDB. On top of that, you use the abstraction layer provided by boto, known as `boto.sdb.db`. This Python module automatically handles many of the nuances specific to SimpleDB, including making things sortable and enabling for indexes for case-insensitive searching. There's only one step required for initializing the database, and that's creating the **domain** that is the SimpleDB equivalent to a database. You can do this using the simple `sdbadmin` script provided by boto:

```
sdbadmin --create -d <domain-name>
```

One of the major limitations of SimpleDB is that each value can be up to only 1,024 characters. If you're a serious blog poster, that's probably not going to be enough. To satisfy this problem, the `boto.sdb.db` module adds a special property known as a `BlobProperty`. This property actually stores the content in S3 and puts a reference in place of the value in SDB. Unfortunately, the property will not be searchable. Because this is a blog, it means you cannot search on the actual content of your blog. There are many possible solutions to full-text indexing, but you don't need to worry about that here.

Because SDB is schema-less, you can technically store whatever you want in the database. In practice, however, this is generally a bad idea because you won't know what's coming out or how to deal with it. As you saw with Figure 8.1, your application needs both a User and a Post object, so you need to define those in code because it can't be defined in the database itself. In boto, this can be done by creating a separate class for each object as shown here.

The User Object

The User object contains all the information about a person. Start by creating a file `blog/resources/user.py`. The artificial schema can be seen next:

```
# File: blog/resources/user.py
from boto.sdb.db.model import Model
from boto.sdb.db.property import *
class User(Model):
    """A simple User object"""
    name = StringProperty()
    username = StringProperty()
    password = PasswordProperty()
    auth_groups = ListProperty(str)
```

As you can see from this example, several properties are available to you that automatically handle many aspects of SimpleDB. The simplest property is the `StringProperty` that does little more than store the value encoded properly for SimpleDB. The next property is the `PasswordProperty`, which simply hashes the value before saving it to the database, so you can't get the raw value out, but you can compare it using the == comparator. The final property used here is the `ListProperty`, which acts just like any of the other properties except that it enables you to store multiple values. In this case, you're saying that `auth_groups` can have multiple strings.

Next, add in a special function to **serialize** this object into XML. Although you can use any serialization method to transmit your object data directly to your client, XML enables you to use XSLT filters as middleware to add in authentication outside of your application layer. It's much easier to put this XML serialization directly into the DB object here so that you don't have to worry about it in all the different places you use an XML format of this object. This will be handled in the `toXML` function defined here:

```
def toXML(self):
    from StringIO import StringIO
    xml = StringIO()
    xml.write('<User id = "%s">' % self.id)
    xml.write("<name>%s</name>" % self.name)
    xml.write("<username>%s</username>" % self.username)
```

```
xml.write("<auth_groups>")
for auth_group in self.auth_groups:
    xml.write("<auth_group>%s</auth_group>" % auth_group)
xml.write("</auth_groups>")
xml.write('</User>')
return xml.getvalue()
```

This XML serialization function just uses a simple method of writing out XML, instead of using a specialized library such as lxml or etree. Most of the slowness in any given application is caused by using one of these libraries. As a simple solution, instead of using one of these libraries, use the StringIO object that seems to increase performance significantly. This can become noticeable when you're creating a list containing more than thousands of items.

Of course, exporting your object as XML is only one half of the equation. You also need to **de-serialize** from XML. This method actually needs to be callable on the class level, so define it as a classmethod:

```
@classmethod
def fromXML(cls, root):
    """De-serialize from an XML string"""
    # If it's a string we need to parse it
    # if not then we assume it's already been parsed
    if type(root) in (str, unicode):
        from lxml import etree
        root = etree.fromstring(root)
    obj = cls()
    if root.get("id"):
        obj.id = root.get("id")
        # If it has an ID, we load in all the values
        # that it previously had
        obj.load()

    if root.find("name"):
        obj.name = root.findtext("name")
    if root.find("username"):
        obj.username = root.findtext("username")
```

```
    if root.find("auth_groups"):
        # Set the auth groups to empty to start with
        obj.auth_groups = []
        for ag in root.find("auth_groups").findall("auth_group"):
            # Add in each auth group in the list
            obj.auth_groups.append(ag.text)
# Return our created object
return obj
```

Here, it's not as important to return things quickly, because you're almost always operating with one object at a time. For simplicity, you've just used the `lxml.etree` module to parse your XML. This function can take either a string or an already parsed XML root node. You set a property only if it's actually sent. This enables you to set only specific attributes and doesn't require your clients to know everything about the object just to set a specific property.

The Post Object

The **Post** object is a little more complicated, containing details about who made the post and when it was created. Create this object in your `post.py` file:

```
# File: blog/resources/post.py
from boto.sdb.db.model import Model
from boto.sdb.db.property import *
from blog.resources.user import User
class Post(Model):
    """A Blog Post"""
    title = StringProperty()
    tags = ListProperty(str)
    content = BlobProperty()
    created_at = DateTimeProperty(auto_now_add=True)
    modified_at = DateTimeProperty(auto_now=True)
    created_by = ReferenceProperty(User,
➥collection_name="created_posts")
    modified_by = ReferenceProperty(User,
➥collection_name="modified_posts")
```

In this example, you introduce several new properties. The first is the `BlobProperty`, which enables you to have an unlimited amount of text as the content for your blog post. Unfortunately, it won't be searchable, so you can add a `tags` attribute that can be used to index any important keywords.

The next property introduced here is the `DateTimeProperty` that has a keyword `auto_now_add` that tells your property to automatically set itself to the current time when the object is created. Then use `auto_now` on the `modified_at` property to specify that the property should be updated *every time* the object is modified.

The last new property type is the `ReferenceProperty`, which has one required argument that is the `Model` that this property must reference. Although you could just use the base `Model` object as the required type, you actually want to make sure that everything in these properties is a `User` object. The next important argument here is a named keyword `collection_name`, which contains the name of the **Reverse Reference** that will automatically be created. Whenever you initialize a class that has a reference property, it will automatically create a reverse link for you. This means that given user `usr`, you can get all the posts created by them by accessing `usr.created_posts`. This is actually an iterator, so you won't get any results until you try to loop over it. You can also filter on this query object or get a number of results by using the `count()` method.

Next, look at your `toXML` function. This is largely similar to the `toXML` function of the `User` class, so we won't go into too much detail here. The dates are stored in UTC time, so you need to use the `isoformat()` function to turn it into an **HTTPDate**. Additionally, instead of adding in the entire XML of the user who created and last modified the post, serialize the ID because it's already loaded for you. To keep things simple, a *lazy* approach is used, and the object's attributes for the reference are not loaded until they are first accessed. If you access only the ID, no additional calls to SDB are required. The XML function for the `Post` object can be seen here:

```
def toXML(self):
    """Serialize to XML, or "xmlize" """
    from StringIO import StringIO
```

```
        xml = StringIO()
        xml.write('<Post id = "%s">' % self.id)
        xml.write("<title>%s</title>" % self.title)
        xml.write('<content href="content"/>')

        xml.write("<created_at>%s</created_at>" %
➥self.created_at.isoformat())
        xml.write("<modified_at>%s</modified_at>" %
➥self.modified_at.isoformat())

        xml.write('<created_by id="%s"/>' % self.created_by.id)
        if self.modified_by:
            xml.write('<modified_by id="%s"/>' % self.modified_by.id)

        xml.write("<tags>")
        for tag in self.tags:
            xml.write("<tag>%s</tag>" % tag)
        xml.write("</tags>")

        xml.write('</Post>')
        return xml.getvalue()
```

The content property is omitted. This is done intentionally because it requires additional queries to pull the full content because it's stored in S3. To make this obvious to the client, you added a special XML tag with an href attribute. Clients can get the body of any post by simply appending /content to the URL for the post.

Finally, look at the fromXML function. Again, this is simple and much like the User class. You need to import only the id, title, content, and tags. The other fields are all automatically set. The fromXML function can be seen next:

```
@classmethod
def fromXML(cls, root):
    """De-serialize from an XML string"""
    # If it's a string we need to parse it
    # if not then we assume it's already been parsed
    if type(root) in (str, unicode):
        from lxml import etree
        root = etree.fromstring(root)
```

```
obj = cls()
if root.get("id"):
    obj.id = root.get("id")
    # If it has an ID, we load in all the values
    # that it previously had
    obj.load()

if root.find("title"):
    obj.title = root.findtext("title")
if root.find("content"):
    obj.content = root.findtext("content")
if root.find("tags"):
    # Set the auth groups to empty to start with
    obj.tags = []
    for tag in root.find("tags").iterfind("tag"):
        # Add in each tag to the list
        obj.tags.append(tag.text)
    for tag in root.find("tags").iterfind("tags"):
        # Add in each tag to the list
        obj.tags.append(tag.text)
# Return our created object
return obj
```

Unlike when you serialize the Post object, when you deserialize it, you can assume the content is right inline in the XML. Typically, this should be in a CDATA tag, but you don't have to worry about that because the lxml.etree module handles that for you.

The Comment Object

Most web-blog systems also have the capability for other people to add comments. This is where your **Comment** object is introduced, with a little extra functionality because you also want to avoid spam. The toXML function doesn't introduce anything new, so you won't go into any depth there about how it's done. The one major new thing you introduce here is the choices parameter for your tag property. This simply restricts the value of that property to one of those specific choices. The following code can be used to describe the Comment object:

```
# File: blog/resources/comment.py
from boto.sdb.db.model import Model
from boto.sdb.db.property import *
from blog.resources.post import Post
class Comment(Model):
    """A simple Comment object"""
    post = ReferenceProperty(Post, collection_name="comments")
    tag = StringProperty(choices=['', 'spam', 'ham'], default='')

    # This is just a string since
    # we don't require them to log in
    # to post
    posted_by = StringProperty()
    content = BlobProperty()
    created_at = DateTimeProperty(auto_now_add=True)

    # We set this so we only process this message once
    processed = BooleanProperty(default=False)

    # This is the chance this post is spam
    spam_chance = IntegerProperty(default=0)

    def toXML(self):
        """Serialize to XML, or "xmlize" """
        from StringIO import StringIO
        xml = StringIO()
        xml.write('<Comment id = "%s">' % self.id)
        xml.write('<post id="%s"/>' % self.post.id)
        xml.write('<content href="content"/>')
        xml.write("<posted_by>%s</posted_by>" % self.posted_by)
        xml.write("<created_at>%s</created_at>" %
➥self.created_at.isoformat())
        xml.write("<spam_chance>%s</spam_chance>" % self.spam_chance)
        xml.write('</Comment>')
        return xml.getvalue()
```

The fromXML method, however, introduces a new deserializer for reference properties:

```
    @classmethod
    def fromXML(cls, root):
        """De-serialize from an XML string"""
        # If it's a string we need to parse it
```

```
# if not then we assume it's already been parsed
if type(root) in (str, unicode):
    from lxml import etree
    root = etree.fromstring(root)
obj = cls()
if root.get("id"):
    obj.id = root.get("id")
    # If it has an ID, we load in all the values
    # that it previously had
    obj.load()

post = root.findtext('post')
if post:
    obj.post = post
content = root.findtext("content")
if content:
    obj.content = content
posted_by = root.findtext("posted_by")
if posted_by:
    obj.posted_by = posted_by
tag = root.findtext("tag")
if tag:
    obj.tag = tag
    if obj.tag == "spam":
        obj.spam_chance = 100
    obj.processed = False
# Return our created object
return obj
```

Next, add the `submit` function to submit the ID of the current
comment object to an SQS queue named `spamfilter`. When a
comment is first entered into the system, it will not show up on
the site because it's `approved` is `False`. Instead of simply sending
out an email to you when a new comment comes in, you'll fire off
a message to your special queue and try to determine automatically if it's spam. Store this as an integer in the `spam_chance` property so that you can easily see which comments were flagged as
spam and appropriately train your system. This is discussed later,
but for now, just note that if the `spam_chance` is more than 1, it's
probably spam and you won't display it. Submitting a comment to
the query can be handled with this function:

```
def submit(self):
    """Submit this comment for approval"""
    import boto
    sqs = boto.connect_sqs()
    q = sqs.get_queue("spamfilter")
    return q.write(q.new_message(self.id)))
```

The last thing to do is override the `put` method. Whenever a new comment is created, it will automatically be submitted. Although you could have combined these two functions into one and just had the entire submit code in the `put` method, it's usually a better choice to split that out because it'll make it much easier to manually resubmit a comment if necessary. Wait to submit the comment until after you call the `Model`'s `put` method because that's where the ID is generated. The modified `put` method can be seen next:

```
def put(self):
    """We override the put (save) method
    to also make sure it's submitted to
    our SQS queue for approval"""
    Model.put(self)
    # We must submit after we're saved since
    # that's when we'll have an ID
    if not self.processed:
        self.submit()
```

Application

Now that you have the storage out of the way, you need to start on your application logic. You need to decouple this layer as much as possible so that if one server fails, it's easy for your system to fail over to another. In your simple blogging application, the only real application logic you need to do is allow users to log in, add a post, modify a post, and delete a post, and allow anyone to view and search posts. You need to ensure that the last functionality, viewing and searching posts, is as low-impact as possible because that's going to be used much more than the others.

Because this is a web application, you need to set up multiple "handlers," for each URL path. Because you follow a REST style interface, you need to define a few simple URL paths: /users, /posts, and /comments.

You can also add an optional index handler at / if you want to show some description of what each URL does. The most supported and flexible object serialization methods are XML and JSON, with XML being mostly preferred because you can then apply XSLT style sheets for authorization.

With Amazon Web Services, you can continue to build your application in much the same way as you created your artificial schema for your database. Depending on what programming language you use, there may already be frameworks available for you to use, but take this approach from scratch and just use a simple **Web Service Gateway Interface (WSGI)** approach.

A Brief Introduction to WSGI

WSGI enables you map a specific URL to a given function, or callable class. In this case, you want to actually use an object because that gives you a lot more freedom. Although you can technically use just all the built-in features of Python for WSGI, you need to install **webob** as well and use the request and response handlers there to make your life a little easier. Although webob is part of **Python paste**, you don't need to use that as your web server. Start with your basic WSGI object shown here:

```python
# File: blog/handlers/__init__.py
from webob import Request, Response
class WSGIHandler(object):
    """Our basic WSGI handler"""
    allowed_methods = []

    def __call__(self, environ, start_response):
        """Handle a WSGI request"""
        resp = Response()
        resp.content_type = "text/xml"
        req = Request(environ)
        # Everything gets wrapped in a giant try block
```

```
        # so we can format exceptions to the user
        try:
            resp = self.handle(req, resp)
        except Exception, e:
            resp.clear()
            resp.set_status(500)
            resp.write(self.fmt_err(500, e.message))
        return resp(environ, start_response)

    def fmt_err(self, code, msg):
        return """<Error>
<code>%s</code>
<msg>%s</msg>
</Error>""" % (code, msg)

    def handle(self, request, response):
        """Dispatch to the appropriate method"""
        method = request.method.lower()
        if method in self.allowed_methods:
            method = getattr(self, "_%s" % method)
            return method(request, response)
        else:
            response.set_status(400)
            msg = "Bad Method %s" % method
            response.write(self.fmt_err(400, msg))
            return response
```

The preceding code splits out the actual handling into a separate function, so this class can be overridden for each specific handler. In the actual __call__ method, you're handling recovering from errors, so an exception that you don't handle elsewhere won't accidentally kill your server. Also specify the specific methods you allow, typically get, post, put, and delete.

Because you're also using a simple WSGIRef server, you also need to create a mapper system to delegate requests to one of the other handlers. To keep this simple, just use something similar to WSGI chaining. Create a WSGIMapper class, as you can see here:

```
# File: blog/handlers/mapper.py
from blog.handlers import WSGIHandler
from blog.handlers.users import UserHandler
```

```
from blog.handlers.posts import PostHandler
from blog.handlers.comments import CommentHandler
class WSGIMapper(WSGIHandler):
    """Handle dispatching requests to different
    handlers based on the config here"""
    wsgi_apps = [
        ('/users', UserHandler()),
        ('/posts', PostHandler()),
        ('/comments', CommentHandler())
    ]

    def handle(self, request, response):
        """Dispatch to the appropriate handler"""
        for cfg in self.wsgi_apps:
            if request.path.startswith(cfg[0])
                return cfg[1](request, response)
```

The DB Handler

The users handler is responsible for enabling users to list all users, get a specific user, create a user, delete a user, or modify a user. As such, you need to implement quite a few methods. Start by declaring the database handler:

```
# File: blog/handlers/db.py
from blog.handlers import WSGIHandler
from lxml import etree
class DBHandler(WSGIHandler):
    """Handle dispatching requests for objects"""
    allowed_methods = ['get', 'put', 'post', 'delete']
    db_class = None
```

You can set the allowed_methods to get, put, and post. This tells the WSGIHandler that these are the methods that you implemented, so any other requests should be automatically denied. You also added a new class level attribute db_class. This enables you to abstract most of the functionality so that you can set this to whatever specific handler you need to and override only specific functions if you need to.

Remember that the WSGIHandler actually forwards these methods along to methods that start with an underscore, so you don't have to worry about overlapping with existing method names. These underscore methods shouldn't be called by anything other than the WSGIHandler. Now add a get function to the database handler:

```
def _get(self, request, response):
    """Get a list of all objects, or a specific one"""
    response.content_type = 'text/xml'
    response.write('<?xml version="1.0" encoding="UTF-8"?>')
    if request.path_info == "":
        return self.list(request, response)
    else:
        return self.fetch(request, response,
➥request.path_info.strip("/"))
```

In this section, you can implemented the GET HTTP method, which is actually forwarded to the _get function in your handler. Remember that this function actually could be a list, a search, or an actual get for a specific object depending on what the full URL is. To keep this example simple, don't allow searching, just listing and fetching. Now add a list function referenced in the _get function:

```
def list(self, request, response):
    """List all the objects"""
    response.write('<%ss>' % self.db_class.__name__)
    for obj in self.db_class.all().order("-created_at"):
        response.write(obj.toXML())
    response.write('</%ss>' % self.db_class.__name__)
    return response
```

The list function simply returns a list of all users as XML. You're sorting in reverse order by created_at so that you always get the most recent item first. You abstracted out the XMLizing into a separate function because this can be used for multiple functions. Following is the fetch function, which simply fetches a single object:

```python
def fetch(self, request, response, id=None):
    """Get a specific object"""
    param = None
    if "/" in id:
        (id, param) = id.split("/", 1)
    obj = self.db_class.get_by_id(id)
    if param:
        response = self.get_param(request, response, obj, param)
    else:
        response.write(obj.toXML())
    return response

def get_param(self, request, response, obj, param):
    """Get a specific parameter"""
    from boto.sdb.db.query import Query
    response.body = ""
    val = getattr(obj, param)
    if isinstance(val, Query):
        response.content_type = 'text/xml'
        response.write('<?xml version="1.0" encoding="UTF-8"?>')
        val.next_token = request.GET.get("next_token", None)
        response.write("<%s>" % param)
        val.limit = 10
        for o in val:
            response.write(o.toXML())
        if val.next_token:
            response.write('<next_token>%s</next_token>' %
➥val.next_token)
        response.write("</%s>" % param)
    else:
        response.content_type = "text"
        response.write(str(val))
    return response
```

This `fetch` function enables you to query against a specific property of an item and the item itself. You can allow users to send a `next_token` for individual properties, so they can continue to fetch more results if there are too many to return in a single batch. The `db` handler makes sure that anyone creating, modifying, or deleting any objects must be logged in. The implementation of the `put` function can be seen here:

```
    def _put(self, request, response):
        """Update an object"""
        if not request.user:
            response.status = "401 Unauthorized"
            response.headers.add(
➡"WWW-Authenticate", 'Basic realm="Blog"')
            response.write(self.fmt_err(401, "Unathorized"))
            return response
        xml = etree.parse(StringIO(request.body)).getroot()
        if xml.tag != self.db_class.__name__:
            response.status = "400 Bad Request"
            response.write(self.fmt_err(400,
➡"This handler only handles %s objects, not %s"
➡ % (self.db_class.__name__, xml.tag)))
            return response
        if request.path_info == "":
            response.status = "400 Bad Request"
            response.write(self.fmt_err(400,
➡"You must provide the ID of the object to update"))
        else:
            obj = self.update(request.path_info.strip("/"), xml)
            obj.modified_by = request.user
            obj.put()
            response.content_type = "text/xml"
            response.write(obj.toXML())
        return response

    def update(self, id, xml):
        obj = self.db_class.fromXML(xml)
        obj.id = id
        return obj
```

You also need to allow for creating new objects, which can be seen here:

```
    def _post(self, request, response):
        """Create a new object"""
        if not request.user:
            response.status = "401 Unauthorized"
          response.headers.add("WWW-Authenticate", 'Basic realm="Blog"')
            response.write(self.fmt_err(401, "Unathorized"))
            return response
        xml = etree.parse(StringIO(request.body)).getroot()
```

```
        if xml.tag != self.db_class.__name__:
            response.status = "400 Bad Request"
            response.write(self.fmt_err(400,
➥"This handler only handles %s objects, not %s"
➥% (self.db_class.__name__, xml.tag)))
            return response
        id = request.path_info.strip("/")
        if id:
            assert(self.db_class.get_by_id(id) == None)
        else:
            id = None
        obj = self.update(id, xml)
        obj.created_by = request.user
        obj.put()
        response.content_type = "text/xml"
        response.write(obj.toXML())
        return response
```

This function is much the same, except it enables you to not send in an ID. If the ID were specified, it should check to make sure that it doesn't already exist. Lastly, allow users to delete objects:

```
    def _delete(self, request, response):
        """Delete an object"""
        if not request.user:
            response.status = "401 Unauthorized"
            response.headers.add("WWW-Authenticate", 'Basic realm="Blog"')
            response.write(self.fmt_err(401, "Unathorized"))
            return response
        id = request.path_info.strip("/")
        if not id:
            response.status = "404 Not Found"
            response.write(self.fmt_err(404, "Object Not Found")
)            return response
        obj = self.db_class.get_by_id(id)
        if not obj:
            response.status = "404 Not Found"
            response.write(self.fmt_err(404, "Object Not Found"))
            return response
        return self.delete(obj)

    def delete(self, obj):
        return obj.delete()
```

The User, Post, and Comment Handlers

Both the User and the Post handlers require little extra code. The Users handler requires nothing other then setting the `db_class`:

```
# File: blog/handlers/users.py
from blog.handlers.db import DBHandler
from blog.resources.user import User
class UserHandler(DBHandler):
    """Handle dispatching requests for the user objects"""
    db_class = User
```

The Post handler requires an additional function override for `get_param`. This takes effect only if the requested parameter is comments, in which case you filter out any spam. Start by declaring the `PostHandler`, which extends your basic `DBHandler` you created earlier:

```
# File: blog/handlers/posts.py
from blog.handlers.db import DBHandler
from blog.resources.post import Post
class PostHandler(DBHandler):
    """Handle dispatching requests for the post objects"""
    db_class = Post

    def get_param(self, request, response, obj, param):
        """Override to make sure we don't return
        spam comments"""
        if param == "comments":
            query = obj.comments
            query.filter("spam_chance <", 50)
            response.body = ""
            response.content_type = 'text/xml'
            response.write('<?xml version="1.0" encoding="UTF-8"?>')
            query.next_token = request.GET.get("next_token", None)
            response.write("<%s>" % param)
            query.limit = 10
            for o in query:
                response.write(o.toXML())
            if query.next_token:
                response.write('<next_token>%s</next_token>' %
query.next_token)
```

```
        response.write("</%s>" % param)
    else:
        response = DBHandler.get_param(self, request, response, obj,
➡param)
    return response
```

The more interesting handler is the Comment handler, which need
to enable creation by nonusers and users. For this to be accom-
plished, you simply need to override the _post method and trim it
down:

```
# File: blog/handlers/comments.py
from blog.handlers.db import DBHandler
from blog.resources.comment import Comment
from lxml import etree
from StringIO import StringIO
class CommentHandler(DBHandler):
    """Handle dispatching requests for the comment objects"""
    db_class = Comment

    def _post(self, request, response):
        """Create a new object, This doesn't require
        a user to be logged in"""
        xml = etree.parse(StringIO(request.body)).getroot()
        if xml.tag != self.db_class.__name__:
            response.status = "400 Bad Request"
            response.write(self.fmt_err(400,
➡"This handler only handles %s objects, not %s"
➡ % (self.db_class.__name__, xml.tag)))
            return response
        id = request.path_info.strip("/")
        if id:
            assert(self.db_class.get_by_id(id) == None)
        else:
            id = None
        obj = self.update(id, xml)
        obj.tag = ""
        obj.put()
        response.content_type = "text/xml"
        response.write(obj.toXML())
        return response
```

This trimmed–down method doesn't require a user; it enables anyone to submit a new comment. The last thing you need to do is override the list function so that you return only nonspam and comments that have been already processed:

```
def list(self, request, response):
    """List all the objects"""
    response.write('<%ss>' % self.db_class.__name__)
    query = self.db_class.all()
    query.filter("spam_chance <" , 50)
    query.order("-created_at")
    for obj in query:
        response.write(obj.toXML())
    response.write('</%ss>' % self.db_class.__name__)
    return response
```

Spam Classification

For the spam classification system, use a **Bayesian** filtering system. This filtering requires you to train the system to be reliable, but after you get a good compliment of what is and what isn't spam, it should be accurate. This training involves giving the system examples of one type or another to let it analyze the data and learn what to describe things as. Bayesian filtering classifies only into categories, so you want to have two categories of comments: spam and ham. Then determine what your chance of spam is by calculating the spam chance and subtracting the ham chance. The larger the number is, the more likely it is spam. Anything below zero is almost assuredly not spam. Fortunately, there's already a simple way to use Bayesian filtering module for Python, **Reverend**.

Because you do things a little differently, you have to store your Spam/Ham database in S3. Start off by creating a nifty set of utilities to handle your spam filtering:

```
# File: blog/utils/spam.py
from tempfile import NamedTemporaryFile
from reverend.thomas import Bayes
import boto
```

```python
class SpamFilter(object):
    """Spam Filter processer class"""

    def __init__(self, bucket, keyname="spam.db"):
        s3 = boto.connect_s3()
        self.spam_db = NamedTemporaryFile()
        self.guesser = Bayes()
        try:
            bucket = s3.get_bucket(bucket)
        except:
            bucket = None
        if not bucket:
            bucket = s3.create_bucket(bucket)
        try:
            self.key = bucket.get_key(keyname)
        except:
            self.key = None
        if self.key:
            self.key.get_contents_to_file(self.spam_db)
            self.spam_db.flush()
            # Load the spam DB
            self.guesser.load(self.spam_db.name)
        else:
            self.key = bucket.new_key(keyname)

    def train_spam(self, text):
        self.train("spam", text)

    def train_ham(self, text):
        self.train("ham", text)

    def train(self, tag, text):
        self.guesser.train(tag, text)

    def save(self):
        """Save to the spam db and upload to s3"""
        self.guesser.save(self.spam_db.name)
        self.spam_db.flush()
        self.key.set_contents_from_file(self.spam_db)
```

```python
    def __del__(self):
        """Before the object is removed, it should be saved"""
        self.save()

    def guess(self, text):
        """Guess the spam/ham ratio"""
        spam = 0
        ham = 0
        value = self.guesser.guess(text)
        for o in value:
            if o[0] == 'ham': ham += o[1]
            if o[0] == 'spam': spam += o[1]
        return int((spam - ham) * 100)
```

Use a special method __del__ that automatically saves the object when it's removed. This helps to avoid the necessity to constantly save the filter after it's been updated. Now make a system to listen on your spamfilter queue and have it perform the appropriate actions. For this, create another simple Python script:

```python
#!/usr/bin/env python
# File: bin/spam_filter.py
import time
import boto
import sys
sys.path.insert(0, '')

def process(sf,q):
    from blog.resources.comment import Comment
    while True:
        m = q.read(visibility_timeout=60)
        if not m:
            time.sleep(30)
            continue
        id = m.get_body()
        print "Got Message: %s" % id
        obj = Comment.get_by_id(id)
        if not obj:
            print "Comment doesn't exist!"
        elif obj.tag:
            print "Comment is already marked as: %s" % obj.tag
            sf.train(obj.tag, str(obj.content))
            print "Training Completed"
```

```
        else:
            print "Guessing type"
            spam_chance = sf.guess(str(obj.content))
            print "Got a spam chance of: %s" % spam_chance
            obj.spam_chance = spam_chance
            obj.processed = True
            obj.put()
        print "Deleting Message"
        print m.delete()

if __name__ == "__main__":
    if len(sys.argv) < 2:
        print "Usage: %s bucket" % sys.argv[0]
        sys.exit(1)
    sqs = boto.connect_sqs()
    q = sqs.get_queue("spamfilter")
    if not q:
        q = sqs.create_queue("spamfilter")
    from blog.utils.spam import SpamFilter
    sf = SpamFilter(sys.argv[1])
    process(sf,q)
```

This simple script is designed for two purposes. First, it checks
to see if there's a tag set on the comment, and if it is, it uses that
tag to train the spam filter. Second, if there isn't a tag, it guesses
the chance of spam and updates the object accordingly. This means
that to flag a comment as spam or ham, all you have to do is set
the tag appropriately, set the processed flag to False, and save.

Presentation

A weblog without any method to present your posts is useless, so
you also need a smooth interface for your visitors to view and
search your blog. Even though you could insert all your posts
directly to your database in HTML or JavaScript, it's probably also
a good idea to give yourself an interface to let you format and post
your content to. Because this is a web application, your entire presentation layer is going to be on the client side, and entirely
untrusted. No matter what you use to develop your client layer,
you can't assume any requests coming from it are valid. Because

there's already a lot of available documentation for how to implement a REST client interface in most languages, you won't go into any depth there. Simply focus on a web-based interface using JavaScript and HTML.

Setting Up the HTTP Proxy

As anyone who's worked with **Ajax** and JavaScript before know that you can't make an Ajax request to another server. For this reason, you need to set up some form of HTTP proxy on your web server to serve up both static content and dynamic data from your server. For this example, use **Apache2** with **Mod Proxy Balancer** and **Mod Proxy HTTP**. You can realistically use any web server that can proxy, but Apache is the easiest to configure, especially if you use an SSL certificate. A simple configuration can be seen here:

```
<Directory "/path/to/your/code/blog/">
    Options Indexes MultiViews FollowSymLinks
    AllowOverride None
    Order allow,deny
    Allow from all
</Directory>

ProxyRequests Off
ProxyTimeout 30

<Proxy *>
    AddDefaultCharset off
    Order deny,allow
    Allow from all
</Proxy>

<Proxy balancer://blog>
    BalancerMember http://127.0.0.1:8080
</Proxy>

<Location />
    DirectoryIndex index.html
    Order allow,deny
    Allow from all
</Location>
```

```
Alias / /path/to/your/code/blog/
ProxyPass /api/ balancer://blog/
ProxyPassReverse /api/ balancer://blog/
```

You need to have `proxy`, `proxy_http`, and `proxy_balancer` enabled. You could also add additional servers into the `Proxy balancer` section if you have a multicore system, and then you would run multiple servers on different ports. It's best to play around with the number of servers you run until you get a decent result without using up all the processing power on your system.

Posts

The first thing to do is make a simple JavaScript library to communicate with your backend. This can be complicated to perfect, but the basics can be handled fairly simply. Start off by creating a base set of commands.

Listing Posts

One of the first things your users will want to do is see a list of blog posts, so that seems like a logical way to begin. Start by making a few functions for listing out generic objects:

```javascript
// File: blog/js/model.js
var Model = {
    path: "",
    name: "",

    //
    // Get all objects
    //
    each: function(fnc){
        var self = this;
        $.get(self.path, function(data){
            var xml = $(data);
            xml.find(self.name).each(function(i,objXML){
                fnc(self.parseXML($(objXML)));
            });
        });
    },
```

```
//
// Parse the XML
//
parseXML: function(objXML){
    var obj = {id: objXML.attr("id")}
    objXML.children().each(function(x, prop){
        if($(prop).children()[0]){
            obj[prop.tagName] = [];
            $(prop).children().each(function(i, p){
                obj[prop.tagName].push($(p).text());
            });
        } else {
            obj[prop.tagName] = $(prop).text();
        }
    });
    return obj;
  }
}
```

You created two empty variables here: path and name. You use these later when implementing the specific instances of each of your models. The each function queries the specified path and returns a parsed version of the returned XML, calling the passed-in function once for every object. Next, create your specific Post implementation:

```
// File: blog/js/post.js
var Post = {
    path: "/api/posts",
    name: "Post",

    each: Model.each,
    parseXML: Model.parseXML,

    // Follow the /content ref
    // to get the content
    getContent: function(obj, fnc){
        var self = this;
        $.get(self.path + "/" +
            obj.id + "/content", function(data){
            fnc(data);
        });
    }
}
```

For the most part, you're just pulling the functions directly out of the `Model` object, but you are also adding a new function `getContent`, which can fetch the actual content of a given post. Remember that the content is stored separately so you need to fetch it separately as well. Because Ajax is asynchronous, this will use a callback function, and you can fetch multiple contents at once.

Next, make some basic HTML for displaying your posts. Start by displaying the most recent posts on your page:

```html
<!DOCTYPE html>
<!-- File: blog/index.html -->
<html>
    <head>
        <meta charset="utf-8"/>
        <link rel="stylesheet" href="style/blog.css" type="text/css"/>

        <script src="js/jquery.min.js"></script>
        <script src="js/model.js"></script>
        <script src="js/post.js"></script>
        <script src="js/blog.js"></script>

        <title>Example Blog</title>
    </head>
    <body>
        <div id="container">
            <div id="header">
                <h1>Example Blog</h1>
            </div>
            <div id="content">
                <div id="posts">
                    <div id="post_template" class="post">
                        <h3>
                            <span class="attr title"></span>
                            <small class="attr created_at"></small>
                        </h3>
                        <hr/>
                        <div class="attr content"></div>
                        <ul>
                            <li class="attr tags"></li>
                        </ul>
```

```
                    <br class="clear"/>
                </div>
            </div>
        </div>
    </div>
  </body>
</html>
```

Here, you defined a template for your posts with the id post_ template. Instead of adding any of the JavaScript code in this HTML file, another file, blog.js, is included:

```
// File: blog/js/blog.js
$(document).ready(function(){
  // Set up the Post Template
  var post_template = $($("#post_template")[0]);
  $("#post_template").remove();
  post_template.attr("id", ""); // Remove the ID

  Post.each(function(obj){
    var p = post_template.clone();
    p.attr("id", obj.id);
    p.find(".attr.title").text(obj.title);
    p.find(".attr.created_at").text(obj.created_at);
    Post.getContent(obj, function(data){
      p.find(".attr.content").text(data);
    });
    var tagTemplate = p.find(".attr.tags").clone();
    var tagParent = p.find(".attr.tags").parent();
    p.find(".attr.tags").remove();
    $(obj.tags).each(function(x, p){
      var tagNode = tagTemplate.clone();
      tagNode.text(p);
      tagParent.append(tagNode);
    });
    $("div#posts").append(p);
  });
});
```

The first thing to do here is to copy the post template into a variable and remove it from the DOM. Then iterate over each post using your Post.each function you created earlier. Each time you get a new object in this function, clone your template, set the ID to the ID of the post, and then start setting attributes. Use the text() function, so any HTML that may have been in the object is escaped, preventing posts from hijacking your site.

Similarly to how you use the post template to create a template in JavaScript and then remove it from the DOM, you can copy out the tags template and then remove it from your node. You can also add a bit of styling, but I'll leave that up to you to decide.

Creating Posts

You can run your server now without any problems and show off your latest posts. The problem you've got now is that you probably don't have any content in your system to view. Now create a simple web form. Start by adding a function to the model.js object called create:

```
// Create a new object
create: function(attrs, fnc){
    var self = this;
    console.log("CREATE: " + self.name);
    var xmlDoc = self.toXML(attrs);
    $.post(self.path, xmlDoc, function(data){
        console.log("Created");
        fnc(self.parseXML($(data)));
    });
},


// Convert to XML
toXML: function(attrs){
    var self = this;
    var xmlDoc = "<"+self.name;
    if(attrs.id){
        xmlDoc += ' id="' + attrs.id + '"';
    }
    xmlDoc += ">";
    for(k in attrs){
        var val = attrs[k];
        if(k != "id"){
            if( (typeof val) == "string"){
```

```
            xmlDoc += "<"+k+">"+val+"</"+k+">";
        } else {
            // Assume it's a list
            xmlDoc += "<"+k+">"
            $(val).each(function(i,v){
                xmlDoc += "<"+k+">"+v+"</"+k+">";
            });
            xmlDoc += "</"+k+">";
        }
    }
}
xmlDoc += "</"+self.name+">";
return xmlDoc;
}
```

Here, you create the XML document by serializing the passed-in attributes into XML. The only problem with this generic method is for lists; you can only use the same property name, not another name for the internal tag name. This comes into play only with tags, but you handled that in your post handler. You don't need to worry about overriding this in your Post-specific handler, so just copy it over using the following code:

```
create: Model.create
```

The last thing to do is make a special creation page so that you can create the post. Just mock up a simple web form on a different HTML page:

```
<!DOCTYPE html>
<!-- File: blog/addPost.html -->
<html>
    <head>
        <meta charset="utf-8"/>
        <link rel="stylesheet" href="style/blog.css" type="text/css"/>

        <script src="js/jquery.min.js"></script>
        <script src="js/model.js"></script>
        <script src="js/post.js"></script>
        <script src="js/user.js"></script>
        <script src="js/comment.js"></script>
        <script src="js/addPost.js"></script>
```

```
      <title>Example Blog</title>
   </head>
   <body>
      <div id="container">
         <div id="header">
            <h1>Example Blog</h1>
         </div>
         <div id="content">
            <form onSubmit="return addPost(this);">
               <label for="tags">Tags: </label>
               <input type="text" name="tags" style="width: 300px;"/>
               <br/><br/>
               <label for="title">Title: </label>
               <input type="text" name="title" style="width: 300px;"/>
               <br/><br/>
               <textarea style="width: 350px;"
➥ rows="20" name="content"></textarea>
               <br/><br/>
               <input type="submit" value="Create Post"/>
            </form>
         </div>
      </div>
   </body>
</html>
```

Now assuming everything is set up correctly, navigate to
/addPost.html on your web server, and you'll be presented with
this form. You can add tags separated by spaces, a title, and body
text for your posts. After you press Create Post, however, you'll
notice a login screen. Because you probably haven't already created
a user, go ahead and do that directly in the database now:

```
>>> from blog.resources.user import User
>>> u = User()
>>> u.username = "foo"
>>> u.password = "bar"
>>> u.put()
```

Now you can log in with your username and password, and you
should be redirected to your front page, which should now be displaying your nice, new post.

Deleting Posts

You already created a deletion method on your servers, so make it possible to delete your posts from your web UI. Although you could make this fancy, for example, by hiding your Delete button from people that can't delete, just keep it simple. Start by adding the following function to your `Model` base class:

```
// Delete an existing object
del: function(id, fnc){
   var self = this;
   $.ajax({
      type: "DELETE",
      url: self.path + "/" + id,
      complete: function(data){
         if(fnc)
            fnc(data);
      }
   });
}
```

Notice that you have to use the basic `$.ajax` method because there's no `$.delete` method for jQuery. This method is fairly self-explanatory, though; send along the actual `DELETE` request. Again, you don't need to do anything except copy this function for the post-specific class, as shown in the following code bit:

```
del: Model.del
```

Next, you need to create a function to use this. Add a simple function to your `blog.js` file. This function refreshes the page after a second, so you don't have to worry about removing the post through JavaScript:

```
// Delete a Post
//
function deletePost(obj){
   var id = $(obj).parents("div.post").attr('id');
   if(confirm("Are you sure you want to delete this post?")){
      Post.del(id, function(){
         setTimeout(function(){
            window.location.reload(true);
         }, 1000);
```

```
        });
    }
}
```

Lastly, add a button into the `<h3>` tag of your post template in blog/index.html:

```
<button onClick="deletePost(this);">Delete</button>
```

Editing a Post

Editing a post requires you to introduce a few nifty, little additions. Use your existing addPost.html template and overload it to allow you to pass in existing data. Start by introducing two new methods to your base Model class:

```
// Get an existing object
get: function(id, fnc){
    var self = this;
    $.get(self.path+"/"+id, function(data){
        var xml = $(data);
        xml.find(self.name).each(function(i,objXML){
            fnc(self.parseXML($(objXML)));
        });
    });
},

// Update an object
put: function(attrs, fnc){
    var self = this;
    var xmlDoc = self.toXML(attrs);
    $.ajax({
        type: "PUT",
        url: self.path+"/"+attrs.id,
        data: xmlDoc,
        complete: function(data){
            if(fnc){
                fnc(self.parseXML($(data)));
            }
        }
    });
}
```

You need both the get and put functions because you have to
load the old data before you can let the user edit it. The get function is little more than the each function, except it also takes an ID
and adds that to the URL.

The put function is mostly the same as the create function,
except you send to the modified URL that includes the id, and
you use the PUT method. Neither of these methods need to be
overridden, so just copy them outright, as seen here:

```
get: Model.get,
put: Model.put
```

Next, borrow this utility to find user parameters in the URL.
This enables you to send users to URLs such as
addPost.html?id=foo and have them automatically load up the
proper post:

```
// File: js/utils.js
function gup(name){
    name = name.replace(/[\[]/,"\\\[").replace(/[\]]/,"\\\]");
    var regexS = "[\\?&]"+name+"=([^&#]*)";
    var regex = new RegExp( regexS );
    var results = regex.exec( window.location.href );
    if( results == null )
        return "";
    else
        return results[1];
}
```

Ensure this is loaded in your addPost.html file as well, so just
add the following line in your <head> tag after importing jquery:

```
<script src="js/utils.js"></script>
```

Next, modify addPost.js file, which enables you to load up a
specific object and submit it via a PUT instead of a POST:

```
// File: js/addPost.js
function addPost(form){
    form = $(form);
    form.find("input[type='submit']")
        .attr('disabled', 'disabled');
```

```
    try {
        var obj = {}
        obj['title'] = form.find("input[name='title']").val();
        obj['content'] = form.find("textarea[name='content']").val();
        obj['tags'] = form
➥.find("input[name='tags']").val().split(" ");
        var id = gup('id');
        if(id){
            obj['id'] = id;
            Post.put(obj, function(obj){
                console.log("Updated Object");
                // Wait a few seconds for the DB to update,
                // then re-direct them to the home page
                setTimeout(function(){
                    window.location = "/index.html";
                },2000);
            });

        } else {
            console.log("Creating Object");
            console.log(obj);
            Post.create(obj, function(obj){
                console.log("Created Object");
                // Wait a few seconds for the DB to update,
                // then re-direct them to the home page
                setTimeout(function(){
                    window.location = "/index.html";
                },2000);
            });
        }

    } catch (e){
        console.log(e);
    }
    return false;
}
$(document).ready(function(){
    var id = gup("id");
    if(id){
        Post.get(id, function(obj){
            $("input[name='title']").val(obj.title);
```

```
        $("input[name='tags']") .val(obj.tags.join(" "));
        $("textarea[name='content']").val(obj.title);
        $("input[type='submit']").val("Update Post");
    });
  }
});
```

Here, you used the new gup function, which Gets a User Parameter (therefore gup) from the URL to determine if you're editing or creating. If you're editing, add in the ID to your object attributes and call Post.put instead of Post.create. The last thing you've done here is automatically load up any existing parameters that are already set. You also change the "Create Post" button to say "Update Post" instead.

Lastly, add a function to send users to that page, and add a button to the front page again for editing. The Edit button can go next to the Delete button, which looks similar:

```
button onClick="return editPost(this);">Edit</button>
```

The code to redirect them is simple. Just set the window.location:

```
function editPost(obj){
   var id = $(obj).parents("div.post").attr('id');
   window.location = "/addPost.html?id=" + id;
}
```

Comments

The Comments section is similar to the Posts model, so you can directly copy over the post.js file with a few modifications for the path and name:

```
// File: blog/js/comment.js
var Comment = {
   path: "/api/comments",
   name: "Comment",

   create: Model.create,
   each: Model.each,
   get: Model.get,
```

```
    del: Model.del,
    put: Model.put,

    parseXML: Model.parseXML,
    getContent: Post.getContent
}
```

Add in a special page to view the post and comments for the post. Replace the original <span> tag on the index page with the following line:

```
<a onClick="return viewPost(this);" class="attr title"></a>
```

Then create a viewPost function that looks similar to the editPost function but goes to a slightly different URL:

```
function viewPost(obj){
    var id = $(obj).parents("div.post").attr('id');
    window.location = "/viewPost.html?id=" + id;
}
```

Next, add another function to your Post.js file to include the ability to fetch related comments. This is almost identical to the getContent function:

```
    // Get all the comments
    getComments: function(obj, fnc){
        var self = this;
        $.get(self.path + "/" +
            obj.id + "/comments", function(data){
                var xml = $(data);
                xml.find("Comment").each(function(i,objXML){
                    fnc(self.parseXML($(objXML)));
                });
            }
        );
    }
```

Copy the idea from your index page, where you listed the posts, and use that to list a specific post and its comments. Create a viewPosts.html file that uses your new functions to display your blog post at the top and the comments related to that blog post below that. This can be done with the following code:

```
<!DOCTYPE html>
<!-- File: blog/viewPost.html -->
<html>
  <head>
    <meta charset="utf-8"/>
    <link rel="stylesheet" href="style/blog.css" type="text/css"/>

    <script src="js/jquery.min.js"></script>
    <script src="js/utils.js"></script>
    <script src="js/model.js"></script>
    <script src="js/post.js"></script>
    <script src="js/user.js"></script>
    <script src="js/comment.js"></script>
    <script src="js/viewPost.js"></script>

    <title>Example Blog</title>
  </head>
  <body>
    <div id="container">
      <div id="header">
        <h1>Example Blog</h1>
      </div>
      <div id="content">
        <div class="post">
          <h3>
            <span class="attr title"></span>
            <small class="attr created_at"></small>
          </h3>
          <hr/>
          <div class="attr content"></div>
          <ul>
            <li class="attr tags"></li>
          </ul>
          <br class="clear"/>
        </div>
        <hr/>
        <div id="comments">
          <div id="comment_template" class="comment">
            <h3>
              <button onClick="return Comment.markSpam($(this)
➥.parents('.comment').attr('id'));"> Spam</button>
```

```
                    <button onClick="return Comment.markHam($(this)
➥.parents('.comment').attr('id'));"> Ham</button>

                        <span class="attr posted_by"></span>
                        <small class="attr created_at"></small>
                    </h3>
                    <hr/>
                    <div class="attr content"></div>
                    <br class="clear"/
                </div>
            </div>


        </div>
      </div>
   </body>
</html>
```

Viewing the Comments

To allow your users to view comments, you need to set up your
viewPost.js script, which will fetch your specific post and comments. Start with fetching the post and comments. Just like with
your posts file, copy the comment template to a variable in
JavaScript and remove it from the DOM. This can be done in the
viewPost.js seen here:

```
// File: js/viewPost.js
$(document).ready(function(){
    var comment_template = $($("#comment_template")[0]);
    $("#comment_template").remove();
    comment_template.attr("id", ""); // Remove the ID

    var id = gup("id");
    if(id){
       Post.get(id, function(obj){
          var p = $(".post");
          p.attr("id", obj.id);
          p.find(".attr.title").text(obj.title);
          p.find(".attr.created_at").text(obj.created_at);
          Post.getContent(obj, function(data){
              p.find(".attr.content").text(data);
          });
```

```
            var tagTemplate = p.find(".attr.tags").clone();
            var tagParent = p.find(".attr.tags").parent();
            p.find(".attr.tags").remove();
            $(obj.tags).each(function(x, p){
                var tagNode = tagTemplate.clone();
                tagNode.text(p);
                tagParent.append(tagNode);
            });
            Post.getComments(obj, function(c){
                var p = comment_template.clone();
                p.attr("id", c.id);
                p.find(".attr.title").text(c.title);
                p.find(".attr.posted_by").text(c.posted_by);
                p.find(".attr.created_at").text(c.created_at);
                Comment.getContent(c, function(data){
                    p.find(".attr.content").text(data);
                });
                $("#comments").append(p);
            });
        });


    }
});
```

Adding Comments

Now instead of creating a separate page just to create these comments like you did with the posts, you add the form directly below the comments. Go back into your `viewPost.html` file and add the following lines below your comments div, at line 50:

```
<form onSubmit="return addComment(this);">
    <label for="tags">Your Name: </label>
    <input type="text" name="posted_by" style="width: 265px;"/>
    <br/><br/>
    <textarea style="width: 350px;" rows="20" name="content"></textarea>
    <br/><br/>
    <input type="submit" value="Add Comment"/>
</form>
```

Next, you need to make your `addComment` function. Put this back in your `viewPost.js` file. This function is similar to the `addPost` function you created earlier, but it automatically sets the post parameter based on the user parameter. This function can be seen next:

```
function addComment(form){
    try {
        form = $(form);
        form.find("input[type='submit']").attr('disabled', 'disabled');

        var obj = {}
        obj['post'] = gup("id");
        obj['content'] = form.find("textarea[name='content']").val();
        obj['posted_by'] = form.find("input[name='posted_by']").val();

        Comment.create(obj, function(obj){
            console.log("Created Comment");
            // Wait a few seconds for the DB to update,
            // then re-direct them to the home page
            setTimeout(function(){
                window.location.reload(false);
            },2000);
        });
    } catch (e){
        console.log(e);
    }
    return false;
}
```

Now you can test out creating comments, and they should be automatically added to your post page. It's important to pass in `false` to the `window.location.reload` function so the form isn't resubmitted again.

Marking a Comment as SPAM or HAM

Now that your users can post comments, you need to make sure you can mark those comments as spam or ham. Remember that normal users can post comments, but only you can modify comments. You also made sure that when a comment is first created, the tag is not set. This means that only a modification can set the tag, so you'll be the only one that can set the tag.

You made two buttons in the comments page: `markSpam` and `markHam`. Both of these functions are just one-liners because all you need to do is set the tag. Add these to your comment object:

```
markSpam: function(id){
    this.put({id: id, tag: "spam"});
},
markHam: function(id){
    this.put({id: id, tag: "ham"});
}
```

Now whenever you click the Spam or Ham button on a comment, it will mark it as such. This then triggers the spam server to use this as training data, helping the system learn what to flag as spam or ham.

Deploying

Up until this point, everything you've been testing on has probably just been running on your local system. Because this application was designed to run entirely within Amazon Web Services, you need to deploy and launch this within AWS. You need to set up a deployment script. Start by developing your EC2 instance, which will house your application server.

Starting the Base Instance

For your purposes, use an existing **ubuntu** image. You can view the latest images available by visiting http://ubuntu.com, choose Cloud, Public Cloud, and then find step 4 that gives a link to the available AMI Identifiers. At the time of this writing, the latest AMI for 32 bit (small) is ami-bb709dd2. Set this AMI as your base and build off of it. To make things simple, build a single-use image.

Assume you've already followed the steps to set up a key-pair and your boto configuration. To start your AMI, use the `launch_instance` command provided by boto:

```
launch_instance -a ami-bb709dd2
```

This command asks you a series of questions about where you want to put the instance, and what security group it should go in, and the key-pair you want to use. You also need to make sure that the security group you choose is open on port 80 to the world.

Next, log into the newly created instance using SSH and your key-pair:

```
$ ssh -i /path/to/your/key.pem ubuntu@ec2-host-name
```

Installing the Software

Start by installing boto from subversion. First check out a copy of it into your local directory:

```
$ apt-get install python-setuptools
$ cd /usr/local/
$ svn co http://boto.googlecode.com/svn/trunk boto
$ cd boto
$ python setup.py develop
```

Then set this up as a **pyami** instance by creating a special /etc/rc.local file and some special scripts in your /root directory:

```
#!/bin/sh -e
# File: /etc/rc.local
# execute firstboot.sh only once
# Note that /mnt only stays with us
# until we're re-bundled, so this is a
# safe place to store this flag
if [ ! -e /mnt/firstboot_done ]; then
    if [ -e /root/firstboot.sh ]; then
        /root/firstboot.sh
    fi
    touch /mnt/firstboot_done
fi

# We run startup regardless of if we've been
# booted before or not, this lets us
# schedule things to be only run on re-boot
if [ -e /root/startup.sh ]; then
        /root/startup.sh
fi
exit 0
```

This makes sure that the `firstboot.sh` is run the first time this
instance is run. Use this script to make sure the `ssh` key is regener-
ated every time a new instance is launched. Because you're not
making this image public, this isn't as big of a deal, but do it any-
way because you're concerned about security. The `firstboot.sh`
script can be seen here:

```
#!/bin/bash
# File: /root/firstboot.sh
# Regenerate the ssh host key

rm -f /etc/ssh/ssh_host_*_key*

ssh-keygen -f /etc/ssh/ssh_host_rsa_key -t
➥rsa -N '' | logger -s -t "ec2"
ssh-keygen -f /etc/ssh/ssh_host_dsa_key -t
➥dsa -N '' | logger -s -t "ec2"

# This allows user to get host keys securely
➥through console log
echo | logger -s -t "ec2"
echo | logger -s -t "ec2"
echo "###################################################" |
➥logger -s -t "ec2"
echo "-----BEGIN SSH HOST KEY FINGERPRINTS-----" | logger -s -t "ec2"
ssh-keygen -l -f /etc/ssh/ssh_host_rsa_key.pub
➥| logger -s -t "ec2"
ssh-keygen -l -f /etc/ssh/ssh_host_dsa_key.pub
➥| logger -s -t "ec2"
echo "-----END SSH HOST KEY FINGERPRINTS-----" | logger -s -t "ec2"
echo "###################################################" |
➥logger -s -t "ec2"

update-motd

depmod -a
/usr/bin/python /usr/local/boto/boto/pyami/bootstrap.py
exit 0
```

Lastly, set up a script to automatically update your system on a
reboot. This is done in `/root/startup.sh`:

```
#!/bin/bash
# File: /root/startup.sh
# Things to run just after the boot process is finished
# On reboot or first boot
#

# Update local packages
apt-get -y update
apt-get -y upgrade

# Update boto, marajo, and botoweb
cd /usr/local/boto;svn up
cd /usr/local/marajo;svn up
cd /usr/local/botoweb;hg pull -u


/usr/bin/python /usr/local/boto/boto/pyami/startup.py

exit 0
```

That's it for boto; next, you start installing your applications.

Installing the Application

Start by installing your prerequisite packages: twisted.web and reverend:

```
$ easy_install twisted reverend
```

Next, copy your entire application directory into /usr/local/blog. Then put in a few symbolic links so that you can access your application from anywhere:

```
$ ln -s /usr/local/blog/blog /usr/lib/python2.6/dist-packages/blog
$ ln -s /usr/local/blog/bin/* /usr/local/bin
```

The last thing to do is modify your startup.sh script to automatically run your server whenever it's started. For your purposes, launch three copies of your application server. Add in the following three lines before the exit 0 line:

```
/usr/local/bin/run_server.py 8080
/usr/local/bin/run_server.py 8081
/usr/local/bin/run_server.py 8082
```

You need to run multiple copies of the server because even though your application is multithreaded, it's not multiprocessed; each copy of the server can use only one core. Most of your EC2 instances have more then one core, and even if they don't, it's often more favorable to run multiple instances of the service for performance reasons. Even if one of these services crashes, there are two others to pick from. Now look at that `run_server.py` script:

```python
#!/usr/bin/env python
# File: run_server.py
def start(appserver, port):
    """Run the WSGI server"""
    from wsgiref.simple_server import make_server
    httpd = make_server("", int(port), appserver)
    print "Listening on http://localhost:%s" % port
    httpd.serve_forever()

if __name__ == "__main__":
    import sys;sys.path.insert(0, "/usr/local/blog")
    from blog.handlers.mapper import WSGIMapper
    start(WSGIMapper(), sys.argv[1])
```

You also need to add the following line to your startup script to automatically launch your spam filter server:

```
/usr/local/bin/spam_server.py
```

That's it! Your application is now set up to run on three ports, and your spam filter will start automatically in the background.

Installing Apache

After you log in, you need to install Apache2 and configure it to work with your system. As with any normal system, use `apt-get` and install it:

```
$ apt-get install apache2
```

Configure and install `mod_proxy` and `mod_proxy_balancer`:

```
$ apt-get install mod_proxy mod_proxy_balancer
$ a2enmod proxy_balancer
```

Next, configure Apache to use your blog application as its proxy and point the directory to your web root. Modify the default vhost file located at /etc/apache2/sites-available/default to the following:

```
NameVirtualHost *:80
<VirtualHost *:80>
  ProxyRequests Off
  <Proxy *>
  AddDefaultCharset off
  Order deny,allow
  Allow from all
  </Proxy>

  <Proxy balancer://blog>
    BalancerMember http://127.0.0.1:8080
    BalancerMember http://127.0.0.1:8081
    BalancerMember http://127.0.0.1:8082
  </Proxy>
  <Directory "/usr/local/blog/www">
    Options Indexes MultiViews FollowSymLinks
    AllowOverride None
    Order allow,deny
    Allow from all
  </Directory>

  DocumentRoot /usr/local/blog/www
  ProxyPass /api/ balancer://blog/
  ProxyPassReverse /api/ balancer://blog/
  ErrorLog /var/log/apache2/error.log
</VirtualHost>
```

Bundling the Image

Bundle the image using the simple bundle_image command provided by boto. This command is relatively verbose, so make sure to follow through the prompts. You need your public and private keys provided to you by Amazon when you first set up your account. You also need an S3 bucket to store the image on and a prefix to

identify your image. Using the `bundle_image` script is quite simple.
Make sure you do this from your local computer, not the instance
you just launched. The bundle image script also provides you with
help if you pass it the `--help` parameter:

```
% bundle_image --help
Usage: bundle_image [options] instance-id [instance-id-2]

Options:
  --version             show program's version number and exit
  -h, --help            show this help message and exit
  -b BUCKET, --bucket=BUCKET
                        Destination Bucket
  -p PREFIX, --prefix=PREFIX
                        AMI Prefix
  -k KEY_FILE, --key=KEY_FILE
                        Private Key File
  -c CERT_FILE, --cert=CERT_FILE
                        Public Certificate File
  -s SIZE, --size=SIZE  AMI Size
  -i SSH_KEY, --ssh-key=SSH_KEY
                        SSH Keyfile
  -u UNAME, --user-name=UNAME
                        SSH Username
  -n NAME, --name=NAME  Name of Image
```

For your Ubuntu-based image, use the following command:

```
% bundle_image -b <my_bucket> \
... -p <my_custom_identifier> \
... -k /path/to/my/key.pem \
... -c /path/to/my/cert.pem \
... -s 10240 \
... -i /path/to/my/ssh-key.pem \
... -u ubuntu \
... -n blog
```

This process may take up to an hour to finish, so now is a good
time to take a break from all this coding. After the processing finishes, you'll be provided with your new AMI ID, which you can
use to launch all your new instances. Make sure you launch at least
one copy of the instance before you terminate your development
instance so that you're sure everything worked.

Creating the Proxy

The last step is to create and set up your proxy system. Use Elastic Load Balancer (ELB) for this, so use the `elbadmin` tool also provided by boto:

```
% elbadmin -l 80,80,http create blog
% elbadmin enable us-east-1a
% elbadmin add blog <instance-id>
```

You probably want to launch a few of these instances and add each one to the load balancer. Also, make sure you set up a CNAME to the address provided to you by the `elbadmin` script, so you can point your users to something more readable.

Summary

Now that you've followed these steps to develop a simple web application, you can take this above and beyond to create other web applications. Of course, if you work on anything bigger than a blog, you probably want a simpler way to handle the more complex aspects of the development. Here, you've taken the raw approach using little help from outside sources for the actual web application so that you can understand the complexities of developing a system in a multitier architecture approach. You used many of the patterns you learned in this book and showed how they can be used with each other to develop a fully functioning system.

9

A Weblog Using Marajo

By now, you should have a firm grasp on all the intricacies of developing a three-tier web blog application the hard way, but what if you want to build anything more complex? Is it feasible to spend hours and thousands of lines of code just to create a simple weblog? What if you want to show/hide things on a page based on whether the user is logged in?

Fear not, cloud developer, you are not alone. When first diving into cloud computing, I struggled with these same exact problems. I searched all over the Internet for a feasible solution to my problems using existing software to no avail. Django seemed to be the closest match, but it didn't support using SimpleDB as a storage engine. I looked at making my own backend for Django but again was halted because of the unique relation-less nature of SimpleDB. It also seemed like Django, pylons, and every other available Python web-application framework was simply too complicated for my simple requirements.

Then something wonderful happened. Google announced Google AppEngine. This new framework seemed like the ideal solution for any developer because you had the ability to use the existing WSGI framework and build your application from there. Although I was not entirely interested in hooking up to Google's servers, this was the turning point for me because it lead to my discovery of Paste and, more important, WebOb. After much research and development work, I created Marajo.

Marajo started off as a clone of the AppEngine framework. I then realized that there was much more functionality I could implement that would make things much easier for me to work with, so it diverged significantly. Eventually, it evolved into a quick framework for spinning up new web services.

At its core, Marajo uses the familiar model-view-control pattern. All three of these sections are run from the same server, sacrificing a bit of speed and performance to make it much faster to develop on. Additionally, using this type of framework takes the browser almost completely out of the picture because you don't have to worry nearly as much about what JavaScript functionality is supported on the browser, just that it's at least modern enough to support HTML and CSS properly. It uses the same template style language as Django and AppEngine, known as **Jinja**. This makes transitioning from Django or AppEngine to Marajo quick and easy.

You previously created a weblog *the hard way*, so now look at how to create that same weblog using the Marajo framework. Focus on the web portion of the app because the spam filter is no different. In this chapter, you learn the basics of how to create the simple hello world example application using Marajo as the framework. This application mirrors the application created in Chapter 8, "A Simple Weblog," but because most of these functions can be abstracted out to the framework, it is much simpler to do, even more complex tasks.

Initializing the Environment

When you first start, initialize your web environment. Start by downloading and installing marajo and all of the prerequisites. First install the development version of jinja2 by running the following command:

```
$ easy_install -U jinja2==dev
```

Next, download Marajo from subversion and install it:

```
$ svn co http://marajo.googlecode.com/svn/trunk marajo
$ cd marajo
$ python setup.py install
```

For your application code, start with a clean root directory for your application. Then create four directories to house your four parts of our code: `handlers`, `resources`, `static`, and `templates`.

handlers

The `handlers` directory houses the individual WSGI handlers. These handlers deal with any special logic that needs to be over-ridden for us. For the most part, every handler extends `marajo.appengine.handlers.db.DBHandler`.

resources

The `resources` directory houses all your persistent data storage models. For your blog application, this stores our `Post` and `Comment` objects. The `User` object is already handled for you by marajo and located at `marajo.appengine.api.users.User`. There's also a user handler available at `marajo.appengine.handlers.user_handler.` `UserHandler` that ensures that you let users modify only their own object and not their authorization group.

static

The `static` directory holds all your static HTML, JavaScript, CSS, and other media. This was previously your `www` directory in Chapter 8, but here you make a special directory under your root because Marajo serves up both static and dynamic content.

templates

The `templates` directory holds all your Jinja2 templates for how to view the data. The template mapper also enables you to create sub-directories that specify the content type requested. Figure 9.1 indicates how the mapper handles these situations.

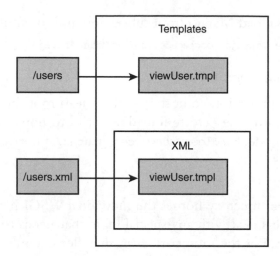

Figure 9.1   The marajo URL mapper.

Creating the Resources

The resources for your new blog system are similar to the application created in the previous chapter, except you don't need to worry about XML serialization. The framework automatically handles all that for you. Start by creating your Post object:

```python
# File: resources/post.py
from boto.sdb.db.model import Model
from boto.sdb.db.property import *
from marajo.appengine.api.users import User
class Post(Model):
    """A Blog Post"""
    title = StringProperty(verbose_name="Title")
    tags = ListProperty(str, verbose_name="Tags")
    content = BlobProperty(verbose_name="Content")
    created_at = DateTimeProperty(auto_now_add=True)

    modified_at = DateTimeProperty(auto_now=True)
    created_by = ReferenceProperty(User,
➥collection_name='created_posts')
    modified_by = ReferenceProperty(User,
➥collection_name='modified_posts')
```

The only major change between this and the application in Chapter 8 is the location of the file, and the location of the User object. Now move on to the Comment object:

```python
# File: resources/comment.py
from boto.sdb.db.model import Model
from boto.sdb.db.property import *
from resources.post import Post
class Comment(Model):
    """A simple Comment object"""
    post = ReferenceProperty(Post, collection_name='comments')
    tag = StringProperty(choices=['', 'spam', 'ham'], default='')

    # This is just a string since we
    # don't require them to log in to post
    posted_by = StringProperty()
    content = BlobProperty()
    created_at = DateTimeProperty(auto_now_add=True)

    # We set this so we only process this message once
    processed = BooleanProperty(default=False)

    # This is the chance this post is spam
    spam_chance = IntegerProperty(default=0)

    def submit(self):
        """Submit this comment for approval"""
        import boto
        sqs = boto.connect_sqs()
        q = sqs.get_queue("spamfilter")
        return q.write(q.new_message(self.id))

    def put(self):
        """We override the put (save) method
        to also make sure it's submitted to
        our SQS queue for approval"""
        Model.put(self)
        # We must submit after we're saved since
        # that's when we'll have an ID
        if not self.processed:
            self.submit()
```

Again, the only difference between the application in Chapter 8 and this is the lack of XML functions and the location of the resources.

Creating the Handlers

When working with marajo, you almost never need to create your own handlers. A simple **CRUD** (Create, Read, Update, and Delete) interface is automatically implemented for you, so it's easy to configure and set up everything. Create one base handler to show your home template:

```
# File: handlers/__init__.py
from marajo.appengine.handlers import RequestHandler
class MainPage(RequestHandler):
    """Simply shows the main page"""

    def get(self):
        self.display("index.tmpl")
```

Additionally, the basic DBHandler doesn't allow nonusers to create anything, so extend it and override the post method:

```
from marajo.appengine.handlers.db import DBHandler
from marajo.exceptions import Unauthorized

class CommentHandler(DBHandler):
    """Override the POST to allow any user to do a create"""

    def post(self):
        """Save or update object to the DB"""
        obj = self.read()
        if obj:
            if not self.user:
                raise Unauthorized()
            obj = self.update(obj, self.request.POST)
        else:
            obj = self.create(self.request.POST)
        return self.redirect("posts/%s" % obj.post.id)
```

Configuring the Application

Configuration for a basic **CRUD** application is quite simple. The entire `app.yaml` file, which is located in your root folder, is written using **YAML** (www.yaml.org/). The first section just defines a few simple variables accessible throughout your templates and handlers:

```
application: blog
auth_db: marajo_users
session_db: marajo_sessions
version: 1
```

Next, configure the handlers subsection of the configuration. This subsection maps the URL patterns to their respective handlers. The mapper enables you to specify either a `handler`, `static_dir`, or `static_file` directive, and then everything else is passed in to the handler as an argument. This is how things, such as the DBHandler, can act to serve up any object depending on what you specify as the `db_class` argument. Now add the following code to the `app.yaml` file you started creating in the previous paragraph:

```
handlers:
- url: /
  handler: handlers.MainPage

- url: /javascript
  static_dir: static/javascript

- url: /images
  static_dir: static/images

- url: /style
  static_dir: static/style

- url: /posts(.*)
  handler: marajo.appengine.handlers.db.DBHandler
  edit_template: viewPost.tmpl
  db_class: resources.post.Post
```

```
- url: /comments(.*)
  handler: handlers.CommentHandler
  db_class: resources.comment.Comment
```

Creating the Templates

We need only a few basic templates to begin. Start with your menu template that will be added to the top of each page. This code uses the typical Jinja syntax to insert variables at specific places. You have access to the current user object if the users are logged in, which can be used to determine if you need to provide them with a login or logout option. Now create the following menu.tmpl file:

```
<!-- menu.tmpl -->
<div id="topmenu">
   <ul class="left">
      <li><a href="/">Home</a></li>
      <li><a href="/posts">All Posts</a></li>
   </ul>
   <ul class="right">
      {%if user%}
      <li><a href="{{logout_url}}">Logout {{user.username}}</a></li>
      {%else%}
      <li><a href="{{login_url}}">Login</a></li>
      {%endif%}
   </ul>
   <br style="clear: both;"/>
</div>
<!-- /menu.tmpl -->
```

It's generally a good idea to add the HTML comments to each template so that when you view the generated source you can figure out where a specific element is coming from. Templates can be tricky to debug if you don't have some sort of reference to where each element was inserted from.

Next, look at your index page. This one doesn't include much, but feel free to expand on it as needed. Now create the following index.tmpl file:

```
{% extends 'base.tmpl' %}

{% block content %}
  <h1>Hello World!</h1>
{% endblock %}
```

This shows the basic concept of making a new regular page to be displayed by a handler. Notice that you always start by extending base.tmpl so that you don't need to retype all the HTML and menu code that's duplicated on every page. This base template defines blocks which you can then override. Here, you override the content block to add in your Hello World comment.

Running the Application

At this point, you have a fully functioning application. You can navigate to your application root directory and run marajo_server.py. You can then navigate to http://localhost:8080 and view your entire application. You should see a login button in the upper-right side of the screen. Marajo uses sessions, so the login happens via sessions, not basic HTTP authentication, so log in before you can post. This is, of course, just a basic setup for a blog, so now look into customizing your templates.

Creating Custom Templates

Now start building some custom templates for your application. The three basic templates that you can override for the database handler are list, edit, and view. For simplicity, you can also combine the edit and view templates into a single template, displaying different items based on whether they're logged in.

The List Template

The list template is the default template that you see when you go to the URL without any arguments. This template is passed in a few arguments, the most notable of which is objects that is an iterable object that enables you to query the objects that should be listed. Look at your list template for your post handler:

```
{% extends "base.tmpl" %}

{% block head %}
    <link rel="stylesheet"
      href="{{static_file('/style/blog.css')}}"
      type='text/css'/>
{% endblock %}



{% block content %}
    <!-- listPosts.tmpl -->
    <div id="posts" class="box">
        {% for obj in objects %}
          <div class="post">
            <h3>
                <a href="{{action_href}}/{{obj.id}}">
➥{{obj.title}}</a>
                <small>{{obj.created_at}}</small>
            </h3>
            <hr/>
            <div class="attr content">{{obj.content}}</div>
            <ul>
                {% for tag in obj.tags %}
                    <li>{{tag}}</li>
                {% endfor %}
            </ul>
            <br class="clear"/>
            <br class="clear"/>
            <br class="clear"/>
          </div>
        {% endfor %}
    </div>
    {% if user %}
        <br class="clear"/>
        <div class="box">
          <form method="POST" class="post">
            <h4>Title</h4>
            <input type="text"
              name="title"
              style="width: 300px"/>
```

```
            <hr/>
            <h4>Content</h4>
            <textarea name="content"
              rows="20"
              style="width: 600px;">
            </textarea>
            <br class="clear"/>
            <hr/>
            <h4>Tags</h4>
            <textarea name="tags"
              rows="10"
              style="width: 600px;">
            </textarea>
            <br class="clear"/>
            <input type="submit" value="Create Post"/>
        </form>
      </div>
    {% endif %}
    <!-- /listPosts.tmpl -->
{% endblock %}
```

Here, a new block called head is introduced, which enables you to insert tags into the HTML head tag. You used this to link to a static file using the static_file function passed into your template. Using this function instead of just passing in the link directly enables you to serve these static files out of CloudFront or S3 if you configure that in your app.yaml file.

The next interesting block of code starts with the {% if user %} tag. This section appear only if the users are logged in, providing them with a mechanism to add an additional post to the blog. As tags are multivalues, Marajo enables you to separate the strings by new lines, so just use a textarea tag. You also don't have to add an action URL to your form because you want to post directly back to the page you're already on.

Next, modify your posts handler config in app.yaml to add the list_template definition. Your new handler section should look like the following:

```
- url: /posts(.*)
  handler: marajo.appengine.handlers.db.DBHandler
  db_class: resources.post.Post
  list_template: listPosts.tmpl
```

The Edit Template

The edit template is called every time the user goes to an object specific URL. This can be also thought of as a view template. If the user is logged in, you can provide him with the form so that he can edit the post, and if the user isn't logged in, you can display the post and allow him to add a comment. The edit template looks like the following:

```
{% extends "base.tmpl" %}

{% block head %}
  <link rel="stylesheet"
  href="{{static_file('/style/blog.css')}}"
  type='text/css' />
{% endblock %}

{% block content %}
  <!-- viewPost.tmpl -->
  {% if user %}
    {% include "editPost.tmpl" %}
  {% else %}
    {% include "displayPost.tmpl" %}
  {% endif %}
  <div id="comments" class="box">
    {% for comment in obj.comments %}
      <div class="comment">
        <h4>{{comment.posted_by}}</h4>
        <hr/>
        <div class="attr content">
        {{comment.content}}
        </div>
        <br class="clear"/>
      </div>
    {% endfor %}
  </div>
```

```
{% if not user %}
    <br class="clear"/>
    <br class="clear"/>
    <div class="box">
        <form method="POST" action="/comments">
            <input type="hidden"
              name="post"
              value="{{obj.id}}"/>
            <label for="posted_by">Your Name: </label>
            <input type="text"
               style="width: 210px;"
               name="posted_by"/>
            <br/><br/>
            <textarea name="content"
               cols="40"
               rows="20">
            </textarea>
            <br/>
            <center>
             <input type="submit"
                value="Add Comment"/>
            </center>
        </form>
    </div>
{% endif %}
<!-- /viewPost.tmpl -->
{% endblock %}
```

Notice that a conditional statement `{% if user %}` is used that signifies the user is logged in. You could also validate that the user is of a specific authorization group by doing `{% if user and user.has_auth_group("auth-group-name") %}` but for now assume that you're the only user. The next directive indicates that you'll include a separate template within the same directory as you are currently called `editPost.tmpl`. This entire section essentially means that if the user is logged in, you'll show them one template, but if they're not, you'll show them another.

The next bit of code shows how to iterate over the comments for your given post using the `{% for comment in obj.comments %}` block. As soon as you call this block of code, it triggers the query against SDB, so expect that to take a little longer to render. You can also add filters or limits to this query by appending them just like you did in the handler code. Because you don't want to see any spam, change that query:

```
{% for comment in obj.comments.filter("spam_chance <", 50) %}
```

Now you'll only show comments with a spam chance of less than 50%. Because the filter returns the query, you can also chain filter, order, and fetch together into one line. Also, add in a limit to show only the last ten comments ordered by date created in descending order:

```
{% for comment in obj.comments .filter("spam_chance <", 50)
➥.order("-created_at").fetch(10) %}
```

The next chunk of code uses logic to show a comment box only if the user isn't logged in. You can assume that if you're logged into the site you're not adding comments to your own posts, so this helps clean up some things that you don't want to see. You're adding another box with your custom form in it that performs a POST operation on /comments. You're setting the post option to the current post's ID so that the comment is automatically attached to this post, and you're letting the users fill in their name and a brief comment. When the users click the Submit button, they'll hit your comment handler that you previously set up, which will redirect them back to this post showing their comment.

Next, look at the displayPost template that shows when the user isn't logged in:

```
<!-- displayPost.tmpl -->
<div id="posts" class="box">
   <div class="post">
      <h3>
         {{obj.title}}
         <small>{{obj.created_at}}</small>
      </h3>
      <hr/>
      <div class="attr content">{{obj.content}}</div>
      <ul>
         {% for tag in obj.tags %}
```

```
            <li>{{tag}}</li>
          {% endfor %}
        </ul>
        <br class="clear"/>
     </div>
  </div>
</div>
<!-- /displayPost.tmpl -->
```

This template is similar to the comments section of the editPost template, where you simply show the details of the post in an HTML format. Now look at the editPost template that will be shown only when the user is logged in. The only major changes to make here are to replace the simple display of the fields with their proper input types:

```
<!-- editPost.tmpl -->
<div id="posts" class="box">
   <form method="POST" class="post">
      <input type="text"
       name="title"
       value="{{obj.title}}"
       style="width: 300px"/>
      <small>{{obj.created_at}}</small>
      <hr/>
      <textarea name="content"
       rows="20"
       class="attr content"> {{obj.content}}</textarea>
      <br class="clear"/>
      <hr/>
      <h4>Tags</h4>
      <textarea name="tags"
         rows="10" style="width: 600px;">
{%- for tag in obj.tags -%}
{{tag}}
{% endfor -%}
      </textarea>
      <br class="clear"/>
      <input type="submit" value="Update Post"/>
   </form>
</div>
<!-- /editPost.tmpl -->
```

Here, use your form with a POST again, but don't set the action URL because you want to post to the current page. You've also set all the forms default values to the post's current values, and now you have a fully functional editing template for your user. In the textarea for the tags, use "-" inside of the {% %} tags. These dashes enable you to remove the whitespace before or after the tag so that you can still make the code readable but not have the tags show up spaced oddly. Don't strip out the whitespace before the {% endfor %} block, however, because you do need one new line after each tag.

Finally, modify your post handler again to add in this template:

```
- url: /posts(.*)
  handler: marajo.appengine.handlers.db.DBHandler
  db_class: resources.post.Post
  list_template: listPosts.tmpl
  edit_template: viewPost.tmpl
```

Summary

For the basic blog example, and for most simple GUI-over-database applications, Marajo is an easy framework for building your application. It uses a simple template language that most people are already familiar with, so switching from Django or Pylons is relatively painless. If you're developing only a web application and don't need to provide an API for external third-party applications, Marajo may be the solution for you.

Glossary

A

Ajax
Asynchronous JavaScript request framework designed to make web browser clients behave more like native desktop applications. This enables you to provide more real-time updates to your clients via browser applications.

Apache
Web server notable for playing a key role in the initial growth of the World Wide Web. Apache is primarily used to serve both static content and dynamic web pages. Programmers developing web applications often use a locally installed version of Apache to preview and test code as it is developed.

asynchronous procedure call
Also called a nonblocking procedure call, this request does not halt other operations while its processing.

ATOM

An XML specification similar to RSS that also provides the ability to page results.

auto-scaling group

A set of instances that all perform the same function, and more instance may be added to scale out. This configuration automatically scales up or down based on a prespecified set of triggers you provide, such as CPU utilization. You can also set limits on these groups to prevent them from scaling out of control.

B

balancer

A software or hardware component that distributes requests among multiple machines.

Bayesian filtering system

Bayesian filtering enables you to train a system with how to classify bits of data, and its most common application is to distinguish illegitimate spam email from legitimate email. Many email clients implement this type of filtering.

C

CAN-SPAM Act

This established the United States' first national standards for the sending of commercial email and requires the FTC to enforce its provisions.

client

An application or system that accesses a remote service on another computer system, known as a server, by way of a network.

cloud

Little more than a cluster of computational and storage resources that has almost limitless expandability. This term has been greatly misused by people and companies alike. The most important aspect of a cloud is the *elasticity* of the service. If it's not *elastic*, it's simply a service, not a cloud.

cloud computing

A specific type of cloud service that provides computational resources.

cloud service

A service provided as a utility to developers or consumers, which has almost limitless expandability and is *elastic* in nature. Similar to water or electric utilities, cloud service offerings are also billed out later based on how much you use, instead of requiring users to pay upfront putting down long-term commitments.

collection
A group of objects; in our case, this usually is synonymous with either a class in object terms, or a table in database terms.

commodity hardware
Consumer grade hardware, not supercomputers, used in traditional large-scale applications.

compute instance
An instance is a single unit of computational power. Most cloud providers refer to this as an instance or virtual machine.

content distribution network
This network had edge locations worldwide and provides you with a single DNS name that automatically chooses the closest point to host files from.

creation request
The user requesting to add a new resource to the collection without specifying a specific ID.

cron
A process that runs periodically, spawning processes as configured.

D

deserialize
To convert from serialize form back into native objects.

DevOp
A term coined by cloud developers that is literally a combination of the term developer and operator. It's used to describe the unique responsibilities of a cloud developer that involves both development of an application and the ongoing operations of said application. The DevOp position has become widely adopted since the idea of using hardware as a service.

disposable instances
The idea that instances are cheap and disposable; therefore, not much effort should be wasted on fixing them.

Django
An open-source web application framework, written in Python, which follows the model-view-controller architectural pattern. Django was created to ease the creation of complex, database-driven websites. It also emphasizes reusability and plugability.

domain
The top-level container in SimpleDB.

DNS Safe
A guideline that requires you to use only lowercase alphanumeric characters, starting with a letter, and dashes. You should not use underscores because they are not supported.

dumb terminal
A special computer that has almost no resources other than to connect to the Internet.

E

Elastic Block Storage (EBS)-backed instance
A type of instance introduced by Amazon that uses a persistent storage device for the root partition. This type of instance can be stopped and restarted without losing information.

Elastic IP
An IP address that you can reserve and attach to any instance.

Elastic Load Balancer (ELB)
Amazon's implementation of a balancer.

entry points
A function provided by Python eggs to add specific metadata along with a bundled package.

ephemeral store
A storage device that is temporary and only for one instance.

eventual consistency
The promise that all data will *eventually* be written to all partitions but may not be written *immediately*. If you query back immediately following a write, you may get a different result than what you just wrote. This often means that writes are performed asynchronously, which means the write process does not block, and you can continue working while the write is performed.

G

GUI-over-database
The simplest form of web application that provides only create, read, update, and delete operations on items in a database.

H

Hadoop
A specific implementation of the Map/Reduce pattern implemented in Java. This application enables you to submit jobs to a cluster of workers.

Hardware as a Service (HaaS)
A term coined by cloud providers that describes offering up hardware directly to the developer as a service, instead of traditional offerings where you pay for hardware as an investment.

To qualify as HaaS, the service must provide low-level access to direct hardware components, such as network, compute, or storage.

highly volatile
Data that is not persistent and may disappear without notice.

horizontal scaling
This method of scaling requires you to add more machines to your application, not add more hardware to the same machine. This is also referred to as scaling out.

HTML5
The latest accepted version of the HyperText Markup Language, this is a standard adopted for conveying how a browser should display information to a user on the World Wide Web. This standard also includes some documentation on local storage that should be provided to the developer of a website via a JavaScript API.

HTTP date
A specific ISO standard date format, which is always represented in GMT and formatted according to RFC 1123.

I

Infrastructure as a Service (IaaS)
A type of Hardware as a Service that specifically provides network hardware. Typically, this involves sharing things such as firewalls or virtual private network hardware.

J

JavaScript
This scripting language is primarily used in the form of client-side, implemented as part of a web browser to enhance user interfaces and dynamic websites; however, it is also used in applications outside web pages.

jQuery
This is cross-browser JavaScript library designed to simplify the client-side scripting of HTML. It was released in January 2006 by John Resig, a former classmate of the author at Rochester Institute of Technology.

JSON
JavaScript serialization format that enables encoding complex object types. This encoding scheme enables you to encode integers, strings, booleans, null values, lists of any supported type, and key-value pairs mapping strings to any other type.

L

LAMP

An acronym for a solution stack of free, open-source software, originally coined from the first letters of Linux, Apache HTTP Server, MySQL and PHP, principal components to build a viable general purpose web server.

local storage option

Introduced along with HTML5, this is a way to store application-level information within the browser. This technology enables you to literally distribute every trusted action between client and server.

lock

A shared resource that prevents other threads from using a shared resources at the same time.

logrotate

A UNIX program that rotates log files to prevent them from becoming excessively large.

ListProperty

This property enables you to store multiple values.

M

machine image

A bundle of an OS, applications, and other code in a single package ready to be cloned and deployed on a compute instance. It's the base of any compute instance and is typically read-only when created. Most cloud venders call this an image or package. This is designed to be the starting point for all your servers.

mapper

A process that takes an input set of data and splits it into manageable chunks.

Mercurial

A highly distributed version control system written entirely in Python. This system enables you to check in changes locally and share those changes with others by pushing or pulling them to a central repository.

MHMessage format

Enables you to encode simple key-value pairs separated by colons. Unlike JSON, this format cannot encode any complex data types.

N

NginX

A lightweight, high-performance web server/reverse proxy and email proxy. This is currently the largest contender to Apache as the free and open web server of choice.

O

oAuth or Open Authorization

An open standard that enables users to share their private resources stored on one site with another site without having to hand out their credentials, username, and password.

Object Relational Mapping (ORM)

A programming technique for converting data between incompatible type systems in object-oriented programming languages. This creates a "virtual object database" that can be used from within the programming language.

open stack

An open-source cloud framework that is used by Rackspace and can be run on any commodity hardware.

P

paging

One of the memory-management schemes by which a computer can store and retrieve data from secondary storage for use in main memory. The operating system retrieves data from secondary storage in same-size blocks called pages.

Platform as a Service (PaaS)

A term coined by cloud providers that describes offering up an abstraction layer on top of hardware. PaaS systems give you the ability to use hardware but not directly as with HaaS. They give you an API into a platform and usually automatically scale for you but also constrain you more than HaaS systems.

process

Any set of instructions that needs to be computed and is composed of one or more threads.

property

A single property or attribute on an instance in object terms or a cell in database terms.

Pyami

A Python framework, provided by boto designed to be run within an Amazon EC2 instance.

Python egg

A packaging format for a Python application similar to Java jar files.

Q

queue

A central system where messages can be stored, retrieved, locked, and deleted.

R

rate limiting
Limits requests against its API by IP address and user accounts. This is used to control the rate of traffic sent or received on a network interface.

reduced redundancy storage
A less reliable and cheaper version of Simple Storage Service (S3) also provided by Amazon.

Relational Data Service
MySQL hosted by Amazon that can be used for high-availability systems, but you are responsible for scaling.

resource
A specific instantiation of a collection, which can be thought of as an instance in object terms, or a row in a table in database terms.

resource deadlock
This occurs when you have no way to recover a lock if the original thread dies before it can release it.

Reverend
A Python package that provides an implementation of Bayesian filtering.

reverse reference
A link to objects defined by a query instead of being explicitly defined within the object.

RTMP or Real Time Messaging Protocol
A streaming protocol to transmit audio or video securely.

Ruby Rails (Ruby on Rails)
This is another popular web application framework, similar to Django, written in Ruby. This framework emphasizes the model-view-control pattern and is widely accepted as one of the best web-based frameworks for Ruby ever created. Its tempting engine enables you to quickly and concisely create simple CRUD interfaces with little-to-no effort. It's well known for the numerous "Create a weblog in 5 minutes" tutorials that use Ruby on Rails.

S

scaling out
See horizontal scaling.

scale upward
See vertical scaling.

self-healing
The capability of a process or instance to recover on its own without any manual intervention.

serialize
Taking an object from the native format and turning it into a format that can be written to disk, or transmitted to another system, often to a different language entirely.

Simple Notification Service (SNS)

A service from Amazon that provides the full functionality for registering and deregistering event listeners, and triggering events and sending them to the appropriate end points. SNS supports email, SQS, and HTTP delivery systems.

Simple Storage Service (S3)

A cloud storage service offered by Amazon. S3 provides you with an API to create, read, copy, and delete file-like "objects" in a centralized repository. It doesn't actually offer you a filesystem directly but simply provides you with a web service to store files. S3 boasts near perfect performance and stability, and is a great service for backing up files that you absolutely need to ensure live on forever. It also offers several advanced features, such as two-factor authentication required for deletions and versioning to prevent you from accidentally overwriting or removing needed files.

syslog

A standard for logging program messages. It enables separation of the software that generates messages from the system that stores them and the software that reports and analyzes them. It also provides devices a means to notify administrators of problems or performance.

T

thin clients

This was actually software that was designed to run on standard computers, not providing much functionality apart from simply connecting to the mainframe.

thread

Also known as a Thread of Execution, this is a single continuous execution of instructions running in sequence. These are used to process and manipulate data.

total failure

A complete breakdown of a system that results in end users not being able to perform any tasks.

U

Ubuntu

A distribution of Linux based off of Debian that provides package management. Many images that run in Amazon's cloud are based off of this distribution.

V

vertical scaling

Scaling a system by adding more hardware to the same machine, or migrating to a new, bigger machine. This type of scaling requires downtime and is not maintainable because there are always limits to how big of a machine you can get.

W

Web Service Gateway Interface (WSGI)

A popular framework for writing web applications that is language-independent. This standard defines how headers, data, and URL parameters are passed into a script no matter what language it's written in.

X

x264

A free software library for encoding video streams into the H.264/MPEG-4 AVC format. This codec has recently become popular due to the increased presence of mobile devices that contain hardware accelerators and decoders that reduce the battery and CPU consumption while playing these videos.

Index

D

PUT method, 60

pyami images, 133

Python

boto python library

downloading, 35

installing, 35

requirements for, 34

software installations (application deployment strategies), 273-275

python eggs, 199

python paste, 241

Reverend, Bayesian filtering systems, 250-253

webob, 241

WSGI, 241

Q

queries

external servers, 138

object queries, boto python library, 46

SimpleDB, 43

queues

description of, 162

example of, 163-170

implementing, 163

message queues, 15

parts of, 161-162

SQS, 165-166

counting messages in queues, 82

creating messages in queues, 81-82

creating queues in, 80

default timeouts, 81

deleting messages from queues, 82

deleting queues, 83

finding queues in, 81

hiding messages in queues, 82

reading messages from queues, 82

usefulness of, 170

using, reasons for, 162

R

Rackspace Cloud, 69

CloudFiles, 112-113

CloudServers, 113

CloudSites, 113-114

rate limiting, Twitter, 141

RDS (Relational Database Service), 95-102

regions (Amazon Web Services), 70, 84

Relational Data Service, data storage in blogs, 231

representation layers, n-tier web clusters, 198

requests

asynchronous requests, 137, 161

commands

description of, 174

example of, 175-179

implementing, 174

reasons for using, 173

usefulness of, 179

example of, 137

Facades, 147

handling requests. *See* architectures

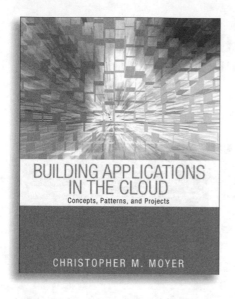

FREE Online Edition

Your purchase of **Building Applications in the Cloud** includes access to a free online edition for 45 days through the Safari Books Online subscription service. Nearly every Addison-Wesley Professional book is available online through Safari Books Online, along with more than 5,000 other technical books and videos from publishers such as Cisco Press, Exam Cram, IBM Press, O'Reilly, Prentice Hall, Que, and Sams.

SAFARI BOOKS ONLINE allows you to search for a specific answer, cut and paste code, download chapters, and stay current with emerging technologies.

Activate your FREE Online Edition at www.informit.com/safarifree

> **STEP 1:** Enter the coupon code: XCSYZAA.

> **STEP 2:** New Safari users, complete the brief registration form.
> Safari subscribers, just log in.

If you have difficulty registering on Safari or accessing the online edition, please e-mail customer-service@safaribooksonline.com